THE HAVEN'S KITCHEN

COOKING SCHOOL

Recipes and Inspiration
to Build a Lifetime of
Confidence in the Kitchen

ALISON CAYNE

ARTISAN | NEW YORK

Library of Congress Cataloging-in-Publication Data

Names: Cayne, Alison, author.
Title: The Haven's Kitchen cooking school / Alison Cayne.
Description: New York : Artisan [2017] | Includes bibliographical references and index.
Identifiers: LCCN 2016038079 | ISBN 9781579656737 (hardback, paper over board)
Subjects: LCSH: Cooking. | Seasonal cooking—United States. | Haven's Kitchen (Firm) |
    LCGFT: Cookbooks.
Classification: LCC TX652.C39 2017 | DDC 641.5/64—dc23 LC record available at
    https://lccn.loc.gov/2016038079

Art direction and cover design by Michelle Ishay-Cohen
Interior design by Erica Heitman-Ford

Artisan books are available at special discounts when purchased in bulk for premiums and sales promotions as well as for fund-raising or educational use. Special editions or book excerpts also can be created to specification. For details, contact the Special Sales Director at the address below, or send an e-mail to specialmarkets@workman.com.

Published by Artisan
A division of Workman Publishing Co., Inc.
225 Varick Street
New York, NY 10014-4381
artisanbooks.com

Artisan is a registered trademark of Workman Publishing Co., Inc.
Published simultaneously in Canada by Thomas Allen & Son, Limited

Printed in Italy
First printing, March 2017

10 9 8 7 6 5 4 3 2 1

To our students, teachers, guests, fans,
and mentors. And to the Haven's Kitchen team,
past and present.

CONTENTS

INTRODUCTION

"I am more modest now, but I still think that one of the pleasantest
of all emotions is to know that I, I with my brain and my hands,
have nourished my beloved few, that I have concocted a stew or a story,
a rarity or a plain dish, to sustain them truly against the
hungers of the world."

—M. F. K. FISHER

Many people don't cook because they never learned how, and they assume it won't come naturally to them. For others, the idea of cooking can be intimidating. For those who do cook, unfortunately it can often feel like a chore. Maybe you've developed a fear of cooking too: of disappointment, of burnt pots and splattered stoves, of the time commitment, the foreign spices, and the ingredients you don't understand. I see all of these types of fears in the students at Haven's Kitchen, my cooking school in the Chelsea neighborhood of Manhattan. Many students take our classes because they want to get over these fears and connect with scratch cooking, or because they lack inspiration and ideas. Sometimes students are in a rut, bored of making the same few dishes that they already know. Some can't quite sync their cravings with what's lingering in their fridge. My guess is some of this feels familiar to you, which is why you've picked up this book.

You might have a strong hunch that even with all of the convenient options and services available to feed us, preparing food with whole ingredients and enjoying a home-cooked meal is a good idea. Cooking from scratch isn't simply a nod to a simpler past. It is increasingly imperative for our well-being, our relationships, our society, and, indeed, our planet. And, above all, cooking can be really fun and rewarding.

If you think about it, there are not a lot of modern-day equivalents of how people have learned to cook for centuries: through spending time in the kitchen at their elders' sides, watching, practicing, and making (and correcting) mistakes. Children helped in the fields and at the hearth, repeating basic tasks like peeling and cutting and roasting and boiling until those steps became automatic. They recognized the smells and sounds and visual clues that signaled when to flip a piece of meat, lower the heat, or add water, or how much longer to simmer a dish. They knew when to cook with fire and when to cook with water, and they knew how to preserve what they would need for a cold winter. Many of us living today didn't have those opportunities. We grew up disconnected from our food sources, and from the kitchen.

At Haven's Kitchen, we aim to reconnect our students with the pride and pleasure of making a meal. I want our students to be able to learn not only to dice and slice, but also to look forward to the processes of gathering ingredients, planning a meal, and preparing and enjoying it. We teach the basics of good sourcing, flavor balance, kitchen skills, and meal composition. Our students learn to understand cooking: what happens to a vegetable when you cut it in a certain way and apply heat to it, what sensory clues to look for when cooking it, and how to prepare it for a final dish. Cooking, as we teach it, is less of a skill set and more of a mind-set—a way of thinking and problem solving that can be applied to any ingredient, dish, or craving. This is why we never give students printed recipes during class. Being liberated from recipes empowers them to really pay attention to what they're doing and *enjoy* the experience. I can't count how many times I've watched as grinning students applaud one another for a well-diced onion or a cleanly filleted fish.

What we really try to do at Haven's Kitchen is create confident cooks who not only feel capable but also relish making meals, experimenting, and feeding people once they return to their home kitchens.

As with any skill, the only path to cooking with confidence involves learning basic techniques and practices. Everyone *can* cook, but the best cooks? They have practiced until they internalized the tips and tricks that make cooking tastier, calmer, cleaner, and more efficient. Habits like cleaning as you go and preparing your ingredients before you cook make for a much more pleasant experience. Little flourishes like a finish of fresh herbs, a tasty sauce, or a good salt can elevate your cooking with relatively little work. Techniques like using an ice bath, tempering, and composition expand your cooking repertoire and make it more rewarding.

I've filled this book with what our students can see, smell, and taste when they take a class at Haven's Kitchen. And though this book may not be able to provide the immediacy of an actual class, the printed page provides other benefits, among them comprehensiveness, easy referencing, and an opportunity to return to the pages and to the recipes again and again.

This cookbook is meant to teach and inspire you: it is not a list of recipes or a photo collage of unattainable food. After making the roasted carrot soup recipe in this book a few times, I hope that you will start to *feel* the best ratio of carrots to liquid, and that you'll begin to play with that recipe, adding spices and finishes that you crave. I hope it is a book that gets read and reread, underlined and annotated, dog-eared and stained and doodled in, well used and passed around. I hope that you will love this book forever but only *need* it for a short while. And I hope, above all, that your kitchen becomes a haven.

HOW TO USE THIS BOOK

"Once you learn the technique, then you can be a creative cook."

—TOM COLICCHIO

At Haven's Kitchen, we teach through hands-on cooking, and this book tries to do the same—albeit at a distance. The goal is to get you in the kitchen as soon as possible. So, after walking you through a few necessary skills and a guide for stocking your pantry, the book moves on to nine chapters of lessons on the key tenets of cooking. Each chapter focuses on an ingredient or a dish that we consider a building block for a lifetime of home-cooked meals. For example, fritter making (see chapter 2) is the best way to explain the art (and importance) of mise en place. Salads (see chapter 6) showcase the secrets of composition and creating a balanced dish.

The recipes in the book—there are more than 100—are not only delicious but educational as well. By learning that the best soups are made by layering flavors, for example, you can eventually make soup anytime, with the ingredients, texture, and flourishes that you crave. Learn to cook a simple bowl of rice, and it will soon become second nature, allowing you to experiment by simmering it in coconut milk or chicken broth and extend your repertoire to other grains. Most of the chapters start with a teaching recipe that breaks down how the recipe works, why certain ingredients are prepared a certain way, and other useful information.

At Haven's, we teach technique as a *means*, not an end. Learning to poach an egg opens up the possibilities for any number of meals. As you gain confidence in preparing sauces, you'll be able to put them together and use them in different ways. Each chapter includes a selection of recipes that are flexible enough for adjustment and good enough that you'll want to continue cooking.

A few last notes of encouragement:

• Write in the book. Your oven temperature might be different from mine. You might like your food saltier. You might prefer different spices.

• Remember, the recipes are guides. Everyone drizzles and sprinkles in his or her own way, and every lemon produces a different amount of juice.

• Improvise! Experienced home cooks don't use ingredients as die-hard "musts"— especially the seasonings. Don't be afraid to experiment.

• Don't let perfection get in the way. Enjoy yourself and have a sense of humor. After all, food is only one part of a meal.

Basic Skills

These are some of the practices that seasoned cooks do almost unconsciously. They make the process of cooking a meal more manageable and enjoyable. Learning them, getting comfortable with them, and mastering them are the first steps to becoming a more intuitive cook. Here are some fundamental skills you will want to have as you begin your cooking practice.

HOW TO READ RECIPES

For confident cooks, recipes are great road maps rather than directives. Well-written recipes give you a clear picture of what ingredients you will need and how to prepare them. They will inspire serving ideas and trigger the imagination. Read carefully, a good recipe can also teach you fundamental techniques and skills. This is why we've annotated them throughout the cookbook.

Here's how to get the most from a recipe.

1. Read it over twice all the way through to get an idea of the dish, what you'll need, timing, and how to serve it.

2. Factor in the time needed to prepare any accompaniment or anything that needs to be precooked. There may be sauces to make ahead of time and ingredients that need to be prepped before the final recipe. Also, formulate a game plan: When is mealtime? Which ingredients take the longest to peel and chop? Which ones take the longest to cook?

3. Read the recipe again as you measure the ingredients and organize your space. Ingredient lists follow the order in which ingredients are used. The recipes in this book show exactly how

and when to prepare the ingredients so you can get organized in advance and be ready to cook.

4. Follow the steps. Keep on hand a tidy cutting board, a few bowls for prepped ingredients, and a bowl for scraps, and clean as you work.

5. Once you've made a recipe a few times, gradually vary it according to your tastes or serve it with other recipes. Make notes on the pages!

6. If you like a recipe, pass it on to someone you love.

HOW TO SEASON WITH SALT

The goal of this book is to teach beginners how to become *intuitive* cooks. I don't ever want a reader to have to measure ¼ teaspoon of salt. Eventually you will understand how to season a dish based on your own preferences.

A pinch of salt can be arbitrary, but generally start with a small pinch of fine sea salt, and add more as needed. Many students undersalt their dishes, and then wonder why they seem to be "missing something."

Salting will become instinctive. It's nice to keep your salt in a small bowl next to your cooking area, adding a pinch here and there as you taste your food. Salt is naturally antibacterial, so it will never spoil if left out. Here are some general guidelines.

A small pinch is what you can hold between thumb and index finger (about ¼ teaspoon).

A large, three-finger pinch equals a scant teaspoon.

A shower of salt should occur just before serving time. When you shower, do so from about eight to ten inches above, which keeps the salting even and well-balanced.

SETTING UP YOUR WORKSPACE

Always make sure your cutting board is secure and has clear space around it. If your cutting board slides around on the counter or wobbles, lay down a damp paper towel first and place the cutting board on top. While you are cutting and cooking, have separate bowls for your scraps and the ingredients. Continuously move what you've cut off your board and into the proper bowls—your mise en place.

STAYING CLEAN AND ORGANIZED

One of the tricks professional chefs use to combat the pressure of putting out complex dishes efficiently and quickly is mise en place (French for "putting in place"). Picture a cooking show chef demonstrating a dish. All of those little glass bowls of premeasured ingredients? That's mise. It's one of the most important skills in cooking (see Fritters). Maintain a clean, organized space and clean up while you cook. Organization is instrumental to good cooking, because not only are the results generally better, but the process is also safer and much more relaxed. The more you organize yourself and prepare your ingredients ahead of time, the more enjoyable the cooking and eating experience—and the less frazzled you'll be.

Knife Skills

Invest in a good knife. The weight, balance, and grip should feel comfortable and manageable to you, and the blade should be sharp enough to slice through a piece of paper at the store.

A sharp knife is essential because it is safer to work with; it also ensures even cuts and requires less force on your part. If it's sharp, your knife should effortlessly glide through everything you slice. We recommend buying a honing rod (also called a sharpening steel) and *learning how to use it*. There are great guides to follow step-by-step online.

A knife should have some heft, but you want to feel in control of it, not vice versa. If treated well, it will last a lifetime. Wash the knife by hand, and dry it off immediately afterward. Do not put your knives in the dishwasher.

THREE ESSENTIAL KNIVES

Every cook should own these three knives:

8-INCH CHEF'S KNIFE

This is a home cook's primary tool. It should have a slight curve to the blade and feel like an extension of your arm when you hold it. You can opt for a 10-inch or even 12-inch blade, but an 8-inch chef's knife is ideal for dicing and chopping.

PARING KNIFE

This is used to trim and peel fruits and vegetables, slice small items, make precise cuts, score meats, and perform countless other tasks for which a larger knife would be ill suited.

BREAD KNIFE

In addition to the obvious job of cutting bread, a bread knife's long, serrated blade is useful for cutting produce with thin skin like tomatoes and eggplant.

KNIFE CUTS

These knife cuts will be used in everything you cook. Mastering them will make your food prep easier and make you feel competent. Keep in mind, though, that a dull knife will make your work more difficult.

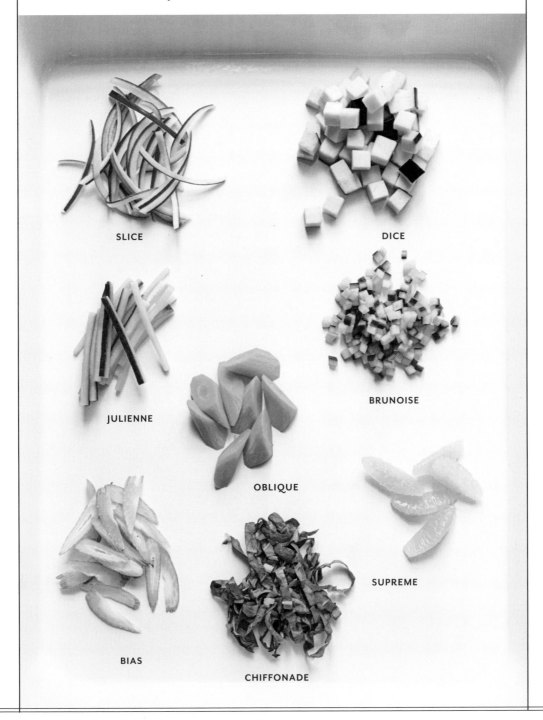

SLICE

DICE

JULIENNE

BRUNOISE

OBLIQUE

BIAS

SUPREME

CHIFFONADE

HOW TO USE A CHEF'S KNIFE

1 Pinch the knife above the bolster on the blade where you best feel the balance between the blade and the handle.

2 Grip the handle with your other fingers.

3 Keep your fingers curled under as you cut. This is called the "bear claw," and it has saved many a fingertip.

4 Always keep the blade in contact with the cutting board, use the whole blade, and work in a steady rocking motion.

HOW TO USE A PARING KNIFE

GRIP. Use a paring knife for more control when slicing small vegetables. Choke up on the knife and use the whole blade in one motion to cut.

SLICING SMALL INGREDIENTS. Create a flat surface so the ingredients are stable on the cutting board. Cut them flat side down.

TRIMMING. Trim the ends off small vegetables like mushrooms by holding them in your hand and carefully pulling the blade toward your thumb.

SUPREMING. Supreming removes the fruit of citrus without the skin, pith, or seeds. Slice the top and bottom off, then cut away the peel from top to bottom. Nestle the citrus in your palm and cut on the insides of the membrane to slice each segment out.

HOW TO DICE AN ONION

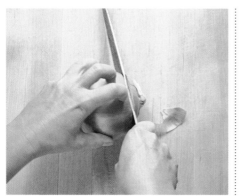

1 Cut off the top of the onion to create a flat surface.

2 With the flat surface on the cutting board, cut through the root to split the onion in half.

3 Remove the peel.

4 Hold down the onion with your nondominant hand. Make horizontal cuts through the onion, taking care not to cut all the way through.

5 Following the natural lines of the onion, slice perpendicular to the root.

6 Rotate the onion and cut it into a small, even dice.

HOW TO PICK AND CUT HERBS

PICKING SOFT HERBS. Unless the herbs are headed for blending, avoid using the stems. Pick the leaves by gently pinching them off the stem. Gently rinse and pat dry before chopping.

PICKING HEARTY HERBS. For herbs on a woody stalk, like rosemary, remove the leaves by sliding your thumb and index finger down the stalk against the grain.

CHOPPING. Bunch up the leaves in a tight pile. Holding the pile with your nondominant hand, slice through it with a sharp chef's knife. Keep the blade flush against the hand holding the pile.

CHIFFONADING. For larger leaves, like mint, sage, or basil, stack them on top of one another. Roll them up and hold them closed. Thinly slice the roll to create thin ribbons.

HOW TO CREATE AN EVEN DICE

1 **CREATE A FLAT SURFACE.** After cutting off the top, slice a thin piece off the side of the vegetable to create a flat, stable surface.

2 **CREATE PLANKS.** With the flat surface on the cutting board, slice the vegetable vertically into planks. The width of the planks will determine the final size of the dice.

3 **CUT INTO BATONS.** Place a few planks on top of one another and slice them into batons that are the same width as your original cut to maintain a square dice.

4 **DICE.** Rotate the batons and make a final cut to slice the batons into a uniform dice.

HOW TO CUT OBLIQUES

1 Slice the vegetable on a steep bias.

2 Rotate the vegetable 90 degrees toward you so the cut surface is facing up.

3 Maintaining the bias, continue to slice and rotate the vegetable toward you.

4 As you cut the wider end of the vegetable, make your cuts thinner to ensure even cooking.

For the Pantry

High-quality, fresh ingredients result in high-quality finished dishes. Look for items with the *fewest number of ingredients and the least amount of processing.* Beware of throwaway terms like "natural," "artisanal," and "quality." When a product is certified as organic it signals that ingredients have been grown without pesticides, growth hormones, antibiotics, and nonorganic feed.

OIL

Choosing the right oil can be overwhelming when there is a whole aisle at your local grocery store offering a multitude of options. We recommend having two or three oils on hand.

Olive Oil
A good-quality extra-virgin olive oil for roasting and sautéing, making dressings, and finishing. Olive oils are not neutral in flavor; they can range from spicy to fruity depending on their origins. The volcanic soil of Sicily produces a luscious green olive oil with a bite whereas most Spanish olive oils tend to be a touch sweeter and more golden. When buying extra-virgin olive oil, do not buy blended oils. Look for the IOC (International Olive Oil Council) or EC (European Community) seal, and a "harvested" or vintage date. When the recipes in the book call for "olive oil," always assume it is extra-virgin, and don't be shy to drizzle it; most dishes benefit from a little richness at the end.

Oil for High Heat
A neutral, refined oil with a high smoke point, such as canola, sunflower, safflower, or grapeseed oil, is also essential. These oils are used for deep-frying because olive oil is not ideal for high-heat cooking. They're also good for when you don't want the herbal flavor of olive oil. An oil's "smoke point" is precisely what it sounds like—the temperature at which the oil shifts from shimmering to smoking. When oil begins to smoke, free radicals release, giving the oil and the food you are cooking a burnt, bitter flavor as well as degrading its nutritional value.

Finishing Oil
One other oil you may enjoy keeping in your toolkit is a finishing oil. Finishing oils are rich. Cooking with these delicate oils alters their flavor, so they should not be used with heat but only as a drizzle to finish a dish or enhance a vinaigrette. Start with hazelnut oil or walnut oil. A lot of Asian-inspired dishes feature toasted sesame oil.

Oils should be stored in a cool, dark place or in the refrigerator. In general, use within a year of purchase. As oils age, they begin to oxidize, which will cause them to become rancid and bitter. More viscous, less-refined oils, such as walnut or toasted sesame, should be stored in the refrigerator for up to eight months after opening.

SALT

Sea salt is the least processed salt available on the market, produced through evaporation of ocean water or water from saltwater lakes. Given its natural production and limited processing, trace minerals and elements from the original water source are often dried into the small flakes, adding flavor, nutrients, and color to the crystals. We recommend using a fine sea salt such as Baleine while cooking and a flaky sea salt like Maldon to finish dishes just before serving.

SPICES

We recommend buying whole spices and grinding them as needed. Buy small amounts of dried herbs like oregano and thyme; spices and herbs lose their flavor over time. When stored in an airtight container, whole spices stay fresh and potent for years, and dried herbs will last for six months.

Peppers

While the black peppercorn may be the most ubiquitous pepper, there are hundreds of other species. The black variety is just pungent and spicy enough to season a food without overwhelming it.

While we keep all of these in our pantry, you may want to build your pepper collection gradually. Start with black whole peppercorns and one of the more zesty options. Buy small quantities and experiment.

• Whole peppercorns—black and white (white pepper is more commonly used in Asian cuisine and has a more earthy, funky flavor; cooks also use it when they don't want little black specks on their food, but it is stronger, so you should use less of it than the black alternative)

• Red pepper flakes (also labeled crushed red pepper, typically made from a few different chiles)

• Pimentón (Spanish smoked paprika), a woodsy, less aggressive paprika

• Cayenne (a lot of heat, not too much depth of flavor)

• Aleppo pepper (a common spice in Middle Eastern dishes; fruity, hot, and funky at the same time)

Other Spices in Our Pantry

• Cumin seeds

• Mustard seeds

• Cinnamon sticks

• Coriander seeds

• Cardamom pods

• Bay leaves

Spice Blends We Frequently Use

• Za'atar, a Middle Eastern spice blend that can include marjoram, oregano, thyme, sesame, and sumac. It's herbal and earthy, but also tart from the sumac.

• Ras el hanout, a North African spice mixture that can include up to twenty or so different herbs and spices (see a simplified version on page 155).

Other Pantry Items

To keep a well-stocked kitchen, have these items in your pantry.

Vinegars

Vinegar improves with age and, unlike oil, has an almost infinite shelf life. Purchase high-quality vinegars without added sugars and flavoring agents. We recommend having a few options in the larder. These are our favorites.

- Apple cider
- Balsamic (but only bottles certified as *Aceto Balsamico Tradizionale*)
- Champagne
- Rice
- Sherry
- White wine or red wine

Sweeteners

When it comes to sweeteners, the less refined the better. Typical white sugar is processed with bleach and other chemicals. When buying sugar, look for "organic" and "cane." It's useful to keep on hand granulated sugar, superfine granulated sugar, and confectioners' sugar. At Haven's Kitchen, we also sweeten sauces and dressings with raw, local honey and maple syrup. Syrups and honey are sweeter than sugar, so you may need less.

Soy Sauce

Soy sauce, Japanese shoyu, and their gluten-free counterpart, tamari, are used frequently in our cooking to add rich umami flavors and salinity. Use them as a base for a dipping sauce or marinade or to add depth to stocks and soups. Most Asian recipes call for soy sauce.

Mirin

Another frequent player in Asian cuisine, mirin is a sweet, light rice wine. Try it sprinkled on blanched broccoli.

Tahini

This creamy, tangy sesame paste is the base for many of our zesty sauces and dips. You'll find it in many Middle Eastern recipes.

Hot Sauce

This versatile ingredient is always good to have on hand. We prefer sambal oelek, a spicy, rich chile paste made from ground chiles, which add a bit of texture to the heat.

Anchovies, Sardines, and Fish Sauce

These shelf-stable fishy foods are the secret flavor boost to many dishes.

Olives and Capers

Cured and preserved via pickling, these pantry staples add flavor, texture, and acid to dressings, sauces, roasted vegetables, grilled seafood, and many other dishes.

Nuts and Seeds

The natural oils in nuts and seeds go rancid within a few months, so buy nuts raw, unsalted, and whole in small quantities and store in sealed containers in a cool, dark place. Once opened, it is a good idea to store nuts and seeds in the refrigerator to keep them fresh longer. Toast in a dry skillet over medium-low heat for a minute or so to release their essential oils and natural flavors before using.

- Almonds
- Cashews
- Hazelnuts
- Peanuts
- Pecans
- Walnuts
- Black sesame seeds (hull intact)
- Pumpkin seeds (pepitas)

Dried Fruit

A sprinkle of sweet, chewy dried fruit on a salad or rice bowl is always a welcome addition.

- Cherries
- Currants
- Figs
- Raisins

Dried Pasta

Look for pasta made from durum wheat (the box might say *grano duro*). Pasta comes in countless shapes and sizes, but if you keep in stock a short and a long noodle, you'll be set for most recipes. A short pasta like penne or fusilli is good with sauces like pesto that cling to the ridges and fill the tubes. Longer, thinner pastas like linguini pair well with thinner sauces; thicker ribbons like fettuccine are best for meaty sauces.

Specialty Pasta

Aside from the multitude of new pastas made from gluten-free flours, these pastas are quick and easy to make. Be aware that gluten-free pastas don't cook the same way as their old-school counterparts, so follow the directions on the box carefully.

- Couscous looks like a grain but is actually tiny little pastas.

- Vermicelli are very thin Italian noodles. Asian vermicelli can be made from rice or mung beans, and are also called cellophane noodles.

Beans

Use dried beans whenever possible. In a pinch, use organic canned. Keep both in the pantry.

- Black beans
- Garbanzo beans (also known as chickpeas)
- Lentils
- White beans (also called cannellini or Great Northern)

Grains

Whole grains spoil more quickly than their refined cousins. Grains can be sprayed heavily with pesticides, so make sure to buy organic varieties. Experiment with different grains and use up the bag or box within a year. Don't run out and buy all of these grains at once. Try them and see which ones you prefer.

- Arborio rice for risotto (extra-starchy Italian variety)
- Barley (nice in soups, quite nutty and chewy, softer than farro)
- Brown rice

- Farro (a hulled wheat variety called spelt, my personal favorite for its chew)
- Millet
- Polenta (stone-ground)
- Quinoa (technically it's a fruit, but it's cooked like a grain)
- Short-grain white rice (polished brown rice) or Basmati (a bit more flavorful)
- Wheat berries
- Whole steel-cut oats

Canned Tomatoes

A few cans of organic Italian crushed tomatoes are good to have on hand for a last-minute sauce or soup.

Flour

For beginning home cooks, we recommend using unbleached, unbromated, all-purpose flour. We also like garbanzo flour for flatbread and rice flour for creating light, crispy batters. If you are up to the challenge, try substituting a whole-grain alternative, like buckwheat (which is also gluten free) or whole wheat flour, for up to half of the white flour in a recipe. Flours milled from whole grains are denser and more flavorful than white flour.

For the Refrigerator

Keeping your fridge stocked with a few fresh staples means always being ready to whip up dinner or a snack. Here are a few items that are nice to have on hand. High-quality ingredients provide the best flavor.

Citrus
lemons, limes, oranges

Garlic, shallots, scallions, and ginger
(you can store ginger in your freezer)

Fresh herbs
parsley, thyme, rosemary, dill, chives, cilantro

Cheese
Buy whole wedges and blocks of cheese rather than the shredded and bagged varieties. Grating them yourself takes less than a minute, saves packaging, and spares you from added preservatives and bland flavor. Keep these two on hand:

• Authentic Parmigiano-Reggiano (from the Emilia-Romagna region of Italy)

• Sharp Cheddar

Plain organic Greek yogurt
Add creaminess to dressings and sauces with yogurt. Buy 2% or full-fat for the best flavor.

Butter
Find butter made from organic milk, from grass-fed cows that is free of growth hormones. Look for sweet, unsalted butter with a high butterfat content.

Eggs
I recommend buying eggs from pastured hens only. Look for large eggs labeled "Certified Humane"; they should be evenly sized in the package.

Miso
A paste often made from fermented soybeans, miso adds mellow but savory flavor to Asian dishes. It comes in a few "strengths" and can be made from other legumes and grains such as adzuki beans and barley, lending a range of colors and flavors from light and sweet to darker and more pungent. Try one at a time and see which you prefer.

Mustard
I like to have both a smooth Dijon and a coarse, grainy version on hand. Again, it's a good idea to figure out what you like.

Tools and Equipment

While I stand by the premise that you don't need a lot of "stuff" to cook well, having some stuff is a good idea. Granted, people had been cooking for thousands of years before anyone invented the slotted spatula or the Y-shaped peeler. But tools like these have made our jobs as cooks more efficient. They are worth the investment.

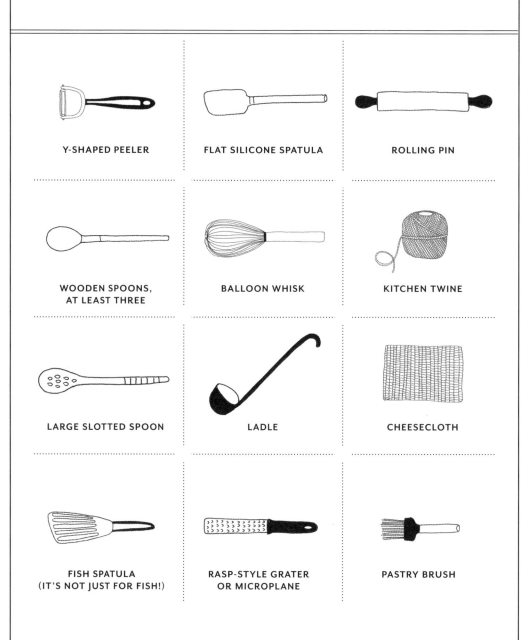

Y-SHAPED PEELER

FLAT SILICONE SPATULA

ROLLING PIN

WOODEN SPOONS,
AT LEAST THREE

BALLOON WHISK

KITCHEN TWINE

LARGE SLOTTED SPOON

LADLE

CHEESECLOTH

FISH SPATULA
(IT'S NOT JUST FOR FISH!)

RASP-STYLE GRATER
OR MICROPLANE

PASTRY BRUSH

PARCHMENT PAPER

MEASURING SPOONS

COLANDER

CUTTING BOARDS,
WOODEN AND PLASTIC

KITCHEN TOWELS,
LOTS OF THEM

FINE-MESH STRAINER

BOX GRATER

ASSORTED STAINLESS STEEL
MIXING BOWLS

SALAD SPINNER

DRY MEASURING CUPS

ASSORTED SMALL
GLASS PREP BOWLS

MORTAR AND PESTLE

THERMOMETERS,
ONE FOR MEAT AND ONE
INFRARED FOR FRYING

KNIVES

TONGS, TWO OR THREE
PAIRS OF VARIOUS LENGTHS

APPLIANCES

Modern appliances have certainly made cooking a faster, easier endeavor. Food processors and blenders quickly pulverize, chop, mix, and liquefy all sorts of ingredients that would have taken our ancestors hours to prepare. As a proponent of home cooking, I would never discourage such shortcuts. If it's a choice between making something quickly and making it the "old-fashioned" way, I vote for just making it.

**VITAMIX OR OTHER
HIGH-SPEED BLENDER**

STAND MIXER

FOOD PROCESSOR

IMMERSION BLENDER

SPICE GRINDER

POTS, PANS, COOKWARE

This is a comprehensive list. Use it as a guide to stock your kitchen shelves, but don't feel you must own every single item. If a recipe calls for a pan or size you don't have, simply use the closest alternative.

SMALL SAUCEPAN
WITH LID, 1-QUART

STAINLESS STEEL SAUTÉ
PANS, 6, 10, AND 14 INCHES,
WITH LIDS

2 WIRE RACKS
FOR COOLING AND RESTING

MEDIUM SAUCEPAN
WITH LID, 4-QUART

NONSTICK FRYING PAN,
8 TO 10 INCHES

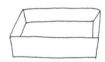

BAKING DISHES,
9 BY 13 AND 8 BY 8 INCHES

LARGE DUTCH OVEN,
6- TO 8-QUART

CAST-IRON SKILLET,
8 TO 10 INCHES

CAKE PANS,
9-INCH ROUNDS

LARGE STOCKPOT
WITH LID, 8- TO 12-QUART

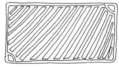

CAST-IRON GRILL PAN

BUNDT PAN

2 OR 3 18-INCH RIMMED
BAKING SHEETS, AKA SHEET
PANS (ALUMINIZED STEEL)

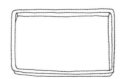

RAMEKINS, 8 OUNCES

GRAINS & BEANS

CHAPTER 1

A LESSON IN
Cooking with Purpose

"The only way to learn to cook is to cook."

—ALICE B. TOKLAS

FOR MANY STUDENTS WHO COME to Haven's Kitchen, the prospect of mushy rice, burned garbanzos, bitter quinoa, and the dreaded scorched pot are scary enough to deter them from cooking at all. Aspiring home cooks want to be creative, to cook more, and to make what they like to eat, but many just don't have the confidence—and so they eventually lose the desire. Grains and beans are often the most daunting ingredients, but are actually the best place to start.

The first lesson of cooking is understanding what you are actually *doing* to ingredients when you prepare them. Knowing the purpose of cooking methods and techniques makes the process less about rigid recipes and mindless steps in a sequence, and more about realizing what you want your final dish to look, taste, and feel like. *Purpose* means knowing what you want to achieve as you chop, heat, and season your food, and those who cook with purpose are more confident and capable in the kitchen.

Cooking grains and beans illustrates the importance of considering exactly what you are doing: in this case, simmering the ingredients *long* enough that the heat and liquid penetrate the interior and render it edible, but *gently* and *slowly* enough that the entire pot cooks at roughly the same pace. Once you start thinking that way—asking yourself, *What am I doing with this knife, pot, oven, spice, and why?*—you will get to that place where cooking becomes part of your muscle memory. Once you've internalized how fundamentals like time and heat and salt work, you'll know your favorite methods and ratios. You'll know when to steam and when to sauté, when to add water or lower the heat, when to dice and when to mince. In other words, you'll be an intuitive cook.

Cookbook author Michael Ruhlman once wrote, "Thinking in the kitchen is underrated." Learning to cook grains and beans is a terrific way to begin doing just that. And once mastered, these simple age-old ingredients open up countless possibilities, from unadorned, back-to-basics rice and beans to steaming-hot breakfast porridge with ancient grains (page 48). You'll be able to whip up versatile quinoa, delicious as the canvas for a grain bowl, and form it into crispy fritters (page 63). Practicing these recipes will loosen your grip on your cookbooks and make cooking less daunting, more creative, and ultimately more fun.

How to Cook Grains

There is no one correct way to cook grains. Ask a hundred seasoned chefs and you'll get close to that many opinions. Ask another hundred grandmothers and you'll get double. There are those who rely on the technology of a rice cooker and those who prefer to set a pot on the stove and use their powers of sight and touch. There are cooks who rinse and soak their rice before they cook it. Some folks swear by keeping the lid on a pot of rice for the entire cooking time; others like to leave the lid off and add more water when needed. The fact that each person adamantly stands by his or her particular method should give comfort: you can relax knowing that there is no single way to do it.

Cooking grains isn't a perfect science because no two grains are alike. Even under the banner of "white rice," there are several varieties. That's why it's helpful to consider a few things about your grain before you set about cooking it. Considering its size, texture, and whether it has been hulled or is still nestled in its outer bran will give you clues about how much liquid and time it will take to cook it. Larger and whole grains like wheat berries and farro need more liquid and simmering time than their refined, pearled, or polished counterparts. The thicker the bran, the more liquid and time it'll need. The smaller the grain, the quicker it will cook.

You will also want to think about how you plan on eating your grains once they're cooked. This will help you figure out the cook times for firmer grains (used in salads; see page 208) or more tender consistencies (as in Farro Risotto, for example, page 53).

Despite their differences, most grains will use between ½ and 3 cups of liquid for every cup of uncooked grain. Many grains taste especially good if toasted in the pot for a few minutes before you add liquid and begin the boiling process. Grains generally benefit from a brief steam, off the heat, after they've finished cooking, before you fluff them. There's a big world of grains available to you; once you get comfortable, try as many as you can.

Teaching Recipe

A BOWL OF RICE

SERVES 4

Cooking rice can be intimidating to new cooks. This is a shame, because knowing how to handily whip up a pot of rice will add exponentially to your cooking repertoire. Once you feel comfortable with it, the world of grains is at your disposal. And remember, humans were making rice long before there were measuring cups and timers. Cooks all over the planet have grown up making rice differently, and because there are thousands of rice varietals, ratios differ. The most reliable ratio is 1½ to 2 cups of liquid for every cup of raw rice. This recipe should calm any rice anxiety you may have and teach you how to consider the purpose of simmering. A pot of unadorned rice is delicious on its own, but you can flavor it as well. My kids love brown rice with a dollop of pesto (see page 302) swirled in at serving time. Or stir in a generous pat of butter and a tablespoon of minced parsley or cilantro. Store cooled leftover rice in an airtight container in the refrigerator for three to five days. You can use leftovers to make fried rice (see page 51).

2 CUPS LONG- OR MEDIUM-GRAIN WHITE RICE	**3 CUPS WATER** **FINE SEA SALT**

MEASURE

❶ Measure the rice.

COOKING NOTES

Grains roughly double their volume from dried to cooked, so work backward based on the amount you plan to serve. Figure roughly ½ to 1 cup cooked grains (¼ to ½ cup dried) per person, depending on the dish.

continued

SOAK AND RINSE

❷ Rinse or soak the rice if you wish.

Soaking rice for 20 to 30 minutes in advance of cooking cuts down on stove time, and some argue that it offers a plumper grain. It's certainly not mandatory, but if you do soak, make sure to cook in fresh water.

If you want the rice to have some stickiness, don't rinse the grains, but if you want the individual grains to be more separate, then do. To rinse, place the rice in a fine-mesh strainer. Rinse thoroughly under running water while rubbing the grains and moving them around in the strainer until the water runs clear, about 2 minutes.

BOIL, THEN SIMMER

❸ Pour the rice and water into a medium pot. Bring to a rapid boil over high heat. Reduce the heat to the lowest setting and cover the pot with a tight-fitting lid so the rice steams as it simmers.

Rice cooks by absorbing the liquid in which it's simmering. The catch is that the ratio of grain to liquid must be proportional so that there's just enough liquid to cook the rice—and none left over. Because white rice no longer has the bran, or outer covering, it doesn't require as much liquid to cook.

Covering the rice allows it to steam as it simmers, plumping the grains as they slowly absorb the liquid. It also prevents the liquid from evaporating too quickly and scorching the rice.

TASTE

❹ After about 15 minutes, observe and taste. Taste a grain to gauge its tenderness: if it's still toothsome, cook for another 3 to 5 minutes, depending on the bite. The grains should look uniformly plump.

Tasting rice is the best way to test for doneness; however, you can also determine if it is cooked through by breaking a grain in half. If the middle is slightly chalky and opaque, cook for a few more minutes. For the most accurate timing guidelines, refer to the packaging—but always defer to your powers of observation and taste.

REST, FLUFF, SEASON, AND SERVE

5 When the rice is done, remove the pot from the heat. Let the rice rest, covered, so it steams for another 5 to 10 minutes.

Steaming the rice off the heat for a few minutes will make for a more evenly cooked pot.

6 Fluff with a fork to air out the grains. If the rice is still a bit too moist, leave it uncovered for 10 minutes so the moisture can evaporate.

Fluffing with a fork airs out the rice and helps separate the grains.

7 Season, and serve as desired.

Add salt or herbs, such as chopped parsley or cilantro.

VARIATIONS

For more flavor, sauté some minced garlic or onion in olive oil before adding the rice. When the garlic or onion softens and just begins to color, add the rice and cook for a few minutes, stirring, until it produces a nutty aroma. Then add the water and cook as usual.

Or, simmer the rice in coconut milk and water or chicken stock. Depending on the liquid, add a spice or herb that will work well, like a cardamom pod, a bay leaf, or a sprig of thyme.

A POT OF QUINOA

MAKES 2 CUPS

Quinoa has a natural coating of a compound called saponin that gives it a slightly bitter and sometimes soapy taste. A good rinse will remove this compound, leaving a subtle, nutty flavor. Serve as a side dish or in a grain bowl like I do on Sundays (see page 42). Make a double batch and use leftovers for Quinoa Broccoli Patties (page 63).

1 CUP QUINOA, WHITE, GOLDEN, RED, OR BLACK	2 SCANT CUPS WATER FINE SEA SALT

❶ Rinse the quinoa thoroughly in a fine-mesh strainer and drain.

❷ Place the quinoa and water in a medium saucepan and add a large pinch of salt. In general, use a 2:1 ratio of water to quinoa, but because the quinoa is already a bit wet from rinsing, hold back on the water slightly.

❸ Bring the quinoa to a boil over high heat, then cover and reduce to a simmer. Cook over low heat for 15 to 20 minutes, until the grains are tender but have a slight bite and all the water is absorbed.

❹ Remove from the heat but keep the lid on for an additional 5 minutes. Fluff with a fork and serve immediately, or let cool and store in an airtight container in the refrigerator for 3 to 5 days.

GRAINS & BEANS

SUNDAY BOWL
page 42

How to Cook Beans

Beans, technically the seeds of a plant, are packed with nutrients and fiber. There are thousands of varieties available, all satisfying and versatile. For such an ancient, humble food, beans can be surprisingly luxurious. I won't get too prosaic about the benefits of buying dried beans in bulk and cooking them from scratch, but it's not as time-consuming as you might think. It's less expensive and gentler on the environment than buying canned beans, and doing the work to cook dried beans will give you a sense of satisfaction.

Unlike rice, which relies on an exact ratio of water to grains, beans cook in ample water, making the process a bit less exacting. Use a larger pot than you think you need: beans roughly double in size from dried to cooked (e.g., 2 cups dried will net about 4 cups of cooked beans).

There is a pretty fierce debate about whether or not to soak beans prior to cooking. I prefer to soak them; soaked beans seem to cook more evenly. Soak them on your counter for at least 8 hours—in a pot or bowl, submerged in at least twice their volume of water. The exceptions are smaller beans like lentils, which do not need a soak. You can also opt for a quick soak:

Place the beans in a pot and add water to cover by at least 2 inches. Bring to a boil, then remove the pot from the heat, cover, and let the beans sit in the hot water for 1 hour before proceeding with the recipe.

In addition to the "soak versus no soak" debate, there is also contention about when to season beans. Some schools argue that adding salt too early in the cooking process toughens the beans; others insist that it tenderizes them. Some even salt during the soaking phase. I like a compromise: Salt *after* the beans have cooked but while they're still simmering in the liquid. This way, the salt won't affect the cooking process, but the flavor has a chance to be absorbed.

How to know when they're done cooking? Different beans have different cook times, about 20 minutes for red lentils to about 1 hour for garbanzos. Simmer them until they're plump, tender, and creamy, adding a bit more water along the way if the beans start looking dry. The centers of the beans should be creamy, not crunchy, and if you are making hummus or another purée, cook them for another 15 minutes after they're thoroughly cooked.

Try different liquids and seasonings in your beans. Instead of using water as your cooking liquid, try stock, coconut milk, or a combination of water and crushed tomatoes. Before adding the liquid and the beans, sauté aromatics like chopped onion, garlic, or jalapeño. And feel free to throw in a citrus peel, a piece of kombu, or a bay leaf while the beans simmer.

Teaching Recipe

JOSÉ'S BLACK BEANS

SERVES 8

José has worked at Haven's Kitchen since the day we opened. He learned to make *moro*, a dish of rice, beans, and vegetables, as a boy in the Dominican Republic. Every family has their own version of *moro*, but no matter the differences, rice and beans is always a comforting, fortifying, and economical meal. Serve this in a bowl with the cooking broth, a dollop of good sour cream, and Tomatillo Salsa (page 312).

1 POUND (ABOUT 2½ CUPS) DRIED BLACK BEANS

EXTRA-VIRGIN OLIVE OIL

1 CELERY STALK, DICED

½ ONION, DICED

2 JALAPEÑO OR FRESNO CHILES, STEMMED, SEEDED, AND MINCED

4 GARLIC CLOVES, MINCED

4 SCALLIONS (WHITE AND GREEN PARTS), THINLY SLICED

¼ BUNCH OF CILANTRO (ABOUT 8 STEMS), ROUGHLY CHOPPED

2 FLAT-LEAF PARSLEY SPRIGS, ROUGHLY CHOPPED

2 OREGANO SPRIGS

FINE SEA SALT

FRESHLY SQUEEZED LIME JUICE

SORT

❶ Sort through the beans, picking out and discarding any pebbles or foreign objects.

COOKING NOTES

After measuring the beans, sort them: there's nothing less pleasant than biting into a rock. The easiest method is to pour them onto a baking sheet so you can quickly scan for and discard any stones, odd clumps, or other foreign objects.

continued

SOAK

❷ In a pot or large bowl, soak the beans for at least 8 hours. Then drain and rinse them and set aside.

Soaking beans cuts down on simmering time and allows for even cooking. If you are lucky enough to find superfresh beans, they rehydrate more quickly and require less soaking time. See Resources (page 366) for my beans of preference, or buy them at your local farmers' market.

BUILD FLAVOR

❸ Heat a large pot over medium heat; then pour in enough oil to cover the bottom of the pot. When the oil begins to shimmer, add the celery, onion, chiles, and a pinch of salt. Add the garlic after about a minute. Sweat until the aromatics have softened but not browned, and the onion is translucent, about 4 minutes. Stir in the scallions, cilantro, parsley, and oregano.

Here you're building flavor with aromatics (see page 150 for an in-depth explanation). Sweating is similar to sautéing but uses a lower temperature, cooking the vegetables gently and not allowing them to brown. It helps to add the garlic a minute or so after the celery and onion.

SIMMER

❹ Stir in the beans and cover with double their volume of water. Bring the pot to a boil, then reduce to a simmer and cook, uncovered, until the beans are tender, adding extra water as needed, about 30 minutes. Add a few large pinches of salt. Continue to cook for 40 to 50 minutes, or until the beans are tender and saucy. Taste the beans and add more salt if necessary.

You'll often see the expression "double their volume" in recipes. It means that if the beans come 1 inch up the side of the pot, the water should come up 2 inches. Add extra water if you notice that most of it has been absorbed and the beans look like they're drying out.

How will you know when they're done? Beans should be creamy in the center but still retain their shape. Bite one: it should be tender but neither mushy nor firm ("toothsome"). When the beans look plump, pick one out of the pot and break it in half. The middle of the bean should have the same color as the outer edges; if the center is white or chalky, they need more time.

SEASON

❺ Remove from the heat. Season with lime juice to taste.

You can serve the beans as is, in their broth, or let them cool in the cooking liquid and then drain them. If you intend to store the beans for later, let them cool in their liquid before refrigerating them, covered, for up to 3 days.

One-Bowl Meals

Learning how to master grains and beans opens up a world of recipes. An inspired grain bowl balances texture, flavor, and color. Use these examples as inspiration.

	BASE	VEGETABLE	HEARTY TOPPER	SAUCE	BONUS
SUNDAY BOWL (photo on page 35)	**Quinoa** (see page 34)	**Sautéed kale** (see page 99) and **sliced avocado**	**Fried egg** (see page 180)	**Green Cashew Sauce** (page 325) or **Tahini Dressing** (page 237)	**Toasted pumpkin seeds**
MEZE BOWL	**Bulgur** or **Mujaddara** (see page 47)	**Fresh spinach**, **chopped cucumber**	**Falafel** (page 83) and/ or **Lamb Kofta** (page 284)	**Greek Yogurt Dressing** (page 240)	**Lemon zest**
THAI-INSPIRED BOWL	**Rice** (see page 31), cooked in half water, half coconut milk (see page 151)	**Carrots, julienned** (see page 9)	**Grilled Chicken Paillard** (page 271)	**Peanut Sauce** (page 324)	**Peanuts**, toasted and chopped; **chopped cilantro** or **Thai basil**
AUTUMN BOWL (photo opposite)	**Wheat berries** (1 cup grain : 3 cups water; start checking for doneness at 30 minutes)	**Sautéed rainbow chard** (see page 99)	**Roasted cauliflower** (see page 112)	**Romesco Sauce** (page 320)	**Toasted almonds** and **chopped parsley**
NORTHERN ITALIAN—INSPIRED BOWL	**Polenta** (see page 56)	**Crispy Sautéed Mushrooms** (page 102)	**Poached egg** (see page 170)	**Fresh Tomato Sauce** (page 307)	**Grated Parmigiano-Reggiano**
HAVEN'S KITCHEN STAFF MEAL BOWL	**White rice** (see page 31) and **José's Black Beans** (page 39)	**Sliced avocado**	**Pork Salsa Verde** (page 289)	**Tomatillo Salsa** (page 312)	**Superquick Pickled Red Onions** (page 111)

AUTUMN BOWL
opposite

BIBIMBAP

SERVES 4

Bibimbap, a centuries-old Korean dish, essentially means "mixed rice" and has an infinite number of variations. You could call it the forerunner of the contemporary grain bowl.

GINGER-GARLIC VINEGAR SAUCE
(PAGE 311)

4 CUPS COOKED RICE, BROWN OR WHITE
(SEE PAGE 31)

GINGER-GARLIC TOFU (PAGE 331) OR
GRILLED CHICKEN PAILLARD (PAGE 271)

1 CUP QUICK PICKLED CUCUMBERS
(PAGE 110), THINLY SLICED

NEUTRAL-FLAVORED OIL,
SUCH AS GRAPESEED OR CANOLA

1 POUND (4 TO 6 CUPS) MIXED MUSHROOMS,
SUCH AS BUTTON, CREMINI, AND SHIITAKE,
TRIMMED AND CUT INTO 1-INCH PIECES

FINE SEA SALT

1 BUNCH OF CHARD, KALE, OR OTHER
WINTER GREENS, DESTEMMED AND
CHOPPED (ABOUT 2 CUPS)

4 FRIED EGGS (SEE PAGE 180)

1 CUP GRATED CARROTS

SESAME SEEDS, TOASTED (SEE PAGE 18),
FOR GARNISH

❶ Make the ginger-garlic sauce.

❷ Prepare the rice, the tofu or chicken, and the pickles. Everything can be made a day in advance and served at room temperature.

❸ Warm a large sauté pan over medium-high heat. Pour in enough oil to generously coat the bottom of the pan. When the oil begins to shimmer, add the mushrooms. Do not crowd the pan, or the mushrooms will steam and not brown. Work in two batches if necessary. Sauté, flipping and tossing the mushrooms, until most of the residual moisture has evaporated and the mushrooms have browned, 12 to 15 minutes. Season with salt. Set aside on a plate and wipe out the pan.

❹ Warm the pan over medium heat. Pour in enough oil to coat the bottom of the pan.

When the oil begins to shimmer, add half of the chard and stir. When the first batch wilts, after 3 or 4 minutes, add the remaining chard and a pinch of salt. Toss for another minute or two, or until all the chard is wilted. Remove from the heat and use a slotted spoon to transfer the chard to a bowl, leaving behind as much of the liquid as possible.

❺ Discard the liquid from the pan, wipe down the pan, and fry the eggs.

❻ To serve, you can set out all the ingredients and have everyone assemble their own bibimbap bowl. Or, equally divide the rice, tofu or chicken, cucumbers, carrots, mushrooms, and chard among four bowls. Top each one with a fried egg. Garnish with sesame seeds and serve with the ginger-garlic sauce.

MUJADDARA

SERVES 6

If there was ever a winner of a recipe, it's mujaddara, a Middle Eastern dish that combines rice, lentils, and delicious crispy onions in one bowl. It's ideal for practicing cooking both grains *and* beans. Eat it hot for sure, but don't be afraid to eat the leftovers cold.

1¼ CUPS GREEN OR BROWN LENTILS

FINE SEA SALT

4 YELLOW ONIONS, SLICED INTO THIN HALF-MOONS

1 CUP ALL-PURPOSE FLOUR

1 CUP NEUTRAL-FLAVORED OIL, SUCH AS GRAPESEED OR CANOLA

2 TEASPOONS CUMIN SEEDS

1½ TABLESPOONS CORIANDER SEEDS

1 CINNAMON STICK

2 TABLESPOONS EXTRA-VIRGIN OLIVE OIL

1 CUP BASMATI RICE

1½ CUPS WATER

¼ CUP CHOPPED MINCED DILL

1 CUP PLAIN GREEK YOGURT

❶ Put the lentils in a saucepan, cover with plenty of water, salt well, and bring to a boil. Reduce to a simmer and cook, uncovered, over medium heat until the lentils are cooked through, 30 to 40 minutes. Drain and set aside.

❷ While the lentils are cooking, fry the onions: In a large bowl, toss the onions in the flour. Set up a station for the cooked onions—place a wire rack inside a paper towel–lined baking sheet. Heat the vegetable oil in a lidded large skillet over medium-high heat. When the oil begins to shimmer, shake any excess flour from the onions and use tongs to lower a handful into the hot oil. Fry until golden, about 5 minutes, Use tongs to transfer the onions to the prepared rack or paper towels. Continue frying in batches, making sure not to crowd the pan. Season the onions with salt. Discard the oil and wipe down the pan.

❸ In the same pan, toast the cumin, coriander, and cinnamon over medium heat until fragrant, about 1 minute. Add the olive oil and rice, stir to coat the grains, and toast for another 30 seconds. Add the water and 2 hefty pinches of salt. Bring to a boil, then cover the pot and reduce the heat to the lowest setting. Cook for about 15 minutes, or until the rice is tender.

❹ Mix in the cooked lentils. Cover the pot once again, remove from the heat, and allow to sit for 10 minutes.

❺ Meanwhile, stir the dill into the Greek yogurt.

❻ Remove the cinnamon stick and gently stir in half of the fried onions. Transfer to a serving plate and garnish with the remaining fried onions and the dill yogurt.

MULTIGRAIN BREAKFAST PORRIDGE

SERVES 6

In this recipe, multiple grains are cooked together to create a thick, creamy porridge. Each grain has a different cooking time, so some end up a bit softer than others, lending a hearty but varied texture. This recipe can be adapted and customized, so explore different grains and garnishes, keeping the grain-to-liquid ratio the same. For a shorter cooking time, soak the grains in a pot with the water and coconut milk and salt overnight in the fridge; when ready to cook, simply transfer to a pot and cook according to the directions below for 20 to 40 minutes. Serve with your desired toppings.

4 CUPS WATER

ONE 15-OUNCE CAN COCONUT MILK

½ CUP WHEAT BERRIES

½ CUP QUINOA

¼ CUP AMARANTH

¼ CUP MILLET

¼ CUP ROLLED OR STEEL-CUT OATS

FINE SEA SALT

¼ CUP UNSWEETENED COCONUT FLAKES

¼ CUP SLIVERED ALMONDS

2 TABLESPOONS HONEY, OR TO TASTE

½ TEASPOON GROUND CINNAMON

¼ CUP DRIED CHERRIES OR DRIED FRUIT OF CHOICE

FLAKY SEA SALT, SUCH AS MALDON, TO FINISH

❶ Combine the water, coconut milk, wheat berries, quinoa, amaranth, millet, and oats with a pinch of fine sea salt in a medium pot. Bring to a boil, then reduce to a simmer and cook, uncovered, over medium-low heat, stirring occasionally, until the grains are cooked, 40 to 60 minutes. The grains should look plump and hydrated.

❷ While the grains are cooking, heat a small sauté pan over medium heat. Toast the coconut flakes and almonds in the dry pan until fragrant and light golden, 30 seconds to 1 minute. Remove from the heat and set aside.

❸ When the grains are cooked, stir in the honey, cinnamon, and fine sea salt to taste.

❹ Serve the porridge in individual bowls and top with the coconut, almonds, dried cherries, and a small pinch of flaky sea salt. Store any leftovers in an airtight container in the refrigerator for 3 to 5 days. Porridge can be reheated over medium heat with a little water or milk.

FRIED RICE

SERVES 4

Fried rice is best made using cold leftover rice. The grains don't clump or get mushy when you fry them. If you are using freshly cooked rice, spread it out on a baking sheet and place it in the fridge for 10 minutes to chill before frying. This recipe works well with most vegetables, so try substitutions. You can serve this alone or with grilled salmon (see page 261) or crispy tofu (see page 331) on top and a drizzle of Ginger-Garlic Vinegar Sauce (see page 311).

2 CUPS COOKED AND CHILLED RICE, SUCH AS BASMATI, SHORT-GRAIN WHITE, OR BROWN RICE (SEE PAGE 31)	4 SCALLIONS (WHITE AND GREEN PARTS), THINLY SLICED
NEUTRAL-FLAVORED OIL, SUCH AS GRAPESEED OR CANOLA	½ TEASPOON MINCED FRESH GINGER
1 SMALL ONION, FINELY DICED	1 TEASPOON SOY SAUCE
1 MEDIUM CARROT, CUT INTO SMALL DICE	½ TEASPOON TOASTED SESAME OIL
½ CUP FRESH PEAS, BLANCHED AND SHOCKED (SEE PAGE 95)	2 EGGS
	FINE SEA SALT
	½ TEASPOON WHITE PEPPER

❶ Transfer the chilled rice to a bowl and gently toss it with your hands to break up any clumps.

❷ Heat a large wok or sauté pan over high heat. Pour in enough vegetable oil to generously coat the bottom of the pan, and heat until the oil begins to shimmer. Add half of the rice and cook, stirring, until the rice is pale brown and toasted, and has a slightly chewy texture, about 3 minutes. Transfer to a medium bowl. Add more oil and repeat with the remaining rice.

❸ Return all the rice to the wok and press it up the sides, leaving a space in the middle. Add another drizzle of oil to the middle of the pan, allow the oil to heat, and then add

the onion, carrot, peas, about three-quarters of the scallions, and the ginger and cook, stirring occasionally, until softened and fragrant, about 1 minute. Pull the rice into the center of the pan and mix it with the vegetables. Add the soy sauce and sesame oil and toss to coat.

❹ Push the rice to the sides of the wok again and add another drizzle of vegetable oil to the center. Break the eggs into the oil and season with a small pinch of salt. Use a spatula to scramble the eggs, breaking them up into small bits. When the eggs are almost set, mix with the rice. Add the pepper and salt to taste.

❺ Top with the remaining scallions.

CLASSIC RISOTTO

SERVES 4

A slowly stirred, Milanese-style risotto makes for soothing yet decadent cold-weather eating. A cross between a porridge and a soup, risotto is a satisfying meal on its own served in a shallow bowl with freshly grated Parmigiano-Reggiano. The key to good risotto is the highly starchy arborio or carnaroli rice. The starches release as the rice cooks, creating a creamy, saucy texture. To avoid gloppy, gooey risotto, stir often and aggressively with a wooden spoon—do not use a whisk. The bonus is that if you have enough left over, it can be transformed into Arancini (page 86). Serve risotto with an arugula salad and Shallot Vinaigrette (page 231), and a glass of crisp white Italian wine.

---

1 TABLESPOON OLIVE OIL

2 SHALLOTS, FINELY DICED

FINE SEA SALT

2 CUPS ARBORIO OR CARNAROLI RICE

1½ CUPS DRY WHITE WINE

4 CUPS CHICKEN STOCK (SEE PAGE 269) OR VEGETABLE STOCK (SEE PAGE 146)

4 TABLESPOONS (½ STICK) UNSALTED BUTTER

½ CUP FRESHLY GRATED PARMIGIANO-REGGIANO

---

❶ Heat a heavy-bottomed pot or Dutch oven over medium heat. Add the oil and shallots and a pinch of salt and cook, stirring continuously, until the shallots are translucent but not yet browned, about 3 minutes.

❷ Stir in the rice and cook until slightly toasted and fragrant, about 2 minutes.

❸ Pour in the wine and cook until almost entirely evaporated.

❹ Add 1 cup of the stock. Cook, stirring often, until the rice has absorbed most of the liquid. Adjust the heat as needed so that the liquid simmers. Add another 1 cup of the

stock and cook, stirring often, until the rice once again absorbs most of the liquid. Repeat to add the remaining stock in two more additions. The risotto is done when the rice is creamy and tender (from the release of the starch during cooking) but still has bite, 20 to 25 minutes total cooking time. If you've used all the stock and the risotto isn't done, add water and continue cooking. Stir often and be careful not to scorch the grains on the bottom of the pot.

❺ Remove from the heat and add the butter and cheese. Once the butter has melted, stir well and taste, seasoning with salt as needed. Serve immediately.

FARRO RISOTTO WITH MUSHROOMS

SERVES 4

Though not a traditional risotto, this version is nutty and creamy, and less demanding in the stirring department. Because of its sturdy bran, farro does not release starches in the same way as arborio rice, but you still get the comforting porridge feel of risotto—just with a heartier texture.

5 CUPS VEGETABLE STOCK (SEE PAGE 146), CHICKEN STOCK (SEE PAGE 269), OR WATER

1 CUP DRIED PORCINI OR SHIITAKE MUSHROOMS

2 TABLESPOONS UNSALTED BUTTER

1 SHALLOT, FINELY DICED

FINE SEA SALT

1½ CUPS FARRO

½ CUP DRY WHITE WINE

2 BATCHES CRISPY SAUTÉED MUSHROOMS (PAGE 102)

½ CUP FRESHLY GRATED PARMIGIANO-REGGIANO

¼ CUP CHOPPED FRESH FLAT-LEAF PARSLEY (OPTIONAL)

❶ In a medium saucepan, combine the stock and the dried mushrooms. Bring to a boil over high heat, then reduce to a simmer and cook for 15 minutes to infuse the water with mushroom flavor. Strain, reserving the liquid and discarding the mushrooms.

❷ In a medium Dutch oven or other heavy-bottomed large pot, melt the butter over medium heat. Add the shallot and a pinch of salt and cook until tender, about 1 minute. Add the farro and toast until fragrant, about 3 minutes, stirring frequently.

❸ Pour in the wine and cook until it is almost entirely evaporated, about 3 minutes.

❹ Pour in the mushroom stock you just made and bring to a boil, then reduce to a simmer and cook over low heat until the farro is tender, stirring frequently with a wooden spoon, about 30 minutes.

❺ While the farro is cooking, sauté the mushrooms according to the recipe on page 102.

❻ When the farro is cooked, remove from the heat and fold in the Parmigiano-Reggiano. Divide among serving plates and top with the sautéed mushrooms and Parmigiano-Reggiano. Sprinkle with parsley if desired.

POLENTA

Polenta is a dish made with medium or coarsely ground cornmeal. This recipe creates the opportunity to build a one-bowl grain-based meal for any time of the day—breakfast, lunch, or dinner. For this recipe, do not use the instant variety of polenta. Instead, take the time to cook it slowly. Serve polenta with sautéed greens (see page 99) or roasted mushrooms (see page 116) with a poached or fried egg (see pages 170 and 180) and Fresh Tomato Sauce (page 307).

5 CUPS WATER OR CHICKEN STOCK
(SEE PAGE 269)

FINE SEA SALT

1 CUP POLENTA OR COARSE
YELLOW CORNMEAL

½ CUP FINELY GRATED
PARMIGIANO-REGGIANO

FRESHLY GROUND BLACK PEPPER

4 TABLESPOONS (½ STICK) UNSALTED
BUTTER OR MASCARPONE (OPTIONAL)

❶ Bring the liquid to a boil and add a large pinch of salt. Whisk in the polenta (whisking prevents clumping and lumps). It should start to thicken immediately.

❷ Reduce the heat to the lowest setting and simmer, stirring frequently so the polenta does not burn on the bottom. As the polenta begins to thicken, switch from a whisk to a wooden spoon. Cook, continuing to stir often, until the polenta has absorbed all the water and is creamy and smooth, 20 to 30 minutes.

❸ Remove from the heat and season with Parmigiano-Reggiano and salt and pepper to taste. For additional richness, finish with butter or mascarpone.

HUMMUS

MAKES ABOUT 3 CUPS

You'll find hummus so easy to make on your own, and so much creamier and tastier than any brands at the grocery store, that you may never go back to store-bought. Some people drop the garlic completely, while I add a generous four cloves; experiment a few times to see how much you like. This recipe makes a lot of hummus, so be prepared: Serve as a dip, or spread on sandwiches of toasted whole-grain bread with sliced cucumbers, peppers, and tomato. Save some for tomorrow's lunch. It'll keep in the refrigerator for a week.

Remember to start soaking the garbanzos the day before you want to make the hummus.

1 CUP DRIED GARBANZOS	¼ CUP EXTRA-VIRGIN OLIVE OIL, PLUS MORE FOR DRIZZLING
FINE SEA SALT	¼ TO ½ CUP COLD WATER
2 TO 4 GARLIC CLOVES	OPTIONAL GARNISHES: A DRIZZLE OF TAHINI, A LARGE PINCH OF ZA'ATAR, ALEPPO PEPPER, OR CHOPPED FRESH CILANTRO OR PARSLEY
⅓ CUP TAHINI	
JUICE OF 1 LEMON	

❶ Soak the garbanzos in about 4 cups water at room temperature for at least 8 hours.

❷ Drain and rinse the garbanzos and place in a medium saucepan. Cover with ample water and bring to a boil. Reduce to a simmer and cook over medium-low heat until the garbanzos are soft and some are almost falling apart, about 1 hour. Remove from the heat, add a large pinch of salt, and let sit for 15 minutes. Drain.

❸ In the bowl of a food processor fitted with the metal chopping blade, pulse the garlic until roughly chopped. Add the garbanzos and pulse until fine and crumbled, about 30 seconds, pushing down the sides with a spatula as needed.

❹ Add the tahini, lemon juice, olive oil, and ¼ cup water. Blend until smooth, about 3 minutes, adding more water and salt as needed.

❺ Place the hummus in a serving bowl, drizzle with some olive oil, and top with the garnishes of your choice if desired.

❻ Store the hummus in an airtight container in the refrigerator if not serving immediately.

FRITTERS

CHAPTER 2 | A LESSON IN

Mise en Place

QUINOA BROCCOLI PATTIES

LATKES

MIXED VEGETABLE TEMPURA

PAKORA

FALAFEL

ARANCINI

APPLE BEIGNETS

"Once you start cooking, one thing leads to another.
A new recipe is as exciting as a blind date."

—BARBARA KINGSOLVER

AT HAVEN'S KITCHEN, WE TEACH students how to make fritters because whether it's a class on Southeast Asian, Spanish, or Middle Eastern food, there's a fritter that embodies the flavors of that region. Around the globe, street vendors and home cooks alike tantalize crowds of eager eaters with some version of a piping hot, delicately crispy fried ball or patty—each with its own spicy, sweet, or savory sauce.

Fritters are remarkably versatile and satisfying over a salad or wrapped in a warm pita, and hearty enough to be the center of attention. They also make a great fridge-cleaner-outer, perfect for those nights when you find yourself with some random parsley, two lone eggs left over from the weekend, and half a bowl of grains that no one knows what to do with.

But teaching frittering serves another purpose too: making them illustrates a fundamental building block of confident cooking—the art of organization and the genius of *mise en place*, the French culinary term meaning "everything in its place." If you've ever been in a professional kitchen or watched a cooking show, you've noticed lots of little bowls and containers holding chopped, diced, pickled, and otherwise prepared ingredients—all measured and properly cut, and placed in a sensible spot adjacent to the stovetop or whatever appliance or gadget they're destined for. They are the solution to a home cook's biggest challenges: time, space, and confidence.

Set yourself up for success with an uncluttered cutting board, an organized staging area where you prep and mix ingredients, a dredging or battering station, and a landing station for cooling near the frying pan. And before you practice, ask yourself the following questions.

☐ Did I read the recipe twice so I know the ingredients and the goal?

☐ Is there anything I need to do to my ingredients ahead of time?

☐ How will I serve my fritters? Do I need to make a sauce?

☐ What's the most efficient way to set up the kitchen?

☐ How am I forming the fritters? Am I battering? Am I dredging?

☐ Do the fritters need to rest or chill before frying?

☐ Am I deep-frying or panfrying?

The more organized your mise en place, the more efficient, tidier, and happier you'll be while cooking.

Tools

The Boy Scout motto "Be prepared" may have been coined for a test in the woods, but it also applies to endeavors in the kitchen. Fritter making illustrates the value of setting up a wire rack in advance, presents a compelling case for a thermometer, and proves the worth of a large, reliable pot. The following list of tools may seem like a lot, but you will use them every time you cook; having the right "stuff" and knowing how to use it will help you feel less stressed and more playful in the kitchen.

LARGE, HEAVY-BOTTOMED SAUTÉ PAN WITH A LID

A large, heavy-bottomed sauté pan is best for shallow panfrying because of its higher vertical sides. About 12 inches across is ideal: big enough to hold four patties at a time without crowding them. A pan made of stainless steel is optimal, although cast iron also works. The heavy bottom will keep the temperature of the cooking oil stable, ensuring more consistent results.

LARGE, HEAVY POT

When deep-frying, it is important to have a large, heavy pot with tall sides. An 8-quart stainless steel pot can hold enough oil to cover whatever you are frying plus 1 more inch, with at least 3 inches of clearance above. Dutch ovens are also excellent for frying as they have a wide base and tall sides and are usually made of cast iron, which regulates heat efficiently. We recommend an 8-quart pot.

THERMOMETER

Use a thermometer to take all the guesswork and anxiety out of fritter cooking, which entails heating the oil to an exact temperature. I suggest an infrared model: it allows you to read the external temperature without having to make physical contact, ensuring a clean and easy process.

FISH SPATULA

When panfrying, a thin, flexible, slotted metal spatula, such as a fish spatula, is the tool of choice for gently placing fritters in the hot oil, flipping them, and then transferring them to a rack.

SPIDER

A spider is the professional kitchen's slotted spoon. A shallow wire basket secured to a handle, it is a great tool for scooping items from the hot oil when deep-frying. (It's also useful for removing vegetables from hot water when blanching.)

BAKING SHEET AND WIRE RACK

Set up a "landing station" beside your deep fryer so you have somewhere to place the fritters as soon as they come out of the oil. A baking sheet lined with a wire rack is ideal because it allows air flow around the entire fritter, ensuring proper drainage of excess oil and helping to maintain crispiness. If you don't have a wire rack, you can instead line a plate or baking sheet with paper towels, but the bottom of your fritters may become slightly soggy.

Teaching Recipe

QUINOA BROCCOLI PATTIES

MAKES 8

Use this fritter recipe as a template for (1) how to set up your mise en place and (2) how to create your own fritter recipe. Notice how the recipe introduction, or headnote, while giving great serving suggestions, is equally excellent at providing clues for preparation. Because of their fairly universal proportions of ingredients, these fritters are easy to customize with different ingredients.

Serve the patties with Fresh Tomato Sauce for dunking, or over a bed of tender green lettuce with wedges of plump, ripe tomatoes, and drizzled with Greek Yogurt Dressing.

FRESH TOMATO SAUCE (PAGE 307) OR GREEK YOGURT DRESSING (PAGE 240) (OPTIONAL)

1 CUP COARSELY CHOPPED BROCCOLI FLORETS, STEAMED

2 CUPS COOKED QUINOA (SEE PAGE 34)

2 LARGE EGGS, WHISKED

FINE SEA SALT AND FRESHLY GROUND BLACK PEPPER

1 CUP PANKO BREAD CRUMBS, PLUS MORE AS NEEDED

½ CUP GRATED SHARP CHEDDAR

2 GARLIC CLOVES, MINCED

ABOUT 8 FLAT-LEAF PARSLEY SPRIGS, CHOPPED

EXTRA-VIRGIN OLIVE OIL, FOR FRYING

FLAKY SEA SALT, SUCH AS MALDON, TO FINISH

continued

ORGANIZE

❶ Make the Fresh Tomato Sauce or Greek Yogurt Dressing, and refrigerate until ready to use.

❷ Prepare the ingredients according to the list above.

❸ Set up your landing station by lining a sheet pan with a wire rack and having a fish spatula handy.

BASE

❹ In a large bowl, mix the cooked and cooled quinoa and the steamed broccoli florets.

BINDER

❺ Whisk the salt and pepper with the egg in a small bowl and add to the broccoli and quinoa mixture. Add the panko and mix to combine.

COOKING NOTES

Organization is instrumental to good cooking and will set you up for success. It's important to think through your recipe and prepare the ingredients accordingly. Be efficient and consider what needs to be made in advance, such as the dressing, quinoa, and broccoli, and the order in which things need to cut, cooked, and ready.

When frying, it's a useful step to set up your landing station and pull out any other tools or equipment you will need for each stage of cooking.

The base is the main body of a fritter. Several things are important to keep in mind when preparing the base: (1) what needs to be made in advance; (2) the ideal size of any chopped pieces and the need to keep them uniform; and (3) how watery the ingredients are—too wet and you won't get crispy fritters.

The binder is the "glue" that holds the ingredients together. In this recipe, the eggs and the bread crumbs are the binder. The panko absorbs any excess moisture, while the eggs are a mortar.

For fritters like Pakora (page 81) or Apple Beignets (page 89), the batter is what binds vegetables or fruit together.

Whisking the eggs and salt and pepper before adding them to the base ensures that the salt is dissolved and is evenly distributed.

BONUS

6 Mix the Cheddar, garlic, and parsley into the quinoa mixture. Refrigerate for 15 minutes, until the panko has absorbed the excess moisture and has a texture like that of wet sand.

Ingredients like herbs, garlic, onions, spices, and cheese build the flavor and texture of a fritter. In this recipe, salt, pepper, and garlic add flavor, Cheddar gives the fritter the right touch of gooeyness, and fresh parsley brightens everything. Avoid pre-grated cheese. It loses flavor rapidly.

Garlic should be smooth, not chunky, for better flavor and texture.

Refrigerating the mixture allows it to set.

FORM THE PATTIES

7 Divide the mixture into 8 equal balls, then press and flatten into ¾-inch-thick patties.

The mixture should be just dry enough to bind together and form a patty. If it is too wet, add more panko, but be careful not to make it too dry.

TOO WET

TOO DRY

JUST RIGHT

FRYING

❽ Place a 12-inch sauté pan over medium-high heat. When it's hot, pour in enough oil to generously cover the bottom of the pan and heat until it begins to shimmer. Add the patties and sear until the edges are golden brown, 2 to 3 minutes. Flip and cook the second side for another 2 to 3 minutes, or until a deep golden brown.

For panfried fritters, heat the oil just before frying, as it takes only a minute or so to heat. As a rule, the thicker and darker the oil, the less amenable it is for frying. A more refined neutral-flavored oil, like grapeseed or canola, is better for high-heat cooking. The fritters in this recipe aren't deep-fried and cook rather quickly, so olive oil is okay.

You are aiming for a crispy fritter, so work in batches. You want an uncrowded pan with enough room to easily flip the patties.

SEASONING

❾ Transfer the fritters to the rack or plate and immediately sprinkle with flaky sea salt. Serve hot with your preferred sauce or dressing if desired.

Hot fritters are the best fritters.

Add salt while the fritters are hot so the flakes stick to the surface.

Tips for Frittering

Let's say you like the recipe for latkes but want to make them with zucchini, or you'd prefer feta instead of Cheddar in your quinoa patty. Perhaps you've got ingredients in your refrigerator that you think would come together nicely in fritter form. Once you get familiar with these tips, you can make a fritter with almost anything. When you do try your own variations, keep the following principles in mind.

THE BASE INGREDIENTS

All the vegetables in the base must be uniformly cut or shredded and small enough to cook all the way through, without burning, in the few minutes it takes for the exterior to turn crisp and golden. For the fritter to cook evenly, all ingredients must cook at the same pace. This means not only making uniform cuts but also parcooking in advance any vegetables that take longer to cook. If you're using grains for the base, or a combination of vegetables and grains, make sure they are cooled down. Hot grains will absorb more moisture and make it more difficult to achieve the right texture.

MOISTURE

The secret to a crispy exterior is eliminating as much water as possible from the base ingredients. A too-moist fritter will steam in the pan (rather than crisping) and splatter (water and hot oil do not mix). How you extract moisture depends on the vegetable and how it's cut; excess liquid can be removed by salting the vegetables (good for potatoes and summer squash), straining them through a fine-mesh strainer, or wringing them out in a clean kitchen towel. Other vegetables that need to be parcooked—like broccoli or cauliflower—as well as cooked beans and grains can be spread out on a clean kitchen towel to absorb excess moisture.

BONUS INGREDIENTS: FLAVOR COUNTERPOINTS

Balance and counterpoints are discussed often in this book (for example, see page 297). In fritters, the bonus ingredients act as counterpoints to the base. As you scan your refrigerator or browse the market, consider your base ingredients and how the flavors you want can enhance them. If your base is 3 to 4 cups of zucchini, for example, the bonus could be ½ cup feta for tanginess and a creamy touch. You might want to include 1 to 2 cups of chopped scallions or another allium like minced onion, shallot, or garlic. You could go in a nutty direction, adding a handful (or about ¼ cup) of pine nuts or chopped almonds. The thing to remember is that your base is still the zucchini and these other ingredients should be added in relationship to your base and one another. Dried spices, herbs, and condiments pack a punch, so use sparingly.

Here are some of our favorite bonus ingredients:

Cheese
Grated or crumbled feta, Parmigiano-Reggiano, or goat cheese.

Flavoring alliums
Raw or sautéed diced onions or shallots or chopped scallions.

Fresh leafy herbs
Chopped herbs, such as parsley, mint, cilantro, tarragon, or dill.

Potent herbs
Fresh oregano, thyme, savory, marjoram, or rosemary; no more than a large pinch.

Dried spices
Za'atar, Aleppo pepper, paprika, or cumin.

Condiments
Mustard, a hot sauce such as harissa, or even ketchup.

Crunch
Sesame seeds, sunflower seeds, or chopped toasted nuts.

BINDER

Patties like the quinoa broccoli fritters (see page 63) need a binder to hold the ingredients together. For 3 to 4 cups of the base, use 2 whisked eggs and at least ½ cup of flour or bread crumbs. The binder also helps to absorb moisture from the base. As you get more comfortable making your own fritters, you'll start to know what you need to achieve the right texture and ratios.

TASTE—AND TEST

The best cooks taste their food and adjust along the way. As you become a more confident cook, you'll know when a dish needs a little more salt, or a touch more spice or acid. You'll start to know what textures to look for, and what ingredients work together. Taste everything, and frequently. In this case, spare yourself from an entire batch of so-so fritters by making a tester. Make one patty, and before shaping and breading the whole batch, fry it and taste it. If the mixture needs adjusting, you haven't wasted any time or ingredients. If your fritter doesn't crisp, raise the oil temperature. If it falls apart, you may need more binder.

Fear of Frying

The mere mention of frying in classes at Haven's Kitchen conjures a host of feelings ranging from delight to fear—delight when the students think about *eating* what they're about to make, and fear when they think about frying in their homes. When our students express their concerns, here's how we respond:

- **Will I burn myself?** Not if you take the time to get organized and use the proper techniques (like gently laying the fritters into the oil) and tools (like a slotted spoon or spider). Remember to always start with a dry pan before pouring in any oil, and use dry hands or utensils to transfer the fritters to and from the hot oil.

- **It's so much oil!** True, it can be a lot of oil. However, if you're cooking at the proper temperature, that oil is not being absorbed by your fritter but simply cooking it.

- **What do I do with the oil after frying?** Oil used for deep-frying at home can be reused; after all, it feels like a waste to discard it after one use. But reusing oil requires carefully straining out all of the little bits of fried batter, taking care not to burn it. If you do plan on reusing the oil, let it cool, strain it, and store it in an airtight container. When you discard the oil, first pour it into an empty can and store it in the freezer; when the can is full, toss it in the garbage. Oil should not go down your sink drain, because it can congeal and clog your pipes, which are connected to a much larger ecosystem. Ideally we want to keep cooking oil from ending up in our rivers, lakes, and oceans.

FRYING OIL

Frying is the only cooking technique capable of achieving that satisfying crunch we know and love. The trick? Hot oil.

And because the oil gets so hot, it is important to select one with a high smoke point—the temperature when the oil starts to smoke.

When oil goes beyond its smoke point, the oil not only turns bitter but also releases chemicals that are considered carcinogenic. Not good for you, not good for your food.

As a rule, the thicker and darker the oil, the lower its smoke point and the less suited it is for frying. A more refined oil is better for high-heat cooking, and also more neutral in flavor. Canola, grapeseed, sunflower, and peanut oil are all great candidates. For thinner patties like latkes, which cook quickly, you can use olive oil.

PANFRYING

This is the ideal method for fritters like Latkes (page 75) or the Quinoa Broccoli Patties (page 63). Heat a large sauté pan over medium heat. Heating the pan first gets the oil hot quicker and prevents it from burning. Pour in at least ¼ inch of high-heat oil. Test for readiness by holding your hand a few inches over the pan—you should be able to hold it there for no more than 10 seconds comfortably. Does the oil shimmer? It's probably ready for your first fritter. When you place in the fritter, it should promptly sizzle; if not, the oil is not hot enough. If you are uncertain, dip the handle of a wooden spoon or a wooden chopstick into the oil to see if bubbles form around it. You don't need a thermometer for panfrying, but make sure the temperature is correct by testing a small piece of whatever you are frying: it should sizzle continuously and turn golden within a few minutes.

DEEP-FRYING

This method is used for frying or anything that needs to be fully submerged in oil to cook. Play it safe by having a deep enough pot to not only cover the fritters in oil but also give you enough space above to avoid dangerous spills and splatters. The ideal temperature for frying is 350°F. However, when you add your fritters, the temperature drops, so slowly bring the oil up to 360°F on medium heat and then adjust the burner to maintain the temperature around 350°F. An infrared thermometer takes all the guesswork out of the process.

If you don't have a deep-frying thermometer, test the temperature by gently placing a 1-inch cube of bread in the oil. When the oil is at the correct temperature, the bread will sizzle and turn golden brown in about one minute. Be patient; it may take a moment for the oil temperature to adjust when you raise or lower the flame.

When you start adding the fritters, you should see lots of bubbles vigorously escaping from them; if you don't see lots of bubbles, your oil is too cool. You will need to continuously adjust the temperature while cooking, lowering and raising the heat as necessary. If the oil gets too hot, the fritter exteriors will burn while the insides remain uncooked. If the oil is too cool, the fritters will absorb oil and be greasy rather than crisp.

WORKING IN BATCHES

You want to fry things in batches because (1) you don't want the oil to overflow, (2) you want to get even cooking and browning, and (3) adding too many fritters will lower the oil temperature too quickly and they will not get crispy, which is the most important reason you fry.

LATKES

The best latkes (the Yiddish word for potato pancakes) have a potato-chip exterior with a mashed-potato interior. Though simple, latkes are great examples of the balance between crunchy and creamy, the duality of salty and sweet. Popularized in the nineteenth century in Eastern Europe and a traditional Hanukkah dish, latkes are great served as a snack with a dollop of sour cream or applesauce, as a side dish for Roasted Leg of Lamb (page 288), or as the main event surrounded by a few slices of smoked salmon and Quick Pickled Cucumbers (page 110), and garnished with some minced dill.

---

3 IDAHO RUSSET POTATOES, PEELED

1 LARGE EGG, WHISKED

FINE SEA SALT

EXTRA-VIRGIN OLIVE OIL, FOR FRYING

FLAKY SEA SALT, SUCH AS MALDON,
TO FINISH

OPTIONAL BONUSES

¼ CUP SLICED OR DICED ONION

¼ CUP CHOPPED FRESH CHIVES

---

❶ Set up a landing station next to your frying area: place a wire rack on a baking sheet and have a spatula handy.

❷ Using a box grater or a food processor fitted with the shredding blade, grate the potatoes into a large bowl. You should have about 4 cups of shredded potatoes. Wrap the potatoes in a kitchen towel and squeeze out the excess moisture; squeezing should generate about ½ cup of liquid. The potatoes may turn a bit reddish-brown. Don't worry—that's okay!

❸ Put the potatoes back in the bowl. Add the egg and a large pinch of salt (the optional onion or chives also could be added at this

point) and mix the ingredients with your hands. (Yes, your hands! Although you can use a wooden spoon if you prefer.)

❹ Heat a large sauté pan over medium-high heat and pour in ¼ to ½ inch of oil. Wait for the oil to shimmer before forming the patties. You can test the temperature by putting the handle of a wooden spoon or a wooden chopstick into the oil; if it's hot, bubbles will form around it.

❺ Using your nondominant hand, scoop up about ⅓ cup of the mixture. Use the side of the bowl to help form the mixture into a patty. Drain any excess liquid into the bowl, and gently lay the patty in the hot oil. Keep your other hand clean and dry so you can use your spatula and grab a towel if needed. Gently press the latke with the spatula until evenly flat.

6 Fry in batches until the edges brown and get lacy, 2 to 3 minutes. Don't crowd the pan, as you will not get the crispiness you seek. Flip the patties and cook for another 2 to 3 minutes. Continually monitor and adjust the temperature of the oil while frying; too-hot oil will result in burnt edges and raw middles.

7 When the latkes are browned on the second side, use the spatula to transfer them to the wire rack, sprinkle with flaky sea salt, and serve hot.

8 Before frying the next batch, check your oil: if it is dark brown, smells, or is filled with burnt bits, ditch it and start with fresh oil. Wipe down the pan with paper towels, taking care not to burn yourself, and then add more oil to coat the bottom again, heat the oil, and fry the remaining patties.

MIXED VEGETABLE TEMPURA

SERVES 4

The keys to delicate, crisp tempura are to not overmix the batter and to keep it cold. There should be lumps and froth—they give tempura its airiness.

Serve with Ginger-Garlic Vinegar Sauce or like they do in Tokyo, with a pinch of flaky sea salt and a squeeze of lemon. You can also mix 1 part mirin, 1 part shoyu or soy sauce, and 4 parts dashi (see page 149) for a traditional *tentsuyu* dipping sauce.

GINGER-GARLIC VINEGAR SAUCE
(PAGE 311)

VEGETABLE OR CANOLA OIL, FOR FRYING

1½ CUPS PLAIN RICE FLOUR

1 TABLESPOON BAKING POWDER

¾ CUP COLD LAGER-STYLE BEER

¾ CUP COLD SPARKLING WATER

24 PIECES (ABOUT 4 CUPS) OF 3 OR 4 DIFFERENT KINDS OF VEGETABLES, SUCH AS BROCCOLI, CUT INTO LARGE FLORETS; ONIONS, SLICED INTO ½-INCH RINGS; SWEET POTATO, CUT ON THE BIAS INTO ¼-INCH-THICK SLICES; GREEN BEANS, ENDS TRIMMED; AND ASPARAGUS, ENDS TRIMMED

FLAKY SEA SALT, SUCH AS MALDON, TO FINISH

❶ Make the ginger-garlic sauce.

❷ Set up a landing station next to your frying area: place a wire rack on a baking sheet and have a spider or slotted spoon and wooden chopsticks or long tongs handy.

❸ Fill a large, heavy-bottomed pot with enough oil to cover the tempura by at least 1 inch. Heat to 400°F over medium heat. (Note the higher oil temperature for cooking tempura.)

❹ While the oil is heating, prepare the tempura: In a large bowl, combine the rice flour and baking powder. While whisking, gradually pour in the beer and sparkling water, mixing just until combined. Be careful not to overmix; there should be lumps in the batter.

❺ When the oil has reached 400°F, use chopsticks or tongs to dip the vegetables into the batter. Allow the excess to drip off before carefully placing them in the hot oil. Dip only as many as will fit without crowding. Keep the oil temperature steady at 400°F.

❻ Fry the vegetables until light golden and crispy, 3 to 4 minutes. Using the slotted spoon or spider, transfer them to the prepared rack. Sprinkle with flaky salt. Fry the remaining vegetables in uncrowded batches, making sure to allow the oil to return to 400°F before starting the next batch.

❼ Serve hot with your favorite sauce.

PAKORA

SERVES 4 TO 6

Pakora are the star of the show at food carts on bustling street corners in Northern India and Pakistan. A savory, crunchy, deeply seasoned fritter, the pakora uses garbanzo flour to get a nutty crunch. The best part about these fritters is the variety of textures and flavors you can get in one bite—sweet, chewy corn; grated threads of starchy potatoes; and dense bites of cauliflower. Traditionally served with chutney and pickles, they are equally tasty dunked in Sweet Chili Sauce.

SWEET CHILI SAUCE (PAGE 308)

VEGETABLE OR CANOLA OIL, FOR FRYING

1¼ CUPS GARBANZO FLOUR

½ TEASPOON BAKING POWDER

FINE SEA SALT

1 CUP COLD WATER

1½ CUPS CHOPPED OR SLICED VEGETABLES, SUCH AS WHOLE CORN KERNELS, GRATED CARROTS, VERY THINLY SLICED POTATOES, SLICED ZUCCHINI, AND CAULIFLOWER FLORETS

1 SMALL TO MEDIUM YELLOW ONION, VERY THINLY SLICED

1 SMALL HOT CHILE PEPPER, SUCH AS JALAPEÑO, STEMMED, SEEDED, AND MINCED

ONE ½-INCH PIECE OF FRESH GINGER, PEELED AND FINELY CHOPPED

2 TABLESPOONS CHOPPED FRESH CILANTRO

1 GARLIC CLOVE, MINCED

❶ Prepare the sweet chili sauce.

❷ Set up a landing station next to your frying area: place a wire rack on a baking sheet and have a spider or slotted spoon handy.

❸ Fill a large, heavy-bottomed pot with enough oil to fully submerge the fritters. Heat the oil to 360°F over medium heat. The ideal frying temperature is actually 350°F, but the oil will cool slightly when you add the fritters. Heating the oil takes longer than you might anticipate.

❹ While your oil is heating, mix the garbanzo flour, baking powder, and a large pinch of salt in a large bowl. Add the water and stir to incorporate. Mix in the vegetables, onion, and chile pepper. Add the ginger, cilantro, and garlic and stir to combine.

continued

5 When the oil reaches 360°F, use a large serving spoon or ladle to scoop up about ¼ cup of the battered vegetables. Press the spoon against the side of the bowl to allow any excess batter to drip off, and then gently drop the fritter into the hot oil.

6 The size of your pot determines how many pakora you can fry at a time. Just make sure that all the fritters are approximately the same size and that the pot isn't too crowded; otherwise they will not cook evenly. Adjust the heat as needed to maintain a consistent oil temperature of 350°F.

7 Do not disturb the fritters for about 30 seconds, until they form a crust. Once the fritters are golden brown around the edges, use the spider or slotted spoon to flip them. Cook for a total of 1½ to 2 minutes, until golden brown all over, then transfer to the prepared rack and season with salt.

8 Serve hot with the sweet chili sauce.

FALAFEL

MAKES ABOUT FIFTEEN 1½-INCH FALAFEL

Falafel is a crowd-pleaser and a good vegetarian protein option. Serve it with Tahini Sauce (page 295) and a salad of chopped cucumbers and tomatoes drizzled with olive oil and lemon and topped with a large pinch of toasted ground cumin seeds.

1½ CUPS DRIED GARBANZOS	1½ TEASPOONS FINE SEA SALT, PLUS MORE FOR SERVING
½ YELLOW ONION, CHOPPED	
1 GARLIC CLOVE	½ TEASPOON BAKING POWDER
2 SPRIGS FRESH FLAT-LEAF PARSLEY	½ TEASPOON GROUND CUMIN
3 SPRIGS FRESH CILANTRO	½ TEASPOON GROUND CORIANDER
3 TABLESPOONS WATER	¼ TEASPOON CAYENNE
1½ TABLESPOONS WHEAT GERM	VEGETABLE OR CANOLA OIL, FOR FRYING

❶ Soak the garbanzos in a large bowl of water for at least 8 hours.

❷ Line a baking sheet with parchment. Drain the garbanzos well and place them in the bowl of a food processor fitted with the metal chopping blade. Add the onion, garlic, parsley, and cilantro. Pulse to finely chop. The mixture should hold together when pressed, but not be mushy. Transfer to a bowl and add the water, wheat germ, salt, baking powder, cumin, coriander, and cayenne. Mix well until uniform.

❸ Using your hands, mold the mixture into golf ball–sized rounds. Place on the lined baking sheet and refrigerate while heating the oil, about 15 minutes.

❹ Fill a large, heavy-bottomed pot with enough oil to fully submerge the falafel. Heat the oil to 360°F over medium heat.

❺ While the oil is heating, set up your landing station next to your frying area: place a wire rack on a baking sheet and have a spider or slotted spoon and salt handy. Remove your falafel from the fridge.

❻ When the oil reaches 360°F, use the spider or slotted spoon to slowly lower the balls into the pot. The size of your pot determines how many falafel you can fry at a time. Just make sure that the pot isn't too crowded; otherwise the oil will cool. Adjust the heat as needed to maintain a consistent oil temperature of 350°F.

❼ Fry the falafel, stirring occasionally, until dark brown and crispy, about 4 minutes.

❽ Remove the balls with the spider or slotted spoon and let them rest on the rack. Season with salt while hot. Serve immediately.

HOW TO MAKE FALAFEL

1 Don't worry about precision when preparing your vegetables and herbs. Let the food processor do the heavy lifting.

2 Pulse the mixture until it is finely chopped and holds together when pressed into a ball.

3 Form uniform balls for even cooking.

4 Look for a deep brown color. It signifies that the falafel is cooked through.

ARANCINI

Arancini are a great make-ahead party fritter, and the perfect use for leftover risotto (see page 52). To make them ahead of time, after forming the balls (see step 2), freeze them on a parchment-lined baking sheet. When you're ready to fry them, they can go straight from the freezer into the hot oil. Serve with Fresh Tomato Sauce and a glass of Italian white wine.

---

4 CUPS CLASSIC RISOTTO (PAGE 52), COOLED

½ CUP FINELY DICED COOKED VEGETABLES, SUCH AS MUSHROOMS, SQUASH, ASPARAGUS, OR PEAS

½ CUP FRESHLY GRATED PARMIGIANO-REGGIANO

ABOUT 2 CUPS PLAIN RICE FLOUR, FOR COATING

FINE SEA SALT

FRESH TOMATO SAUCE (PAGE 307)

VEGETABLE OR CANOLA OIL, FOR FRYING

---

1 Purée about one-third of the risotto in the bowl of a food processor, and then mix it back in with the remaining cooled risotto. Stir in the vegetables and cheese.

2 Put the rice flour in a shallow bowl and set a large plate next to it. Using a tablespoon measure, scoop a rounded portion of the risotto mixture and use your hands to shape it into a ball. Roll it in the rice flour to coat, shake off the excess, and place on the plate. Continue with the remaining risotto. Place in the refrigerator while heating the oil.

3 Fill a deep, heavy-bottomed pot with enough oil to fully submerge the arancini and heat it on medium to 360°F. The ideal frying temperature is actually 350°F, but the oil will cool slightly when you add the fritters.

4 While the oil is heating, set up a landing station next to your frying area: place a wire rack on a baking sheet and have a spider or slotted spoon handy.

5 When the oil reaches 360°F, working in batches, use the spider or slotted spoon to lower the arancini into the pot. Fry, rotating the arancini occasionally, until golden brown, 4 to 6 minutes. Transfer to the landing station and sprinkle with salt. Fry the remaining arancini, adjusting the heat as needed to maintain a consistent oil temperature of 350°F.

6 Let cool slightly and serve warm with tomato sauce.

FRITTERS

APPLE BEIGNETS

MAKES TWELVE 2-INCH BEIGNETS

It feels a little rebellious to toss in a sweet dish here, but these French-influenced delicacies are quintessential fritters that deserve attention. The dough binds juicy bits of tart apple, and the heat of the fritter gently melts the sugar coating.

VEGETABLE OR CANOLA OIL, FOR FRYING

2 CUPS ALL-PURPOSE FLOUR

⅓ CUP GRANULATED SUGAR

1½ TEASPOONS BAKING POWDER

1 TEASPOON FINE SEA SALT

1 TEASPOON GROUND CINNAMON

¼ TEASPOON GROUND NUTMEG

2 LARGE EGGS

2 TABLESPOONS UNSALTED BUTTER, MELTED

¾ CUP APPLE CIDER

2 LARGE GRANNY SMITH APPLES (OR OTHER TART VARIETY), PEELED AND CUT INTO ¼-INCH DICE

½ CUP CONFECTIONERS' SUGAR

❶ While the oil is heating, set up a landing station next to your frying area: place a wire rack on a baking sheet and have a spider or slotted spoon handy.

❷ Fill a large, heavy-bottomed pot with enough oil to fully submerge the fritters. Heat the oil to 360°F over medium heat. The ideal frying temperature is actually 350°F, but the oil will cool when you add the fritters.

❸ Combine the flour, granulated sugar, baking powder, salt, cinnamon, and nutmeg in a medium bowl and mix well.

❹ In a large bowl, whisk together the eggs, butter, and apple cider. Using a silicone spatula or large spoon, fold the dry ingredients into the egg mixture. Mix until just incorporated, and then fold in the apples. (Adding the dry ingredients to the wet prevents dry clumps.)

❺ When the oil reaches 360°F, ladle about ¼ cup of the batter into the hot oil. Make the beignets the same size and don't crowd them. Adjust the heat as needed to maintain a consistent oil temperature of 350°F.

❻ Fry the beignets for about 2 minutes, or until brown around the edges. Flip them and fry for another 2 minutes. Using the spider or slotted spoon, transfer the beignets to the rack and let cool.

❼ Once the beignets have cooled slightly, sprinkle them with the confectioners' sugar and serve.

VEGETABLES

"When you are chasing after the best flavor,
you are chasing after the best ingredients,
and when you're chasing after the best ingredients,
you are in search of great farming."

—DAN BARBER

AS CONSUMERS, WE'VE GROWN accustomed to eating what we want when we want it. Unfortunately, what we've gained in convenience we've lost in flavor. I promise you, that first bite of tomato deserves to be eaten at a farm stand under summer's blazing sun. And the molasses flavor of a yam simply will not shine in June. Knowing your local farmers and their produce builds your understanding of when vegetables are at their best, when to buy them, and how to cook them. Buying local is also an act of support for farmers who are committed to growing real, nurturing food in a responsible and ethical way. Keep these points in mind when purchasing produce.

Support family-owned farms.

Small and medium-sized farms are critically important. They keep alive food-crop farming (as opposed to commodity crops like soy or corn); preserve the skills, products, and wisdom of traditional agriculture; safeguard the fertility of farmland; and help ensure our collective food security. Support nonindustrial farms by shopping at farmers' markets, requesting local produce at your grocery store, and joining a community-supported agriculture program.

Explore and cook with as many varieties as possible.

When shopping at farmers' markets, you'll see Brussels sprouts streaked deep purple and carrots in varying shades of crimson. You'll undoubtedly find varieties of vegetables you never see in the grocery store. Try them all! Biodiversity is essential to personal nutrition *and* global food security: eating more varieties of local vegetables is important to prevent crop diseases and keep the earth fertile.

Buy more.

Eat vegetables at every meal—and, as often as possible, *as* a meal. Don't get me wrong: I enjoy a good steak as much as the next person, but vegetable-focused meals are good for the environment as well as for our health.

Waste less.

In our busy lives, it's easy to let fresh produce languish in the fridge and toss it out with Thursday's garbage. But try to avoid waste by buying exactly what you need, buying from local growers, and eating it. Use the whole vegetable whenever possible—sauté beet greens, make carrot-top pesto! It takes only about ten minutes to make quick pickles or assemble a salad, and less than thirty to make a vegetable soup. Don't be afraid of ugly fruits and vegetables. Sometimes a less-than-perfect zucchini is even sweeter.

Knife Cuts and Tools

Practicing your knife skills results in several benefits: You build confidence in the kitchen, speed up prep time, waste less, and create better-tasting, more appealing food. With vegetables, in particular, good knife skills allow you to achieve uniform shapes, such as a dice (see page 14), a chiffonade (see page 9), or an oblique (see page 15). Consistent cubes and strips and wedges not only make for easier eating (ever had to tackle a jumbo broccoli spear with only a fork?) but also ensure that everything cooks evenly, sparing you a pan of half-burnt, half-undercooked veggies. Plus, the more cuts you master, the more you will be able to keep the presentation interesting.

CUTTING TIPS

1. The cooking method you plan on using will dictate the knife cut you choose. When roasting root vegetables, for example, it's nice to cut them on the bias to create a larger surface area for browning and caramelization, which is the best part of eating roasted root vegetables. Thai Cabbage Slaw (page 222) requires julienning (see page 9) so the cabbage absorbs the dressing and is easy to eat on a picnic. When braising cabbage (see the recipe on page 118), however, quartering it preserves the shape of the cabbage while it cooks.

2. Always create a flat surface on the vegetable before cutting. Slice a thin, lengthwise layer off the bottom of potatoes, zucchini, and the like so they don't roll on the cutting board. For globes, like cabbages, first cut them down the middle, creating two flat-bottomed halves, and then cut as needed. This will make chopping, slicing, and dicing infinitely easier and safer. For more about knife skills, see page 8.

3. Cut all pieces the same size. This is a blanket rule that applies to all cooking methods. Cutting vegetables in uniform sizes ensures that they cook evenly. If you've ever eaten a vegetable dish that had undercooked pieces mixed in with burnt bits, you know why this is good to avoid.

Y-SHAPED PEELER

Peeling is a matter of preference. Most vegetables have skins that are edible and nutritious—the exceptions being onions and tough-skinned vegetables like hearty winter squash. Just be sure to wash vegetables thoroughly, taking care to clean any cracks and crevices. While you can certainly use a paring knife to peel most vegetables, a smooth Y-shaped peeler will limit waste and injury. Hold the peeler in your dominant hand and the vegetable in the other, and peel *away* from your body.

8- TO 10-INCH CHEF'S KNIFE

A chef's knife is best for cutting vegetables into the appropriate size for the cooking technique: to slice green beans into bite-sized pieces before blanching, to dice an onion for sautéing, to cut a turnip for roasting, and so forth. When using a cutting board, a chef's knife is generally the best tool for the job.

PARING KNIFE

One general rule is to use a paring knife when cutting things while holding them in your palm: hulling strawberries, trimming the ends of asparagus, or peeling apples—delicate work for which a chef's knife would be unwieldy. A paring knife also works well for scoring vegetables before roasting or grilling them. Scoring (making hatch marks) on thick cuts of vegetables like eggplant and zucchini speeds up the cooking time and allows heat and salt to penetrate, creating more flavor all the way through.

HOW TO CUT CAULIFLOWER AND BROCCOLI

When cutting broccoli or cauliflower, use the entire vegetable. The stalks and core are edible too.

1 Set the cauliflower on a cutting board. Cut off the leaves. Cut a circle around the core and remove it, along with the florets from the stem. Continue cutting and pulling away the rest of the florets.

2 Cut the larger florets into smaller pieces. All the florets should be uniformly sized to ensure that they cook evenly. Then cut the core in half lengthwise, then into 5 or 6 smaller pieces.

1 Pull or cut away any leaves from the stalk and hold it down on a cutting board with your nondominant hand. Cut away the outer layer of florets. Continue cutting off the rest of the florets.

2 Halve or quarter the larger florets into smaller pieces if needed, and cut away the woody outer skin from the stalk. Slice the stems into thin strips.

Ways to Cook Vegetables

Some vegetables love penetrating, hot sun. Others enjoy the cool, moist dirt underground. Some do well with frost, and some wither in it. All of them will be at their best within a few days of being harvested. That's why broccoli that has traveled thousands of miles will never be as delicious as the head that grew a few hundred miles from your kitchen.

It follows that the ways to cook produce vary as well. Tender spring vegetables need less heat and flourish with lighter-touch cooking methods like blanching, whereas heartier root vegetables are enhanced by a good, hot roast. Summer grilling coaxes out the ripe flavors of peppers and eggplant, and braising softens and sweetens more fibrous greens in the fall. While this is not a comprehensive list of all cooking methods, it illustrates a range of fundamental techniques that any home cook can master.

BLANCHING

Blanching is a technique that submerges vegetables briefly in boiling water, and then "shocks" them in an ice bath to stop the cooking process. The goal of blanching is to cook the vegetable just enough to bring out its best flavor or, in some cases, to tenderize it just enough to finish by sautéing. Small or thin vegetables, like peas and green beans, can be blanched as is, but larger ones like carrots are best cut into even, bite-sized pieces before blanching. Green beans fare especially well with this technique as it leaves them crunchy but tender enough to sweeten up and brighten to a deep emerald hue. Heartier vegetables, such as broccoli florets, are often blanched before being sautéed because they need to be parcooked before getting tossed into the hot sauté pan.

BLANCHING TIPS

• **What to blanch:** Spring and summer vegetables, like green beans in their many varieties, asparagus, broccoli, broccoli rabe, carrots, cauliflower, and peas.

• **Stop the cooking.** Prepare the ice bath in advance by filling a deep bowl or other vessel about halfway with water and ice.

SPRING PEA AND MINT SALAD

SERVES 4 AS A SIDE

Fresh peas don't need a lot of cooking, but they do need a good dunk in salted boiling water to take off their waxy edge and bring out their true flavor. You can actually see the sweetness coming through as the peas' color transitions from dull to a bright emerald green. The shoots of the peas are the delicate, snappy stems that eventually produce a pod, and eating the peas and their shoots together is a springtime treat. The pep of the mint and the sharpness of the cheese act as counterpoints to the earthiness of the peas. Sunflower seeds provide a contrast in texture. This salad is a lovely side dish for a simple piece of grilled fish (see page 261). Let the peas shine.

½ TEASPOON FINE SEA SALT, PLUS MORE FOR THE BLANCHING WATER

2 CUPS SHELLED GREEN PEAS (ABOUT 2 POUNDS UNSHELLED)

1 CUP PEA SHOOTS

¼ CUP CHOPPED FRESH MINT

1 TABLESPOON EXTRA-VIRGIN OLIVE OIL

GRATED ZEST AND JUICE OF 1 LEMON

¼ TEASPOON FRESHLY GROUND BLACK PEPPER

1 HEAD OF BUTTER OR GEM LETTUCE, LEAVES TORN

½ CUP SHAVED FRESH PECORINO ROMANO OR PARMIGIANO-REGGIANO

¼ CUP SUNFLOWER SEEDS

❶ Fill a large saucepan with water. Salt the water heavily; it should taste like the sea. Bring the water to a rapid boil over high heat. While the water heats, prepare an ice bath (see page 95).

❷ When the water is boiling, add the peas and cook for 1 minute. As soon as the peas turn a superbright green, pull them off the heat.

❸ Using a fine-mesh strainer, scoop out the peas and immediately plunge them into the ice bath until cold, about 2 minutes. This halts the cooking process so the vegetables

don't get mushy; it also preserves the vibrant color.

❹ Drain the peas, removing any ice, and place them on a clean kitchen towel to dry.

❺ Combine the peas, pea shoots, and mint in a large bowl. Toss with the olive oil, lemon zest and juice, salt, and pepper. Gently toss with the lettuce and arrange on individual plates. Garnish with the cheese and sunflower seeds.

SAUTÉING

Vegetables that cook quickly, like snap peas, green beans, zucchini, and dark leafy greens, do very well with this method, which means "to jump" in French. Sautéing cooks vegetables in a small amount of oil or butter over high heat, just enough to make them easier to eat and impart flavor. If you want to sauté larger vegetables, or denser ones like Brussels sprouts or cauliflower, first cut or shave them into smaller pieces or blanch and shock them whole, and then continue with the sauté.

SAUTÉING TIPS

- **What to sauté:** Bok choy, broccoli, broccoli rabe, Brussels sprouts, green beans, mushrooms, rainbow chard, snap peas, spinach, zucchini, and kale or other dark, leafy greens.

- **Heat the pan, then add the oil.** Warm the pan before pouring in the oil. Let it heat until it begins to shimmer and then add the vegetables quickly. The longer oil sits in a hot pan, the more likely it is to smoke and turn bitter.

- **Cook the vegetables in small batches.** Don't crowd the pan—that causes the vegetables to steam and wilt, and you won't get any of that nice caramelized flavor and texture. As with all things, there is an exception: leafy greens can be crowded, as your goal is to wilt and tenderize them.

- **Let them sit for a moment.** Allow the vegetables to sizzle and brown in the hot oil for several seconds before stirring them.

- **Taste while cooking.** Taste the vegetables periodically while cooking them; sautéed vegetables should retain a bit of bite. When the vegetables have achieved the desired degree of doneness, turn off the heat and remove the pan from the burner so the vegetables stop cooking.

- **Eat them quickly.** Sautéed vegetables are best when they're hot and vibrant.

SAUTÉED GREEN BEANS WITH GARLIC

SERVES 4 TO 6 AS A SIDE

Julia Sullivan, the opening chef at Haven's Kitchen, taught me the trick to this recipe. One night, I was sautéing beans in my usual way and Julia said, "Save some of your minced garlic to throw in at the very end." I did, and my usual way was forever altered. Finely minced raw garlic becomes creamy when melded with the steaming beans, and the raw flavor adds a spark to the finished dish.

You can substitute snap peas, asparagus, or blanched broccoli rabe for the beans. Or try long beans—ask your farmer for them or look for them at an Asian specialty grocer. Skinny and longer than green beans, they are worth hunting down. Serve the beans on top of a bowl of rice (see page 31) or under a few slices of Ginger-Garlic Tofu (page 331).

EXTRA-VIRGIN OLIVE OIL	FINE SEA SALT
1 POUND GREEN BEANS, ENDS TRIMMED	¼ CUP WATER
3 GARLIC CLOVES, MINCED	GRATED ZEST AND JUICE OF 1 LEMON

❶ Heat a large sauté pan over medium-high heat.

❷ Add enough oil to coat the pan, about 1 tablespoon. When the oil begins to shimmer, add half of the beans. Sauté, moving the beans around in the pan occasionally until tender, about 4 minutes. Add one-third of the garlic, a pinch of salt, and 2 tablespoons of the water. Cook for another 30 seconds and transfer the beans to a serving bowl.

❸ Repeat with the second batch.

❹ To serve, toss the beans with the remaining raw garlic and the lemon zest and juice.

CRISPY SAUTÉED MUSHROOMS

MAKES ABOUT 2 SERVINGS, DEPENDING ON THE TYPES OF MUSHROOMS USED

These mushrooms—especially just out of the hot pan—are excellent toppers for a spinach salad. The cooking oil wilts the leaves a bit and, with a splash of red wine vinegar and salt, makes a rich dressing. The mushrooms sauté quickly, and finishing them with butter gives them a caramelized flavor. You could also serve them as a side dish for Roast Chicken (page 268) or piled on top of a bowl of warm grains.

EXTRA-VIRGIN OLIVE OIL	1 THYME SPRIG
1 POUND (4 TO 6 CUPS) MIXED MUSHROOMS, SUCH AS CREMINI, SHIITAKE, AND OYSTER, CUT INTO 1-INCH PIECES	1 GARLIC CLOVE, SMASHED
	FINE SEA SALT
2 TABLESPOONS UNSALTED BUTTER	FRESHLY GROUND BLACK PEPPER

VEGETABLES

❶ Heat a large sauté pan over medium-high heat and pour in enough olive oil to generously coat the bottom of the pan—2 to 3 tablespoons. When the oil begins to shimmer, add the mushrooms. Do not crowd the pan or the mushrooms will steam and not brown. Work in batches if necessary. Sauté, flipping and tossing the mushrooms, until most of the residual moisture has evaporated, about 10 minutes.

❷ Add the butter, thyme, and garlic and salt and pepper to taste. Cook, stirring occasionally to distribute the butter and the flavors, until the butter stops foaming. This means that the water from the butter has evaporated, allowing the fats to brown. Continue cooking until the mushrooms are nicely browned, 5 to 6 minutes.

MUSHROOMS

Mushrooms are technically not plants, nor are they actually vegetables—they're fungi. They're a fun ingredient to explore because there are so many varieties ranging in flavors, shapes, and textures. The most common varieties are white buttons, tan creminis, and their bigger, meatier cousins portobellos. But try them all! Buttery chanterelles and slightly smoky shiitakes crisp up when sautéed with butter, and maitakes, considered a terrific healer in Chinese medicine, make an excellent main course when roasted. Mushrooms add earthiness and a good hint of funk to soups, stews, fried rice, and omelets.

Fresh, thinly sliced button mushrooms are an elegant, clean subject for a drizzle of extra-virgin olive oil, a squeeze of lemon, and a dash of salt. Roasted maitakes (also known as hen of the woods) seasoned with lime, salt, and black sesame seeds are great as is or served on top of polenta or rice. Don't wash mushrooms by submerging them in water—that will just make them soggy. Rather, rub off any dirt with a damp paper or kitchen towel.

GRILLING

If there is a smell of summer, it's the aroma of fire meeting meats and vegetables on the grill. Grilling uses intense, direct heat to char vegetables and create a sharp, lush flavor. If you don't have an outdoor grill, substitute a stovetop grill pan.

GRILLING TIPS

- **What to grill:** Sturdy, dense vegetables, such as asparagus, bell peppers, cabbage, corn, eggplant, larger mushrooms like king oyster and portobello, onions, romaine, summer squash, and zucchini. Try grilling wedges of heartier lettuces like Romaine or radicchio as well.

- **Heat is essential.** The most important part of grilling is the temperature. Always make sure that the grill is appropriately hot before starting to cook. Remember that the grill temperature will go down once you add food. When you flip vegetables and meats, we suggest moving them to a part of the grill that has not had food on it, as that area will be hotter.

- **Consider your cut.** In general, cut your vegetables on the larger side so they don't fall through the grates. For example, make thicker slices of eggplant and cut your zucchini lengthwise. Larger cuts lower your odds of overcooking and burning.

- **Grill first.** Marinating the vegetables before they hit the fire makes for a soggy final product. So grill first and flavor afterward.

- **Practice.** Grilling isn't complicated, but it takes some practice to know how to cook the vegetables thoroughly without burning them. Depending on the distance from the flame and the temperature of your grill, which can be difficult to control, cooking times for different vegetables vary.

GRILLED SUMMER VEGETABLES WITH ROMESCO SAUCE

SERVES 4 TO 6

Try serving any or all of these gorgeous, glossy, jewel-toned vegetables on a platter next time you host a barbecue. Vegetarians won't be the only ones making a beeline for them. And make extra romesco; it has a way of converting even the most bird-like eaters.

---

1 CUP ROMESCO SAUCE (PAGE 320)

2 SMALL TO MEDIUM SUMMER SQUASH, CUT LENGTHWISE, OR QUARTERED IF ROUND

1 EGGPLANT, CUT INTO ½-INCH-THICK SLICES AND SCORED (SEE PAGE 105)

1 HEAD RADICCHIO, QUARTERED

3 TO 4 SPRING ONIONS

8 TO 10 ASPARAGUS, ENDS TRIMMED

1 RED BELL PEPPER, HALVED AND SEEDS REMOVED

2 TABLESPOONS EXTRA-VIRGIN OLIVE OIL

FINE SEA SALT

---

❶ Clean the grill by heating it for at least 15 minutes and then brushing the rack with a grill brush. The rack is easier to clean when it's warm. Do not add cooking spray or oil. Then heat the grill for an additional 30 minutes until it's hot and you're ready to cook.

❷ While the grill heats, make the romesco sauce and set aside.

❸ In a large bowl, toss the squash, eggplant, radicchio, onions, asparagus, and red bell pepper with the olive oil and salt to taste.

❹ Check to see if the grill is ready: when you hold your hand 3 inches or so over the grill, you should feel a burning heat. Place the vegetables directly on the grill. Leave undisturbed for at least 2 to 3 minutes. Using long-handled tongs, flip the vegetables and grill the other side.

❺ When all sides are tender and charred, remove the vegetables from the grill. Depending on the vegetable, it will take anywhere from 5 to 10 minutes total to cook—for example, about 10 minutes for the zucchini and 5 minutes for the pepper. Slice the larger vegetables into portions. Serve on a platter, topped with romesco sauce.

QUICK PICKLING

Long before the invention of refrigeration and jet airliners, societies that lived in climates too cold to grow produce year-round relied on pickling to preserve vegetables. Pickling kept people fed through the lean season, and had the added benefit of imbuing vegetables with new flavors.

These recipes are for *quick* pickles, otherwise known as refrigerator pickles. In this method, a combination of vinegar, water, sugar, and spices is heated and poured over raw, uncooked vegetables. This method is not designed to preserve vegetables for years, but imparts flavor and extends the life of produce that might otherwise go to waste. It's also a nice way to eat red onions, keeping their essential crisp bite and flavor but softening them enough to prevent watery eyes.

PICKLING TIPS

- **What to pickle:** Almost anything can be pickled. Vegetables such as beets, carrots, cauliflower, celery, cucumbers, fennel, green beans, okra, peppers, radishes, and red onions, as well as firm, tart fruits like apples and quince, are especially good candidates.

- **Impart flavor through vinegars and spices.** At Haven's Kitchen, we often use champagne vinegar for pickling because it lends good flavor without being overwhelming. Give pickling liquids further complexity by adding whole dried peppercorns; spice seeds such as coriander, mustard, cumin, caraway, or fennel; and/or herbs such as dill.

QUICK PICKLED CUCUMBERS

MAKES 2 CUPS

Adjust this recipe to your taste by using different vinegars and spices. It's an excellent starter recipe for a range of vegetables, especially cauliflower, carrots, radishes, and jalapeños. Bear in mind that certain flavors go well together: champagne vinegar and fennel seeds or rice vinegar and coriander, for example. It may take some experimenting to understand complementary flavors.

1½ CUPS CHAMPAGNE VINEGAR	1 GARLIC CLOVE
¾ CUP WATER	1 BAY LEAF
5 TABLESPOONS SUGAR	1 TABLESPOON WHOLE SPICES, SUCH AS CORIANDER SEED, FENNEL SEED, PEPPERCORNS, ETC.
1 TABLESPOON FINE SEA SALT	
2 THYME SPRIGS	2 PERSIAN CUCUMBERS, CUT INTO ¼-INCH-THICK SLICES
2 DILL SPRIGS	

❶ In a small pot, combine the vinegar, water, sugar, salt, thyme, dill, garlic, bay leaf, and assorted spices. Bring to a simmer over medium heat and cook until the sugar and salt are fully dissolved, 4 to 5 minutes.

❷ While the pickling liquid simmers, place the cucumbers in a pint-sized glass jar with a lid. Tightly pack the cucumbers in the jar, leaving about an inch of headspace at the top.

❸ When the pickling liquid is ready, pour the solution over the vegetables, submerging them completely. Cool to room temperature.

❹ Screw on the lid and refrigerate the pickles for at least 2 hours before eating. The longer the vegetables soak in the pickling liquid, the deeper the flavors and the softer the texture. After you've eaten the pickles, save the liquid and mix it into Bloody Marys or add a dash to salad dressings for some kick. The pickles will keep in the refrigerator for up to 2 weeks.

SUPERQUICK PICKLED RED ONIONS

MAKES ½ CUP

There are nights when you may crave a zingy red onion to top a salad—but not in its raw state. So on those occasions, try this recipe.

¼ CUP CHAMPAGNE OR WHITE WINE VINEGAR	2 TEASPOONS DRIED CURRANTS ½ RED ONION, THINLY SLICED

❶ Pour the vinegar into a small bowl and add the dried currants for some sweetness.

❷ While the currants steep, stir the red onion into the pickling liquid. Let it sit.

❸ When you're ready to serve the salad, simply strain out the currants and the onion and sprinkle them over the greens prior to dressing. You can refrigerate for a day or so, but the onions will lose their crispness.

ROASTING

Roasting is the best cooking method for the hearty, starchier vegetables of the fall and winter, especially root vegetables. In the dry, high heat of the oven, vegetables undergo something called the Maillard reaction, a magical sequence of chemical changes responsible for other heavenly aromas like baking bread and roasted lamb. Whether it's working its wonders on dough, meat, or vegetables, the Maillard reaction rearranges amino acids under the intense dry heat of the oven, browning and creating the heady, rich, savory flavors that techniques like boiling simply cannot produce.

ROASTING TIPS

- **What to roast:** Asparagus, beets, broccoli, Brussels sprouts, carrots, cauliflower, eggplant, fennel, mushrooms, parsnips, potatoes, summer squash, sunchokes, sweet potatoes, and winter squash.

- **Preheat the oven.** Don't cut corners: preheating ensures that the entire oven is hot enough. If you have a convection function on your oven, use it: heat circulation cooks the vegetables faster, more evenly, and with more browning. In general, roast vegetables at 425°F; the exception is mushrooms, which you can cook at 375°F.

- **Line the pan.** Parchment paper creates a moisture-resistant, nonstick surface. It also saves cleanup time; no need to scrub the pan.

- **Create more surface area.** Cut root vegetables, such as carrots, potatoes, and parsnips, on a strong bias to increase the surface area that will brown and form a flavorful crust. Leave asparagus stalks whole, trimming away the woody bottoms; summer squash and eggplant should be cut ½ inch thick on the bias or lengthwise.

- **Sauté first, roast second.** A professional tip I've learned from our culinary director, David Mawhinney, is to sauté smaller cuts of vegetables before roasting them in the oven. The hot, direct heat jump-starts the caramelization process, creating crisp, golden vegetables. Use the same pan, so it is already superhot when it goes into the oven, and the subsequent roasting proceeds more quickly. Make sure to leave space between the vegetables so they don't steam, as this would defeat the purpose of roasting, which relies on dry heat.

ROASTED SWEET POTATO WITH HAZELNUT GREMOLATA

SERVES 4 TO 6 AS A SIDE

Earthy root vegetables, such as sweet potatoes, parsnips, and squash, roast beautifully because of their natural sugar content. Dressing the vegetables with an herby hazelnut gremolata (a play on our Sesame Gremolata) creates a harmonious dish. This one never fails to please.

---

3 SWEET POTATOES, SLICED INTO ¾-INCH DISKS

EXTRA-VIRGIN OLIVE OIL

FINE SEA SALT

FRESHLY GROUND BLACK PEPPER

HAZELNUT GREMOLATA (SEE PAGE 301)

---

❶ Preheat the oven to 425°F. Line a baking sheet with parchment paper.

❷ In a large bowl, toss the sweet potatoes with olive oil and season with salt and pepper to taste.

❸ Place the sweet potatoes in a single layer on the prepared pan. Roast for 30 to 40 minutes, rotating the pan after 20 minutes.

❹ When the sweet potatoes are evenly brown and tender, transfer them to a serving platter and drizzle with gremolata.

ROASTED MUSHROOMS

MAKES 2 TO 4 SERVINGS, DEPENDING ON THE TYPES OF MUSHROOMS USED

Mushrooms are spongy, which means they cook quickly but absorb oil easily. So they can roast at a lower temperature, 375°F, than other vegetables.

It's a pleasure to eat a variety of mushrooms because each has its own unique flavor and texture. But when you're cooking several types together, it can be challenging to get them all evenly cooked because you're working with different shapes, sizes, and densities. Be mindful of this and check on the mushrooms every 5 minutes. Remove those that are crispy and browned, and let the remaining ones continue to roast. Serve these over a grain bowl or salad, dressed with Shallot Vinaigrette (page 231).

1 POUND (4 TO 6 CUPS) MIXED MUSHROOMS, SUCH AS CREMINI, SHIITAKE, OYSTER, AND MAITAKE	ABOUT ¼ CUP EXTRA-VIRGIN OLIVE OIL FINE SEA SALT

❶ Preheat the oven to 375°F. Line a baking sheet with parchment paper.

❷ In a large bowl, toss the mushrooms with the olive oil and salt to taste.

❸ Arrange the mushrooms on the baking sheet in a single, uncrowded layer. Roast for 15 to 20 minutes. Check to see if the mushrooms have an even brown color, and taste to assess the texture. If they aren't quite crispy, continue to roast, checking every 5 minutes.

BRAISING

Braising involves two cooking methods: vegetables are first browned in butter or oil over high heat and then partially covered with wine or stock and cooked slowly over low heat. They emerge supple and full of flavor. Braising is a useful technique for cooking winter root vegetables and chicories like endive and escarole because over low, slow heat, the liquid gradually breaks down tougher fibers to tenderize the vegetables while preserving their shape. Leeks, which you might not necessarily eat on their own, love a buttery bath and transform into an almost creamy dish. Because braising concentrates liquids like chicken stock, blander, fibrous vegetables like cabbage absorb a lot of flavor, leaving them savory and silky, but never mushy.

Not to be confused with stewing, which also cooks "slow and low" with liquid, braising highlights a single vegetable, three-quarters submerged in liquid. Stewing uses an array of different ingredients fully submerged to create a hearty, soupy, one-pot dish.

BRAISING TIPS

- **What to braise:** Artichoke hearts, cabbage, chard, collards, endive, kale, leeks, onions, parsnips, radicchio and other chicories, and squash.

- **Choose your liquid.** The braising liquid flavors as well as cooks the vegetables. After the vegetables have browned, pour in the braising liquid, leaving the top quarter of the vegetables exposed. Bring the liquid to a boil and reduce the heat to low. Cover the pan and simmer the vegetables until tender. You can also add aromatics like bay leaves, thyme, or spices.

- **Braise year-round.** These melt-in-your-mouth vegetables aren't solely for the chilly months. You can also braise baby spring vegetables and summer squashes.

IDEAS FOR BRAISING

SEASON	VEGETABLE	BRAISING LIQUID	AROMATICS
WINTER	Endive	Endive	Bacon, whole peeled garlic clove
SPRING	Turnips with greens	Vegetable stock (see page 146), finished with butter	Kombu, ginger, lemon zest, scallions
SUMMER	Zucchini or summer squash	Extra-virgin olive oil, water	Whole peeled garlic, thyme sprigs
FALL	Parsnips (see page 121)	White wine, butter	Bay leaf, vanilla bean

BRAISED CABBAGE

SERVES 4

Cabbage has acquired a sad, drab reputation, and that strikes me as unfair. This dish brings out cabbage's best assets: its ability to withstand heat without turning into mush, and its readiness to absorb flavor even while holding its own. This recipe transforms a down-to-earth plant into something rich and decadent. Serve it as a side to Roast Chicken (page 268) on a cold evening.

4 TABLESPOONS (½ STICK) UNSALTED BUTTER

1 CARROT, PEELED AND CUT INTO 2-INCH OBLIQUES (SEE PAGE 15)

1 HEAD OF GREEN CABBAGE, QUARTERED

FINE SEA SALT

3 GARLIC CLOVES, PEELED

1 SHALLOT, PEELED

2 BAY LEAVES

1 CUP DRY WHITE WINE

1 CUP CHICKEN STOCK (SEE PAGE 269) OR VEGETABLE STOCK (SEE PAGE 146)

❶ Melt the butter in a large, deep saucepan or Dutch oven over medium heat until completely melted but not browned. Add the carrots and the cabbage. Sear, rotating the cabbage occasionally, until all sides are golden, 2 to 4 minutes.

❷ Season the cabbage with salt. Add the garlic, shallot, bay leaves, wine, and stock. Bring the liquid to a boil and then reduce to a simmer, cover the pan, and cook until tender, 20 to 25 minutes. The cabbage will be a little translucent, but it will keep its shape.

❸ Remove from the heat, uncover the pan, and let cool slightly. Use a spoon to transfer the vegetables to a serving platter. Drizzle the remaining liquid over the cabbage, and serve.

BRAISED PARSNIPS WITH WHITE WINE AND VANILLA

SERVES 4 TO 6 AS A SIDE

Parsnips, vanilla, and white wine complement one another to make a warm, buttery braise that can be served with your Thanksgiving turkey, a savory ham, or some other festive roast. Or, make them for a random Wednesday night dinner with just about anything to make the meal feel special.

---

2 POUNDS PARSNIPS, PEELED

EXTRA-VIRGIN OLIVE OIL

4 TABLESPOONS (½ STICK)
UNSALTED BUTTER

½ CUP DRY WHITE WINE

½ CUP CHICKEN STOCK (SEE PAGE 269) OR
VEGETABLE STOCK (SEE PAGE 146)

2 BAY LEAVES

1 VANILLA BEAN, SPLIT IN HALF LENGTHWISE

FINE SEA SALT

2 TABLESPOONS ROUGHLY CHOPPED
FRESH FLAT-LEAF PARSLEY LEAVES

---

❶ Cut the parsnips into 2-inch-thick obliques (see page 15). Depending on the size of the parsnips, each one should yield 3 to 6 pieces.

❷ Heat a large skillet or Dutch oven with a tight-fitting lid over high heat. Pour in enough oil to generously coat the bottom of the pan. When the oil begins to shimmer, add the parsnips. Sauté, stirring occasionally, until the edges begin to caramelize and all sides are golden brown, 4 to 5 minutes.

❸ Add the butter, wine, stock, bay leaves, vanilla bean, and 2 pinches of salt and bring to a boil. Reduce to a simmer and cover. Simmer until tender and easily pierced, 8 to 10 minutes, depending on the size of the parsnips.

❹ Add the parsley and toss to coat. Transfer to a serving plate and drizzle with the braising liquid.

FRYING

There are two methods of frying: deep-frying and panfrying (see page 73). Deep-frying, in which vegetables are fully submerged in hot oil, is the preferred method for making French fries, tempura, and fritters such as falafel. Panfrying uses less oil—a generous pour in the pan—and requires rotating the vegetables to ensure that they brown and cook evenly. Vegetables sit in the piping-hot oil, producing a crispy texture on the outside and a tender inner core.

FRYING TIPS

- **What to fry:** Artichoke hearts, broccoli, Brussels sprouts, cauliflower, eggplant, potatoes, and sweet potatoes. Small pieces, cooked in batches, work best.

- **Tools for frying:** We recommend a heavy-bottomed sauté pan for panfrying and a large heavy pot or Dutch oven along with an infrared thermometer for deep-frying. For a more comprehensive list, check out the tools list in the Fritters chapter (see page 58).

- **Add crunch.** For extra-crispy vegetables, try dunking slices or wedges into 2 eggs whisked with a pinch of salt, and then dredging them through a shallow plate of flour or bread crumbs. In hot oil, panfry the vegetables in batches for 1 to 2 minutes on each side on medium-high heat, until they are browned, crisp, and cooked through. Using a slotted spoon or a fish spatula, remove the vegetables from the pan and place on paper towels or a wire rack to drain the extra oil.

CLASSIC FRENCH FRIES

SERVES 6

Really, what could be better than crispy, salty fries? Belgians are still disgruntled that their arguably greatest offering to the world, the *frite*, has been attributed to their southern neighbor. Twice frying is the secret here, and please don't be afraid to fry. It takes some planning, but the technique is one that a home cook can master, and the folks at your table will be grateful for it. Try these fries, period. But if you're looking for a "main" dish, then nod to the past and start with Belgian Moules (page 256) and a bowl of Roasted Garlic Aioli (page 315). Note: The initial fry can be done up to a day ahead and the parcooked potatoes kept in the refrigerator.

6 IDAHO RUSSET POTATOES	FINE SEA SALT
NEUTRAL-FLAVORED VEGETABLE OIL, FOR FRYING	

① Scrub or peel the potatoes. Cut lengthwise into ¼-inch-thick slices, then stack the slices and cut lengthwise into ¼-inch-thick "logs." To prevent them from turning brown, place the cut potatoes in a bowl of cold water until you are ready to fry.

② Drain the potatoes and pat dry. Set up your fry station: fill a large, heavy-bottomed pot (such as a Dutch oven) with enough oil to cover the fries by at least 1 inch. Do not fill the pot more than halfway. Set a wire rack on a baking sheet and have a slotted spoon or spider handy.

③ For the first fry, slowly heat the oil over medium heat to between 275°F and 300°F. Using an infrared thermometer, check the temperature periodically. Fry a batch of 1 large or 2 small handfuls of potatoes for

4 minutes. The potatoes won't be brown and might still be raw in the middle. Using the slotted spoon or spider, transfer the potatoes to the prepared rack to drain off the oil. Let the oil return to between 275°F and 300°F before frying the next batch. Continue frying the rest of the potatoes in uncrowded batches. Let cool completely, about 20 minutes. (The fries can be made up to this point and stored, covered, in the refrigerator for 1 day.)

④ To finish, heat the oil to 360°F over medium-high heat. Working in batches, fry the potatoes a second time until they turn golden brown, 3 to 4 minutes. Using a slotted spoon, transfer the potatoes to the wire rack.

⑤ Season with salt and serve immediately.

EDAMAME MISO DIP

MAKES 1½ CUPS

This recipe is a refreshing spring and summer dip. The miso adds a salty, deep umami flavor. If you can't find whole fresh edamame still in the pod, use 1½ cups of shelled frozen edamame. Follow the directions below but blanch for only 2 to 3 minutes, until bright and tender.

FINE SEA SALT	1 TABLESPOON WHITE MISO
4 CUPS (1 POUND) EDAMAME IN THE SHELL	1 GARLIC CLOVE, SMASHED
¼ CUP EXTRA-VIRGIN OLIVE OIL PLUS ½ TABLESPOON FOR DRIZZLING	JUICE OF 1 LIME
	½ TEASPOON TOASTED SESAME OIL
2 TABLESPOONS FRESH MINT, CHOPPED	¼ CUP COLD WATER, OR AS NEEDED

❶ Fill a medium stockpot with water. Add about ¼ cup salt; it should taste like the sea. This may seem like a lot of salt, but the salted water absorbed by the vegetables is the primary seasoning agent. Bring the water to a rapid boil. Meanwhile, prepare an ice bath (see page 95).

❷ When the water boils, add the edamame and cook for 3 to 5 minutes. When the edamame can be easily popped out of the shell, turn off the heat.

❸ Drain the edamame and plunge them into the ice bath until cold, about 2 minutes. This halts the cooking process so they get soft but not mushy; it also preserves their vibrant color.

❹ Drain the edamame, removing any ice. Using your fingers, pop the beans out of their shells and place in the bowl of a food processor.

❺ Add the ¼ cup olive oil and the mint, miso, garlic, lime juice, and sesame oil. Purée until almost smooth, about 3 minutes, adding salt to taste and water as needed.

❻ Place in a serving bowl and drizzle with ½ tablespoon olive oil. Serve with raw vegetables, with crackers, or as a spread on a sandwich.

SMASHED CUCUMBER SALAD

SERVES 4 AS A SIDE

A favorite appetizer served at Chinese restaurants was the inspiration for this cucumber salad. It's especially delicious with Chinese black vinegar, which is made from glutinous rice and malt and likened to balsamic. You can use the vinegar straight up as a dipping sauce for Grilled Whole Fish (page 261) or to flavor sautéed greens (see page 99 for sautéing). If you don't want to purchase this specialty ingredient, rice vinegar works as well.

4 SMALL TO MEDIUM PERSIAN CUCUMBERS (ABOUT 1 POUND)

FINE SEA SALT

½ TEASPOON SUGAR

2 TABLESPOONS CHINESE BLACK VINEGAR OR CHINKIANG VINEGAR

1 TABLESPOON LIGHT SOY SAUCE

2 TEASPOONS TOASTED SESAME OIL

¼ TEASPOON WHITE PEPPER

4 GARLIC CLOVES, MINCED

1 TEASPOON HOT CHILI OIL (OPTIONAL)

¼ CUP CHOPPED FRESH CILANTRO, BOTH STEMS AND LEAVES

❶ Using the flat side of a cleaver or a rolling pin, lightly smash or roll the length of each cucumber until it splits. This allows the dressing to absorb into the core of the cucumber quickly. Cut them lengthwise and then into 1-inch diagonal slices.

❷ Put the cucumber slices into a bowl, add a large pinch of salt and the sugar, mix well, and set aside for 10 minutes.

❸ While the cucumbers are marinating, make the dressing. In a small bowl, mix the black vinegar, soy sauce, sesame oil, white pepper, garlic, and chili oil, if using.

❹ Drain any liquid from the cucumbers that accumulated during salting. Add the dressing and mix well.

❺ Toss with the cilantro and serve immediately.

ROASTED ROOT VEGETABLES WITH BROWN BUTTER

SERVES 6

This recipe may be part of my not-so-hidden agenda to lure you to your local farmers' market in November. It combines cauliflower, Brussels sprouts, fennel, celery (yes, you can roast it!), and a few types of squash—all stars at the late fall market. Delicatas and Kabochas are stellar squash varieties because they don't need to be peeled, cut rather easily, and roast to become sweet and velvety. The vegetables cook at different speeds, so roast them on separate baking sheets, and then combine. If you want to save time and cleanup, opt for fewer vegetables—it will still taste wonderful.

2 FENNEL BULBS, CUT INTO 6 WEDGES

1 SMALL HEAD CAULIFLOWER, CUT INTO FLORETTES (SEE PAGE 94)

1 POUND (ABOUT 4 CUPS) BRUSSELS SPROUTS, TRIMMED AND CUT IN HALF

3 CELERY STALKS, CUT INTO 3-INCH PIECES

1 ACORN SQUASH, CUT INTO 8 WEDGES

1 DELICATA SQUASH, CUT LENGTHWISE, SEEDS REMOVED, AND SLICED INTO ½-INCH-THICK HALF-MOONS

EXTRA-VIRGIN OLIVE OIL

FINE SEA SALT

FRESHLY GROUND BLACK PEPPER

¼ POUND (1 STICK) UNSALTED BUTTER, AT ROOM TEMPERATURE

1 TABLESPOON SHERRY VINEGAR

¼ CUP ROUGHLY CHOPPED FRESH FLAT-LEAF PARSLEY

❶ Preheat the oven to 425°F.

❷ Line three baking sheets with parchment paper.

❸ In a large bowl, separately toss each vegetable with about 1 tablespoon olive oil, a large pinch of salt, and freshly ground black pepper and place on a parchment-lined baking sheet. Repeat with each batch of vegetables. Place all the pans in the oven and roast until golden and tender, 15 to 25 minutes. If you cannot fit all the pans in your oven, work in batches. Place the roasted vegetables on a serving platter.

❹ Fifteen minutes before you are ready to serve, make the brown butter. In a small, heavy-bottomed saucepan, melt the butter over medium heat, swirling the pot, until large bubbles form, about 2 minutes. Swirl the pot constantly while the butter foams up.

continued

After another minute or so, the large bubbles will subside and a small layer of white foam will appear on the surface. Reduce the heat to low and continue to swirl the pan for about 1 minute, until the bubbles disappear and the butter is amber in color and nutty in aroma. The time it takes to brown the butter will vary based on the size and thickness of your pan and the heat level. Transfer to a clean, cool bowl to stop the cooking.

❺ Toss the roasted vegetables with the brown butter, sherry vinegar, and parsley. Taste, season with additional salt if needed, and serve.

RATATOUILLE

SERVES 6 TO 8

Eggplants, when cooked down and seasoned, will literally melt in your mouth. This ratatouille functions as a sauce, a stewy braise, or a filling. Serve it as a bed for a fillet of grilled fish (see page 261) or as a spread on Grilled Flatbread (page 333). Try it spooned into your Scrambled Eggs (page 174) or Polenta (page 56).

EXTRA-VIRGIN OLIVE OIL

1 YELLOW ONION, CUT INTO ½-INCH DICE (ABOUT 1 CUP)

FINE SEA SALT

2 RED BELL PEPPERS, CUT INTO ½-INCH DICE (ABOUT 1 CUP; SEE NEXT PAGE)

6 ROMA (PLUM) TOMATOES, CUT INTO ½-INCH DICE (ABOUT 2 CUPS)

2 GARLIC CLOVES, SMASHED

2 OREGANO SPRIGS

2 THYME SPRIGS

1 MEDIUM EGGPLANT, CUT INTO ½-INCH DICE (ABOUT 4 CUPS)

2 ZUCCHINI, CUT INTO ½-INCH DICE (ABOUT 2 CUPS)

¼ CUP CHOPPED FRESH FLAT-LEAF PARSLEY OR TORN BASIL LEAVES

❶ Heat a large Dutch oven over medium heat. When the pan is hot, pour in oil to coat the bottom, about 1 tablespoon. Add the onion and a large pinch of salt and sweat until it begins to soften, about 1 minute. Add the bell peppers and sweat for an additional minute. Add the tomatoes, garlic, oregano, and thyme and another large pinch of salt. Cook, stirring occasionally with a wooden spoon, until most of the water has cooked out of the tomatoes, about 10 minutes.

❷ While the tomatoes cook down, heat a large sauté pan over high heat. Pour in enough oil to coat the pan. Working in small batches to avoid crowding the pan, sauté the eggplant. Cook each batch until golden on all sides, about 4 minutes. Transfer to a bowl.

Cook the zucchini in the same way, allowing the pan to return to a high heat between batches and adding oil as needed. When each batch is golden, set aside with the eggplant.

❸ Add the eggplant and zucchini to the Dutch oven. Continue to cook over medium-low heat until the flavors come together and all the vegetables are tender, about 10 minutes.

❹ Taste for salt and adjust the seasoning as needed. Remove the garlic cloves and thyme and oregano sprigs. Transfer to a serving dish or serve out of the Dutch oven. Garnish with parsley or torn basil.

HOW TO SLICE A BELL PEPPER

1 Using a chef's knife, cut the top and bottom off the pepper and reserve.

2 Holding the pepper vertically, make a slice from the top to the bottom.

3 Unroll the pepper and use your knife to remove the pith and seeds.

4 Cut the pepper into thin strips and then into dice. Slice or dice the reserved tops and bottoms.

SOUPS

"Let things taste of what they are."

—ALICE WATERS

HOME COOKS ACROSS THE AGES
have known that when the family needs
comfort and strength, when there's only one
pot or one potato, make soup. And yet we've
all had lame soups: tasteless, tepid, flat, and
oversalted in a last-ditch effort to save the
batch. Hopefully, you've also experienced
soup at its finest: rich and comforting,
all the flavors and ingredients perfectly
harmonious. The difference between an
uninspired soup and one that is deeply
satisfying lies in the process of *layering
flavors*—building up your broth so that each
spoonful is completely the essence of the
produce, not water with some stuff in it.

Layering flavors doesn't necessarily
mean adding *more* ingredients; it means
consciously infusing your soup from the
moment you begin. Start with aromatics or
roast the vegetables before puréeing them.
Tossing in a Parmigiano-Reggiano rind or
a spice sachet as the soup simmers adds
a boost of flavor. Giving it more time on
the heat allows it to reach its richest, most
potent result. Don't forget to top it off with
a shot of acid and fresh herbs.

When thinking about what soup to make,
consider the following questions:

- What's in season? Or, what is the season?

- What do you have in the fridge or pantry?
  If you have a bunch of carrots, carrot soup
  it is. If you see a stalk of broccoli and a
  bunch of chard, try minestrone. Stale
  bread? Ribollita!

- How much time do you have to create the
  flavor layers? This may determine if you
  need to use a quick flavor base such as
  miso, dashi, dried mushrooms, or bouillon.
  Maybe you have enough time to make a
  stock or to steep flavor into your liquid
  using a spice sachet. Or maybe you will just
  roast some vegetables and make a purée.

- Do you want something brothy or on
  the heartier side? If you are in a stick-to-
  your-ribs mood, then think about adding
  potatoes, beans, grains, more vegetables,
  or meat.

Start by considering what you want your
soup to taste like, and then enhance and
fortify it along the way by adding ingredients
to achieve that result. Once you understand
the idea of layering flavors, your soups will
take on more life and complexity. Even a
clear broth can be deeply satisfying with the
benefit of time and layered flavors.

Tools

Making soup doesn't require more than a big stockpot and a wooden spoon, but a high-speed blender or an immersion blender will work wonders for your puréed soups. A ladle makes for much cleaner serving, and while any pot will do, a few are considered first in class.

HEAVY-BOTTOMED STOCKPOT

An 8-quart heavy-bottomed stockpot is an essential item in a home cook's kitchen. It's big enough to boil a pound of pasta, two lobsters for a romantic dinner, or an entire chicken carcass for a savory broth.

DUTCH OVEN

A 6- to 8-quart Dutch oven is ideal for making stews, chilis, and other hearty soups. It's good for anything that needs to move from stove to oven or vice versa. It is one of the most versatile cooking vessels: we use a Dutch oven to bake breads, roast chickens, make casseroles, and fry fritters.

Note that a metal spoon will scratch a Dutch oven's enamel sides, so it's a good idea to have a few long wooden spoons in your arsenal.

LADLE

A ladle allows you to serve soup straight from the pot.

FINE-MESH STRAINER

A fine-mesh strainer that can rest inside a larger bowl makes it easier to first drain the broth and then scoop out tidbits of meat or vegetables.

HIGH-SPEED BLENDER

A high-speed blender (Vitamix or other) is a worthwhile investment for many purposes, but especially for making purées. It's our secret to creamy soups made without the aid of cream.

When puréeing hot soups and liquids, fill the blender only halfway, vent the top so hot air can escape, and hold a kitchen towel over the vent to prevent splatters.

IMMERSION BLENDER

An alternative tool for puréeing soups is an immersion blender. Although it doesn't offer the same smooth, creamy consistency as a high-powered countertop version, it is an affordable, compact option. Just be careful, as hand blenders can cause splatters and burns. Always put the device into the pot *before* you turn it on, start blending at the bottom, and move upward as you observe the soup puréeing—keeping the head fully immersed the whole time to prevent hot splatters. Then turn it off before pulling it out of the pot.

Teaching Recipe

RIBOLLITA

SERVES 8 TO 12

Two seemingly disparate things are able to comfortably coexist: everyone's grandmother can have a "secret" soup recipe *and* every one of those recipes likely follows a similar fundamental pattern. This ribollita recipe illustrates one such pattern, as it shows how to build a soup from the bottom up, beginning with a foundation of sautéed aromatics and gradually adding depth of flavor, texture, and color with other ingredients.

EXTRA-VIRGIN OLIVE OIL

2 CELERY STALKS, DICED

1 YELLOW ONION, DICED

1 FENNEL BULB, DICED

FINE SEA SALT

2 LARGE GARLIC CLOVES, MINCED

9 CUPS VEGETABLE STOCK (SEE PAGE 146) OR CHICKEN STOCK (SEE PAGE 269)

ONE 28-OUNCE CAN CRUSHED TOMATOES

2 BAY LEAVES

5 THYME SPRINGS AND 5 FLAT-LEAF PARSLEY SPRIGS TIED TOGETHER WITH TWINE

1 CUP DRIED CANNELLINI BEANS, SOAKED OVERNIGHT, OR ONE 15-OUNCE CAN CANNELLINI BEANS

2 OR 3 PIECES OF PARMIGIANO-REGGIANO RIND, EACH A FEW INCHES

PINCH OF RED PEPPER FLAKES

FRESHLY GROUND BLACK PEPPER

3 SLICES OF STALE COUNTRY-STYLE BREAD, CUT INTO ½-INCH CUBES AND TOASTED (ABOUT 2 CUPS) OR ABOUT 2 CUPS OF CROUTONS (PAGE 143)

1 SMALL BUNCH LACINATO (AKA DINOSAUR, AKA TUSCAN) KALE, STEMMED AND CHOPPED

CHOPPED FLAT-LEAF PARSLEY, FOR GARNISH

1 LEMON

continued

AROMATICS

❶ Heat a large Dutch oven or stockpot over medium-high heat. Pour in enough oil to cover the bottom of the pan. When the oil is warm, add the celery, onion, and fennel. Season with salt and cook, stirring occasionally, until the onion is translucent and aromatic, 4 to 5 minutes. Add the garlic and cook until the garlic has softened, about 1 minute.

Soups that have a brothy base like ribollita are best when you build a foundation by sweating aromatics: a medley of celery, onion, fennel, and garlic.

Add garlic later; it cooks more quickly because it is minced.

LAYERING FLAVOR

❷ Add the stock, crushed tomatoes, bay leaves, herb bundle, dried beans (if using canned beans, you'll add them later), Parmigiano-Reggiano rinds, and red pepper flakes. Season with salt and black pepper. Bring to a simmer and cook on low heat, stirring frequently to prevent the rinds from sticking to the bottom of the pot, for 30 to 45 minutes.

Layering flavor is the key to a soup that satisfies all of your senses. Here you build the flavor into the broth with aromatics, a savory liquid, herbs, and, in this case, the cheese rind.

Note that you add the soaked dried beans at this point because they take longer to cook; canned beans get added later. Dried beans will add more starch to the ribollita and you'll end up with a thicker dish, but canned beans offer the desired texture as well.

HOMEMADE
CROUTONS

Make homemade croutons by cutting or tearing leftover crusty bread into cubes, tossing with olive oil, salt, and herbs, and baking at 350°F until crunchy, 10 to 15 minutes. Croutons last a week or so stored in an airtight container.

BUILDING TEXTURE

❸ Add the bread cubes or croutons (and canned beans, if using) and simmer until the bread has absorbed the broth, the beans are soft and plump, and the soup begins to thicken, 20 to 30 minutes.

Build texture and body into the soup with the beans and bread.

Stale country-style bread is a key ingredient here. Preferably, use a day-old bread like ciabatta. Toasting the bread helps it keep its texture. Because canned beans are precooked, you want to add them at this stage so they will not get too mushy.

ADDING GREENS

❹ Add the kale and continue to simmer until the greens are just cooked, about 5 minutes.

Hearty greens like kale hold up to the heat of soup, retaining their texture and color.

TASTE

❺ Taste the soup and add more black pepper and salt, if needed. Discard the cheese rinds, bay leaves, and herb bundle.

Always taste your soup before serving.

SERVING

❻ Serve each bowl of soup garnished with some chopped parsley and a squeeze of lemon juice.

Parsley is so much more than a frilly garnish. The flat-leaf variety used here adds color and flavor. Finish the soup with a squeeze of lemon; it offers a hint of acid, bringing the whole bowl together.

The best soups have a finisher to top off the bowl.

VEGETABLE STOCK

MAKES 4 QUARTS

This vegetable stock is one of our secrets to making great soups. Use it as your liquid for a deeper, more flavorful soup. Make a big pot of it when you have a free afternoon. Let it cool until lukewarm. Line a jug or pitcher with a 1-quart ziplock freezer bag, ladle the stock into the bag, and seal it. You should be able to fill four bags. Freeze them for up to six months by laying them flat in the freezer. That way, defrosting them takes less time.

3 CELERY STALKS, CHOPPED	4 GARLIC CLOVES, SMASHED
3 CARROTS, CHOPPED	¼ BUNCH OF FLAT-LEAF PARSLEY
1 LARGE ONION, CHOPPED	5 THYME SPRIGS
½ FENNEL BULB, CHOPPED	½ TEASPOON BLACK PEPPERCORNS
1 TABLESPOON EXTRA-VIRGIN OLIVE OIL	2 BAY LEAVES, PREFERABLY FRESH

❶ In the bowl of a food processor fitted with the metal chopping blade, pulse the celery, carrots, onion, and fennel until the mixture is chunky with pea-sized bits.

❷ Place a large stockpot over medium heat. Add the olive oil and heat until it begins to shimmer. Add the vegetable mixture and cook, stirring occasionally, for 3 to 5 minutes.

❸ Pour in 4 quarts water. Add the garlic, parsley, thyme, peppercorns, and bay leaves. (The stock will be strained later, so a sachet is not necessary.) Bring to a boil over high heat, and then simmer over low heat for 45 minutes.

❹ Set a fine-mesh sieve or a colander lined with a kitchen towel or cheesecloth over another large pot and strain the stock. This step takes the murkiness out of the stock, which gives it a nicer mouthfeel and also extends the stock's shelf life. Discard the pulp. If not using it immediately, let cool to room temperature, and then pour into freezer bags or lidded containers, cover, and refrigerate or freeze. Tightly sealed, the stock will keep for 5 days in the refrigerator and up to 6 months in the freezer.

A SPICE SACHET AND
A BOUQUET GARNI

Aromatics can be added to soup in the form of a spice sachet or a bouquet garni. To build a spice sachet, place loose whole spices on a 6-inch square of muslin and tie it into a sachet with a piece of unwaxed kitchen string. For a bouquet garni, use kitchen twine to tie together herbs like fresh parsley stalks, thyme sprigs, and bay leaves. These techniques make it easier to remove the aromatics after the soup is done.

DASHI

MAKES 1 QUART

Dashi (Japanese for "stock") is one of Japan's oldest culinary secrets. Dried seaweed and bonito flakes (dried, smoked flakes from the bonito fish) infuse the stock with a delicate and savory flavor. Japanese cooks use dashi as the base for many recipes, including miso soup, noodle dishes, and even salad dressings. It takes less time to make than vegetable stock but will imbue your soups with flavor just the same. You can also enjoy a hot bowl of dashi all by itself.

THREE 2-BY-3-INCH PIECES OF KOMBU (DRIED KELP)	1 CUP (1 OUNCE) BONITO FLAKES

❶ Pour 1 quart water into a medium pot and add the kombu. Bring to a simmer over medium heat and then reduce to a bare simmer for 20 to 30 minutes. Skim any foam that floats to the top of the water.

❷ Increase the heat to high; when the water reaches a boil, remove the pot from the heat. Use a slotted spoon to remove the kombu. Add the bonito flakes and let sit until all the flakes have absorbed water and sunk to the bottom of the pot, about 5 minutes.

❸ Set a fine-mesh sieve or colander lined with a coffee filter over another pot or bowl and strain the broth.

❹ Discard the bonito pulp. If not using the broth immediately, let cool to room temperature, pour into a container or freezer bag, seal, and refrigerate or freeze. You can also pour dashi into ice cube trays and freeze for later use. Tightly sealed, the stock will keep for 5 days in the refrigerator and can be frozen for up to 1 month.

VARIATIONS

• Season with a dash or two of mirin and soy sauce to add salinity and depth.

• Add 1 to 2 tablespoons miso at the end and the soup can serve as a simple meal or as a first course. (Make sure to add the miso *after* the dashi is off the heat.) A range of miso pastes, from white to deep terra-cotta red, are available; the lighter the color, the sweeter and lighter the flavor. Try the white first; if you like it and seek deeper flavor, move toward the darker shades.

• Add ½ cup thinly sliced fresh shiitake mushrooms, 1 cup cubed tofu, ¼ cup (about 3) slivered scallions, and a 1-inch piece of ginger, peeled and cut into fine julienne (see photo, opposite).

Tips for Layering Flavors

There are many ways to build a soup. Sweating aromatics creates a sweet, deep foundation that allows the other ingredients to shine. You can also build a broth with savory ingredients like bonito flakes or Parmigiano-Reggiano rinds. Puréeing a vegetable at its prime with sea salt coaxes out its essence. These techniques are used in soups and stews around the world. As you begin to create your own recipes, use them to build deeply satisfying soups.

BROWN MEAT FIRST

If you're adding meat to your soup or stew, browning proteins like meat or fowl, especially with skin, is an important step for building flavor and rendering fat. Heat your pot over medium-high heat and coat the bottom with oil. When the oil begins to shimmer, add the meat. When it's evenly browned, set the meat aside and use the rendered fat to cook the aromatics. Proteins like fish and other seafood should be added later, as they cook more quickly and do not need to be browned.

BUILD A FOUNDATION WITH AROMATICS

An onion gives a soup what it needs and then, after leaving its mark, quietly fades into the background. Soups around the globe are built on onions and their cohorts in the allium family: leeks, garlic, shallots, and scallions. Combined with diced, deeply flavored vegetables, they create the foundation for well-rounded soups. The combination of preferred aromatics changes depending on the region:

- French recipes rely on *mirepoix*: a compound of celery, carrots, and onion softened in butter.

- Traditional Italian recipes use *battuto*: a base of parsley, onion, and lard, with garlic added later so it doesn't burn.

- The Spanish foundation of choice is *sofrito*: onion, garlic, and tomatoes cooked in olive oil.

- Southeast Asian soups are grounded by a mix of garlic, ginger, and chiles cooked in peanut, palm, or coconut oil.

USE THE APPROPRIATE LIQUID

What makes soup, soup is the liquid. Choose a liquid that supports the other ingredients. For example, a rich duck stock should not be used for a puréed pea soup; you would use water to make sure that the pea flavor shines through. The primary liquids to use are the following:

Stock
A good stock cooks for a long time to absorb flavor and minerals from its ingredients. A vegetable-based stock (page 146) or stocks made from fish and meat bones (see the chicken stock on page 269) create a concentrated flavor base.

Quick Broths
Dried and pungent ingredients like miso, tomato paste, mushrooms, and bonito flakes quickly flavor a broth.

Water
This is a perfectly acceptable liquid to use, especially for puréed soups.

Flavoring Liquids
Try using liquids like coconut milk, which is what we use for our Green Curry with Chicken (page 162).

ADD SUPPORTIVE INGREDIENTS (AT THE RIGHT TIMES)

The order in which you add your ingredients depends on their cooking times. Add ingredients that will take longer to cook first, such as dried beans, browned meat, and grains like farro. Greens should always go in last because they cook quickly, and you want to preserve their bite and vibrant color.

FINISH THE SOUP

Something as straightforward as a squeeze of citrus or a healthy grating of Parmigiano-Reggiano can make a seemingly simple dish feel special and decadent. Here are some other finishing options:

Large Croutons
Croutons add wonderful crunch (see page 143).

Crème Fraîche or Greek Yogurt
Mixed with a squeeze of lemon juice and za'atar, a dollop looks lovely against a deeply hued soup.

Sherry Vinegar or Olive Oil
Try adding a dash or drizzle to finished soups.

Fresh Herbs
Tender herbs like cilantro and dill work best.

Ras el Hanout
(see page 155)

Making Soup Purées

The best puréed soups—from carrot to celery root to mushroom—have a smooth, lush texture. Inevitably when we serve them at Haven's Kitchen, our guests ask if we're *positive there is no cream* in the soup. A few people have even demanded to ask our cooks directly, and having confirmed with our kitchen team that, indeed, there is not one ounce of dairy in the soup, inquire about the "secret" ingredient. Here it is: finish the blending process with a good shot of olive oil, which provides the texture people associate with cream.

In general, you should opt for water rather than stock when making puréed soups. A water base allows the flavor of the vegetable to shine: shouldn't a broccoli purée taste like broccoli? And why would you want corn soup to taste like anything but corn? Another beautiful thing about purées is that they allow you to use the slightly bruised and battered produce that otherwise might have gone to waste.

PREPARE AND COOK THE BASE VEGETABLE

When prepping vegetables for a puréed soup, you want to cut them into small, uniform sizes so they cook evenly. To determine your knife cuts, consider how you will be cooking your vegetables. If you are cooking them in water (which will net a cleaner flavor than cooking them in stock), then simply chopping the vegetables is fine. Roasting hearty root vegetables before making them into soup concentrates the taste and adds depth, so you'll want to maximize their flavor by cutting them on the bias to create more surfaces to caramelize. Tender vegetables like peas and asparagus are best blanched before being blended, whereas potatoes should be simmered and softened up. But don't simmer for too long—vegetables should be cooked through, but not broken down so much that they lose flavor.

Roasting

When roasting root vegetables like carrots, cut them on the bias to increase the surface area that will caramelize (see page 15). Preheat the oven to 425°F. Toss the vegetables in a large bowl with olive oil and salt. Arrange the pieces on a baking sheet in an even layer and roast until golden and tender. The time will vary depending on the vegetable.

Blanching or Simmering

If blanching or simmering, bring a large pot of water to a boil and season with salt. Add the vegetables and cook until tender. Strain the vegetables, saving the cooking liquid for later. When using the cooking liquid to thin your soup, remember that it's already seasoned with salt, and taste before adding more.

PURÉE

Transfer the cooked vegetables to a blender. Pour in hot water or their cooking liquid—you want enough to completely cover them. Use the cooking liquid with moderation, given that it was salted.

Start blending on the lowest setting. Gradually increase the speed every few seconds to the highest level and purée for 2 to 3 minutes total. Observe the texture as you blend, and add more liquid as needed to achieve the desired consistency.

With the blender on high, slowly add the olive oil—about 1 tablespoon per cup of purée—to emulsify the soup. If the mixture looks too thick, slowly add more hot water while blending.

FINISH THE SOUP AND SERVE

Finish your soup with a light drizzle of a nut oil, like walnut, or pumpkin seed oil—something that will complement your soup—or a garnish of fresh herbs. It's always pretty to garnish a purée with a few cooked pieces of the primary vegetable: top pea soup, for instance, with crème fraîche and a few petite peas. It's a small detail that adds a touch of charm.

ROASTED CARROT SOUP

SERVES 4 TO 6

The goal when making a puréed soup is to coax a vegetable's flavor to shine through. One way to accomplish that is to roast the vegetables before you purée them. Roasting adds depth and highlights natural flavors. Adding the olive oil while blending creates a velvety texture.

3 POUNDS CARROTS	FINE SEA SALT
¼ CUP EXTRA-VIRGIN OLIVE OIL	RAS EL HANOUT (RECIPE FOLLOWS)

❶ Preheat the oven to 425°F. Line a baking sheet with parchment paper.

❷ Cut the carrots on the bias into 1-inch pieces. The angle increases the surface area that will brown and caramelize.

❸ Place the carrots in a large bowl, drizzle with about 2 tablespoons of the olive oil, and season with salt. Toss the carrots until evenly coated. Spread the carrots on the prepared baking sheet, spacing them evenly. Roast until the edges start to brown, 15 to 20 minutes.

❹ Transfer the carrots to a large stockpot. Pour in water to cover, about 5 cups. Bring to a boil over high heat, then reduce to a simmer and cook until the carrots are soft, 20 to 25 minutes.

❺ Working in batches, use a blender to purée the carrots and the cooking liquid. Fill the blender no more than halfway full and take care not to burn yourself. While blending, add the remaining 2 tablespoons olive oil. Add water as needed to reach the desired consistency.

❻ Taste and season with salt and ras el hanout and serve.

VARIATIONS

CARROT GINGER
When blending the carrots, add a 2-inch piece of fresh ginger, sliced.

MISO GINGER
Replace the water with dashi (see page 149), and while blending add 1 to 2 tablespoons red miso paste and a 2-inch piece of fresh ginger, sliced. Omit the ras el hanout.

COCONUT CURRY
Before adding the liquid, mix in 1 to 2 tablespoons of red curry paste. Replace 2 cups of water or stock with one 15-ounce can of coconut milk. Omit the ras el hanout.

Ras el Hanout

The name of this spice blend translates to "head of the shop," or "top shelf" for English speakers. There are infinite variations on ras el hanout. Some people add saffron; some recipes include the floral notes of dried rosebuds. Ras el hanout adds a warm, earthy flavor to dishes. You can also mix it into yogurt as a garnish for roasted vegetables like squash, sweet potatoes, and carrots, or try it as a rub.

1 TEASPOON CUMIN SEEDS, TOASTED AND GROUND

1 TEASPOON GROUND GINGER

1 TEASPOON FINE SEA SALT

½ TEASPOON SAFFRON

½ TEASPOON TURMERIC

½ TEASPOON GROUND CINNAMON

½ TEASPOON CARDAMOM PODS, TOASTED AND GROUND

½ TEASPOON CORIANDER SEEDS, TOASTED AND GROUND

½ TEASPOON GROUND NUTMEG

½ TEASPOON FRESHLY GROUND BLACK PEPPER

Whisk all the ingredients together in a small bowl. Store in a sealed container for up to a year.

PEA SOUP, CHILLED AND HOT

SERVES 6 TO 8

Chilling a warm soup in an ice bath preserves its color and flavor and is an easy technique to practice at home: fill a large bowl with half ice and half water, place a slightly smaller bowl on the ice, and pour in the soup in batches, whisking it until it is chilled throughout.

FINE SEA SALT	½ CUP FRESH FLAT-LEAF PARSLEY LEAVES
8 CUPS FRESH OR FROZEN GREEN PEAS, A FEW RESERVED FOR GARNISH	¼ CUP EXTRA-VIRGIN OLIVE OIL, PLUS MORE FOR DRIZZLING
½ CUP FRESH MINT LEAVES, PLUS A FEW FOR GARNISH	CRÈME FRAÎCHE (OPTIONAL)

❶ Prepare an ice bath and set a slightly smaller bowl in it.

❷ Fill a medium pot with about 4 quarts water, bring to a boil over high heat, and salt generously. You want to be able to taste the salt in the water, but it shouldn't quite taste like the sea because you will be using this water to thin the soup.

❸ When the water comes to a boil, add the peas (reserving a few for a garnish) and cook until tender, about 30 seconds. Add the mint and parsley leaves and cook for an additional 10 seconds, or until the herbs turn bright green.

❹ Remove the pot from the heat. Strain the peas and herbs but reserve the cooking water.

❺ Place the peas, mint, and parsley in a blender and add just enough cooking water to cover. Blend on high for about 30 seconds, adding more cooking water as needed to reach a smooth consistency. Continue to blend while slowly streaming in the olive oil.

❻ If you prefer to eat your soup hot, skip step 7.

❼ For cold soup, pour the soup into the bowl you've set in the ice bath. If you desire an even smoother consistency, strain the soup through a fine-mesh sieve as you pour it into the bowl. Whisk until thoroughly chilled. Once the soup has cooled, taste it and season with more salt as needed. It's important to do the final seasoning after the soup has cooled, as cold soups need a little more salt than hot soups.

❽ Pour the soup into serving bowls. Finish each bowl with crème fraîche if desired, a drizzle of olive oil, a few cooked peas, and torn mint leaves.

FISH CHOWDER

SERVES 6 TO 8

Like many creamier soups, this one is thickened with a roux. To make a roux, heat butter, oil, or another fat; stir in flour until well blended and toasty. In this case, fat is used to sauté the aromatics, and then the flour is added later. Smoked paprika, or pimentón, adds a subtle smokiness that lends warmth, which is welcomed on a cold night.

4 TABLESPOONS (½ STICK) UNSALTED BUTTER

1 LARGE YELLOW ONION, CHOPPED

1 CELERY STALK, CHOPPED

2 LEEKS, WHITE AND LIGHT GREEN PARTS ONLY, CLEANED AND THINLY SLICED

1 LARGE CARROT, CHOPPED

1 FENNEL BULB, CHOPPED

FINE SEA SALT

3 BAY LEAVES

2 GARLIC CLOVES, MINCED

1 TEASPOON PIMENTÓN, OR SMOKED PAPRIKA

3 TABLESPOONS ALL-PURPOSE FLOUR

4 CUPS WATER OR FISH STOCK, OR 2 CUPS WATER AND 2 CUPS CLAM JUICE

1 CUP DRY WHITE WINE

2 CUPS HEAVY CREAM

3 IDAHO RUSSET POTATOES, PEELED AND CUT INTO 1½-INCH DICE

1½ POUNDS FIRM WHITE FISH, SUCH AS COD, CUT INTO 1- TO 1½-INCH PIECES

FRESHLY GROUND BLACK PEPPER

JUICE OF ½ LEMON

2 TABLESPOONS FINELY CHOPPED FRESH CHIVES

2 TABLESPOONS FINELY CHOPPED FRESH FLAT-LEAF PARSLEY

❶ In a large, heavy-bottomed pot or Dutch oven, melt the butter over medium heat. Add the onion, celery, leeks, carrot, and fennel plus a large pinch of salt. Cook, stirring often, until tender, about 5 minutes. Add the bay leaves, garlic, and paprika, and cook for another minute.

❷ Create a roux by using a wooden spoon or spatula to stir the flour into the vegetables, until smooth. Add the water, stock, or clam juice and the wine and stir constantly, scraping the bottom of the pan, until the mixture returns to a simmer.

❸ Add the cream and potatoes and bring to just under a boil, or what is known as a "hard simmer." Cover the pot, leaving the lid slightly ajar. Cook until the potatoes are just tender, about 20 minutes.

❹ Reduce the heat to low and add the fish. Cover the pot and cook until the fish is opaque and cooked through, about 5 minutes. Remove from the heat. Season with salt, pepper, and lemon juice to taste. Divide among serving bowls and garnish with the chives and parsley.

GREEN CURRY WITH CHICKEN

SERVES 4 TO 6

The definition of curry has evolved over the ages, from an Indian dish seasoned with garlic, ginger, and turmeric to South Asian, Southeast Asian, and Caribbean potages and their colonial variations. This recipe is a good lesson in learning how to make your own curry paste.

3 GARLIC CLOVES

ONE 2-INCH PIECE OF FRESH GINGER, PEELED AND CHOPPED

2 JALAPEÑOS, STEMMED, SEEDED, AND CHOPPED

1 BUNCH OF CILANTRO, LEAVES AND STEMS, COARSELY CHOPPED, SOME RESERVED FOR GARNISH

2 TABLESPOONS NEUTRAL-FLAVORED OIL, SUCH AS GRAPESEED OR CANOLA

FINE SEA SALT

¼ CUP WATER

2 TABLESPOONS COCONUT OR GRAPESEED OIL, PLUS MORE AS NEEDED

1 WHOLE CHICKEN, CUT INTO 14 PIECES: 2 LEGS, 2 THIGHS, 2 WINGS, AND 4 PIECES CUT FROM EACH BREAST; OR 2 TO 3 POUNDS OF A COMBINATION OF THIGHS, BREASTS, AND LEGS, SKIN-ON

1 YELLOW ONION, THINLY SLICED

ONE 13.5-OUNCE CAN FULL-FAT UNSWEETENED COCONUT MILK

FRESHLY SQUEEZED LIME JUICE

❶ Make the curry paste: In the bowl of a food processor or blender, purée the garlic, ginger, jalapeños, cilantro (setting aside some for garnishing), grapeseed oil, and salt. With the machine running, slowly pour in the water and continue blending to create a smooth paste. Set aside.

❷ Heat the coconut oil in a large pot or Dutch oven over medium-high heat. When the oil begins to shimmer, add about half of the chicken, skin side down, or as many pieces as will fit in a single, uncrowded layer. Sear for about 4 minutes, until golden. The goal is to render the fat to flavor the aromatics in the next step. Turn the chicken pieces over and sear for another 4 minutes, and then transfer to a plate. Sear the remaining chicken pieces, working in batches.

❸ Reduce the heat to medium and add more oil, if necessary, to cover the bottom of the pot. Add the onion and a pinch of salt. Cook, stirring occasionally, for about 2 minutes, or until the onion is translucent. Add the chicken and the curry paste and stir for a minute. Stir in half of the coconut milk, mixing well to fully incorporate, then add the rest.

❹ Bring the soup to a boil. Reduce to a simmer and cook the soup, uncovered, for about 45 minutes.

❺ Season with salt and lime juice to taste. Garnish with chopped cilantro.

AJO BLANCO

SERVES 4

David introduced us to this Andalusian variation of gazpacho, made with almonds, garlic, and bread. It is a refreshing change from the usual tomato version. Try blanching your own almonds, but if you're looking for a shortcut, you can purchase them already blanched. Garnish it as David does: with a brunoise of cucumbers, halved green grapes, and sliced almonds.

1 CUP EXTRA-VIRGIN OLIVE OIL	1 ENGLISH CUCUMBER, PEELED AND CUBED; RESERVE ½ INCH TO BRUNOISE FOR GARNISH
6 GARLIC CLOVES, PEELED	
2 LARGE SLICES OF SOURDOUGH BREAD, GRILLED OR TOASTED, CRUST REMOVED, CUBED (ABOUT 1½ CUPS)	1½ CUPS WATER, PLUS MORE AS NEEDED
	1 TABLESPOON SHERRY VINEGAR
½ CUP MARCONA OR BLANCHED ALMONDS; RESERVE ¼ CUP FOR GARNISH	FINE SEA SALT
	½ CUP GREEN GRAPES, HALVED

❶ Prepare an ice bath and set a slightly smaller bowl in it.

❷ To make a garlic confit, combine the olive oil and garlic in a small saucepan and warm slowly over the lowest heat possible until the cloves turn light brown, about 15 minutes. Lift out the garlic with a slotted spoon and set aside; reserve the oil. You'll use it to drizzle on the finished soup. Store any remaining oil in the refrigerator for up to 1 week and use it in salad dressings and marinades.

❸ Using a blender, purée the bread, ¼ cup of the almonds, the cucumber, cooked garlic, and ½ cup of the water until a coarse meal forms. Gradually add the remaining 1 cup water and continue blending until smooth, adding more water—a few tablespoons at a time—if needed to loosen it up. Add the vinegar and then slowly drizzle in ½ cup of the reserved oil from the garlic confit, blending until the mixture has a smooth and silky texture. Add more water if needed to thin the soup to the desired consistency. Taste and season with salt.

❹ Pour the soup into the prepared bowl in the ice bath. For a very smooth texture, strain the soup through a fine-mesh sieve into the bowl set in the ice bath.

❺ While the soup is chilling, prepare the garnish. Toast and chop the remaining almonds and brunoise the cucumber (see page 9).

❻ When ready to serve, stir the soup until thoroughly chilled. Transfer to serving bowls and drizzle with garlic olive oil. Garnish with toasted, chopped almonds, cucumber brunoise, and halved grapes.

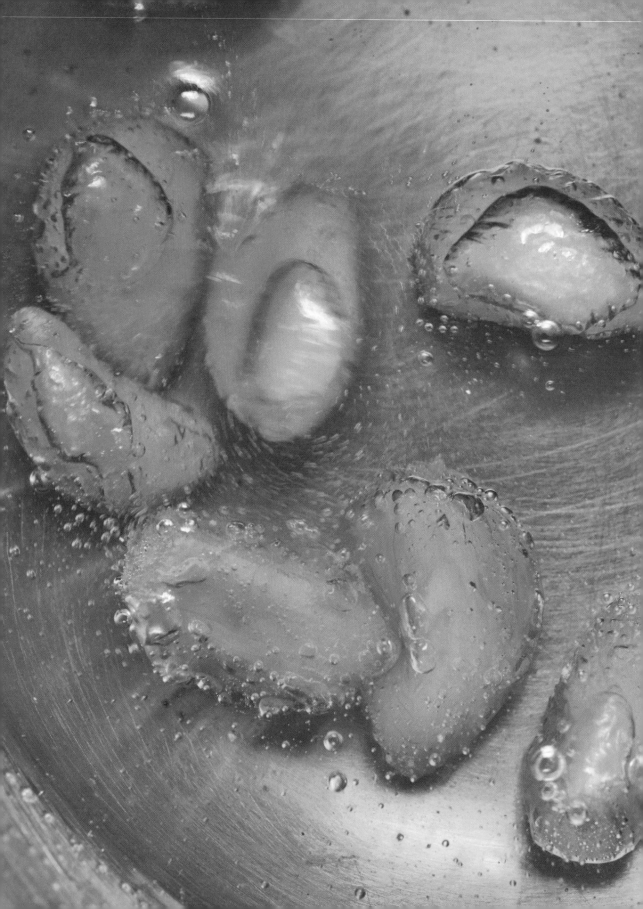

EGGS

"I had no idea this is what scrambled eggs could taste like."

—SYLVIA, HAVEN'S KITCHEN STUDENT

EGGS ARE THE MOST HUMBLE
ingredient. They are complete on their own, yet they are at their best when adding flavor, texture, and appeal to other dishes. You have to admit, it's amazing that one little ovoid can be capable of transforming, and being transformed into, so many different dishes.

There are very few meals that wouldn't be better with an egg involved. Salads drizzled with vinaigrette adorned with luscious poached eggs. Bowls of hot beans and rice crowned with lacy fried eggs. The opportunities are endless.

Learning to cook eggs teaches the fundamentals of how time and temperature affect your finished product. For example, an egg scrambled quickly over high heat will emerge from the pan quite different from one stirred slowly over low heat. And consider the flavor and texture of eggs boiled for just a few minutes compared with those of eggs boiled for a solid ten (or the unfortunate fifteen). As with most skills, repetition is the secret. Luckily, eggs are mostly foolproof and economical. Buy a dozen. If you mess up, they'll still taste pretty good—and there will always be more eggs in the fridge, so you can try again without too much regret.

Tools

SILICONE SPATULA

A heatproof 12-inch silicone spatula is all you really need for egg flipping, folding, and plating.

BALLOON WHISK

A balloon whisk aerates eggs and adds a fluff factor. Whisks come in several shapes and sizes; we recommend an 8-inch.

NONSTICK OVENPROOF SKILLET

A 10- to 12-inch nonstick ovenproof skillet is a boon to egg cooking and cleanup because of its rounded sides. For almost all other cooking, use stainless steel or cast iron, but nonstick is helpful in releasing eggs cleanly from the pan. You can certainly make do without a nonstick pan, but you will need to add more fat to the pan when cooking.

Preparations and Tips for Egg Making

There are as many preferences for how to cook eggs as there are egg eaters. By learning about heat and timing, you'll find techniques you love to get your poached eggs more custardy than runny, or make the delicate, lightly crisped edges around an over easy. Once you know how to boil, poach, scramble, and fry, the possibilities for how you can eat your eggs are infinite.

TIPS

- Eggs cook quickly no matter how you cook them, so they require careful observation.

- Look for "Certified Humane" eggs from grass-fed, free-range chickens raised on local farms. Healthier and happier chickens lay eggs with yolks that are bright yellow veering on orange.

- Temper your eggs. Let them come to room temperature for up to a half hour before cooking or baking. Tempered eggs cook more evenly, and when you need them for baking or Pavlovas or pancakes, they whip up better, adding more volume to the final product. If you don't have half an hour to wait, you can quickly temper eggs by placing them in a bowl of hot tap water for 3 to 5 minutes before using.

- Uncertain if that egg is still fresh? An older egg floats in a bowl of water; a fresh egg sinks.

POACHED EGGS

Contrary to what many people say, poaching eggs does not require special tools or a dash of vinegar. The only secret is getting the water hot enough to set the egg, but not so hot that the egg rips apart when you drop it in.

HOW TO POACH EGGS

1. Fill a large pot with enough water to cover the eggs by at least 4 inches. Some recipes call for adding vinegar during this step, but we prefer not to; vinegar makes the whites set more quickly but also leaves them rubbery.

2. Bring the water to a boil over high heat, and then reduce to a simmer. Look for a gentle stream of bubbles rising to the top. You want to avoid a violent boil. Continue adjusting the temperature while cooking so the water never comes back to a boil.

3. Crack the eggs one at a time into a small dish or bowl and gently slide each one into the water, as close to the surface as possible. The goal is to make sure the egg whites hold together.

4. Once the eggs are lying on the bottom of the pot, let them settle undisturbed until the whites are set, about 30 seconds. Gently stir the water once—without touching the eggs—so they don't stick to the bottom.

5. When the whites are cooked through and opaque, 1½ to 2 minutes, use a slotted spoon to remove them from the water one at a time.

6. If you are not eating the eggs immediately, place them in an ice bath (see page 95). If you won't be eating them for a few hours, place them (still in the ice bath) in the refrigerator until ready to serve. To reheat the eggs later, heat a pot of water just until it's too hot to leave your fingers in. Remove the pot from the heat and place the eggs in the water for 1 minute.

SERVING SUGGESTIONS

Poached eggs are the star of brunch fare like Eggs Benedict (page 186) or a bistro lunch like Salad with Poached Eggs (page 189).

Poached eggs are also an apt topper for our Toasted Farro with Roasted Winter Vegetables (page 216).

SOFT BOIL
4 minutes—a runny yolk with a just-set exterior

MEDIUM BOIL
6 minutes—a set exterior yolk, but a slightly runny center

MEDIUM-HARD BOIL
8 minutes—a custardy yolk

HARD BOIL
10 minutes—a firm, chalky yolk

BOILED EGGS

Boiling eggs is a fairly simple task. Boiling eggs so that the yolk has partly set in some places but remains golden and gooey in others is a whole different story.

Cooks disagree about whether you should start your eggs in cold water and bring to a boil or gently lay the eggs in water that's already boiling. I've made great eggs with both techniques, but the latter makes for easier peeling.

How long you boil your eggs is a matter of personal taste. Some people enjoy thoroughly hard-boiled eggs with crumbly yolks; some, a barely set yolk. Try different boiling times and get to know how many minutes it takes to get the yolk you want. Regardless of the cooking time, use older eggs, as superfresh eggs are more difficult to peel; temper them first; and don't forget the ice bath at the end, as it helps to separate the shell from the cooked egg inside.

HOW TO BOIL EGGS

1. Before boiling your eggs, temper them for half an hour. If you don't have time for that, place them in hot tap water for 3 to 5 minutes before boiling them. Tempered eggs will not crack when they go into boiling water.

2. Fill a large pot with enough water to cover the eggs by at least 1 inch. Bring to a rolling boil—big bubbles, turbulent water.

3. Gently lay the eggs in the water by resting them on a slotted spoon and sliding them in. The amount of time they boil will depend on what type of egg you desire.

4. Use a slotted spoon to scoop the eggs out of the pot and place them in an ice bath (see page 95) for about 3 minutes, or run them under very cold water for about 1 minute.

5. To open a soft-boiled egg, use the back of a spoon to gently tap the top. Remove the top section and scoop the egg directly from the shell. To open a medium- or hard-boiled egg, crack the bottom (the chubbier end of the oval), where there is a little air pocket, against a hard surface and peel.

6. If you are not eating the eggs immediately, place them in an ice bath. To reheat later, heat a pot of water just until it's too hot to leave your fingers in. Remove from the heat and place the eggs in the water for 1 minute.

SERVING SUGGESTIONS

Try sprinkling boiled eggs with za'atar or Aleppo pepper or douse them with Romesco Sauce (page 320) or Chimichurri (page 300). You can also use boiled eggs for Gribiche (page 314) or slice them for a salad.

SCRAMBLED EGGS

In the world of scrambled eggs, there are purists like Jacques Pépin who remain loyal to tiny curds of scrambled eggs cooked with ample butter, low heat, and constant stirring. On the other end of the spectrum are those like my high school friend Vicki, who cooked her eggs in about 10 seconds over high heat by mixing them in a rather flamboyant zigzagging motion until they were cooked to a crisp. Both methods are equally delicious. This method follows the Jacques Pépin school because it demonstrates how taking the time to stir eggs over low heat produces the creamiest, most delicate scrambled eggs many of our students have ever had.

The secret is removing the eggs from the heat just at the moment when they "set" and no longer look liquid. The residual heat in the pan finishes the cooking process. The most important instruction is to *watch* so you know when the eggs hit that magic point.

HOW TO SCRAMBLE EGGS

1. In a bowl, whisk 3 eggs with a splash of water or milk and a pinch of salt until the yolks and whites are fully blended.

2. Put ½ tablespoon butter in a room-temperature nonstick skillet—a 6- to 8-inch pan is best so the eggs will be concentrated and won't overcook. Set over low heat. Once the butter has melted, add the whisked eggs.

3. Use a silicone spatula to stir continually, gently folding the eggs curdling around the edges into the center of the pan, so the uncooked eggs can reach the heat. Even if you do not see action, don't be tempted to raise the heat!

4. When the eggs begin to set but are still slightly runny, fold in a pat of butter, gratings of cheese, or a couple tablespoons of herbs.

5. When the eggs are glistening and porridge-like in texture, about 5 minutes, lift the pan off the burner—but don't remove the eggs yet. You want the residual heat from the pan to finish the process; the eggs will need about 30 more seconds to fully set. Serve hot.

SERVING SUGGESTIONS

Soft scrambled eggs are an admirable and complete meal on their own. Make the dish decadent by adding a dollop of crème fraîche. They are comforting on buttered toast with chopped parsley or chives, or serve them with warm tortillas, José's Black Beans (page 39), and Tomatillo Salsa (page 312).

OMELET

There is something elegant about a chef-made omelet, with its symmetrical folds and its melted cheese and spinach so well contained. My omelets, in contrast, were always a little haphazard and unkempt. Fine tasting, but with a few stray leaves or onions most definitely out of place. With a bit of practice, you will eventually master the trifold with all the pieces tucked in.

HOW TO MAKE AN OMELET

1. Prepare the filling (optional). One-quarter cup of filling suffices for a 3-egg omelet. Cut your ingredients into uniform bite-sized pieces. Sauté uncooked ingredients like vegetables and meats until tender. Do not cook herbs or cheese. Set aside.

2. Combine 3 large eggs with a splash of water or milk, a pinch of salt, and 1 tablespoon cold butter cut into tiny cubes. Whisk together until the yolks and whites are fully blended.

3. Place a serving plate next to the stovetop so it's ready to receive the omelet as soon as it's done. Put 1 tablespoon butter in an 8- to 10-inch nonstick skillet and set over high heat.

4. When the butter has just melted—but is not yet brown—add the eggs. While moving the pan back and forth on the heat, work a silicone spatula around the edges of the pan and fold the eggs to the center to cook; they should look like drapey folds rather than scrambled curds. When the bottom of the egg is set but the top is still a little runny, remove the pan from the heat.

5. Arrange the prepared filling, if using, in the middle of the eggs. Sprinkle any cheese so it melts first.

Don't overstuff, or the omelet will not fold over nicely. Let it sit for a few seconds to melt the cheese.

6. Fold the omelet in thirds, like a letter. Use the spatula to fold a third of the egg over the middle. While sliding the omelet off the pan onto the plate, roll the omelet over so the folded sides are on the bottom.

Filling Options:
Crispy Sautéed Mushrooms (page 102) and Comté cheese

Pancetta, shallot, and Gruyère

Spring onions and asparagus

SERVING SUGGESTIONS

A plain omelet, a salad of baby spinach dressed with good extra-virgin olive oil and a dash of salt, and a crisp glass of Chablis makes for a filling and refined meal for one. If you're feeling intimidated, start by adding different cheeses, and work your way up to more complicated fillings as you get more comfortable with your skills.

HOW TO MAKE AN OMELET

1 Place butter in a skillet set over high heat.

2 Pour in the eggs while moving the pan back and forth to spread them out.

3 Using a silicone rubber spatula, keep folding the eggs into the center of the pan.

4 Work the spatula around the edges of the pan, coaxing the eggs toward the center.

5 Add the filling to the middle of the eggs. Don't overstuff.

6 Let the omelet sit for a few seconds while the cheese melts and softens the filling.

7 Fold the omelet into thirds, bringing each side into the middle.

8 Roll the omelet out of the pan onto a plate, folded side down.

FRIED EGGS

Even when they go it alone, a pair of fried eggs makes for a quick and gratifying meal in a pinch.

FOR SUNNY-SIDE UP

1. Heat a nonstick skillet over medium-low heat. (The size of your pan depends on how many eggs you are frying.) Put about ½ tablespoon unsalted butter per egg in the pan.

2. When the butter melts and starts to sizzle, crack the eggs into the pan. Do not disturb for 45 seconds, or until the whites set. There will still be some uncooked whites around the yolk. Remember, if you start at a higher temperature, the eggs may set more quickly.

3. Cook for another 45 seconds to 1 minute. Gently shake the pan while cooking to release the eggs from the bottom of the pan.

4. For extra flavor, spoon melted butter from the pan over the eggs while they're cooking.

FOR EGGS "OVER"

1. Heat a nonstick skillet over medium-low heat. Put about ½ tablespoon unsalted butter per egg in the pan.

2. When the butter melts and starts to sizzle, crack the eggs into the pan. Do not disturb for at least 45 seconds, until the whites set.

3. Once the whites set, use a silicone spatula to flip the eggs.

For over easy, cook for another 15 to 30 seconds.

For over medium, cook for another 1½ minutes.

For over hard, cook for another 2 minutes.

4. Gently shake the pan while cooking to release the eggs from the bottom of the pan.

5. For extra flavor, spoon melted butter from the pan over the eggs while they're cooking.

6. Use the spatula to gently remove the eggs from the pan, keeping the yolks intact.

SERVING SUGGESTION

While most people put fried eggs on top of something, consider placing them on the *bottom*. Set an over-medium egg on a plate and then top it with baby arugula and Superquick Pickled Red Onions (page 111). The egg blends with an acidic vinaigrette, creating nature's best sauce.

MY DAD'S FRIED EGG

My father has recently opened up to me a lot about his younger days: the war, the women, the *food*. I grew up watching him make these eggs, but it wasn't until last year that I asked him why he makes them this way. The answer? Because he wanted his whites supercrispy and his yolk superrunny. The hot butter and heat from the bottom crisp up the whites, while steam from the splash of water ensures that the yolks don't overcook.

1. Heat a small nonstick skillet over medium-low heat. Add 1 tablespoon unsalted butter and swirl it around so it covers the entire pan.

2. When the butter melts, crack the egg into the pan and raise the heat to high.

3. Sprinkle as much water as you can hold in your hand (about a teaspoon) into the pan and then cover it tightly. Cook the egg for about 1 minute.

4. Remove the pan from the heat and season the egg with salt and pepper.

Serving Suggestion
This egg is best served old-school: laid atop a half-burnt, heavily buttered slice of thin seeded rye toast. Break the yolk and add more salt to your liking.

FRITTATA

A frittata is a dependable dish for entertaining as it can be made ahead of time. Complete the recipe through step 5. Once the frittata is out of the oven, instead of plating it on a serving dish, put it on a foil-lined baking sheet, wrap, and refrigerate.

When you're ready to serve, unwrap it and pop it under the broiler for 3 to 5 minutes, checking frequently, until the frittata is warm and the cheese bubbles. Transfer to a serving plate.

HOW TO MAKE A FRITTATA

1. Preheat the oven to 325°F.

2. In a large bowl, combine 12 large eggs with ⅓ cup half-and-half and about 1 teaspoon fine sea salt. Whisk until well blended. Set aside.

3. Heat a 10-inch ovenproof nonstick pan over medium-high heat and pour in 1 tablespoon neutral-flavored oil (such as grapeseed or canola). Add 1 cup chopped vegetables—no more or the frittata won't hold its shape—and a generous pinch of sea salt. Sauté until the vegetables are tender.

4. When the vegetables are cooked and their residual liquid has evaporated, pour in the egg mixture. Using a silicone spatula, gently fold the eggs from the edges into the center. Stir constantly so the eggs on the bottom do not overcook. Remove the pan from the heat when the eggs begin to set in drapey folds and the top is still a little runny.

5. Sprinkle with grated cheese—Gruyère is nice—and place in the oven. Cook until the top is set, about 6 minutes.

6. Remove the pan from the oven and set it on a wire cooling rack; let the frittata cool for at least 5 minutes. Holding the pan with your nondominant hand, work a silicone spatula around the edges and beneath the frittata to gently release it, then slide it out onto a cutting board or serving platter. Serve warm or at room temperature.

Filling Options:

Red peppers, scallions, Manchego

Mushroom, pancetta, Parmigiano-Reggiano

Leeks, cauliflower, Gruyère

HUEVOS DIVORCIADOS

SERVES 4

This is a fun, brightly colored egg dish that the father of our kitchen manager, Zoe Maya Jones, taught her. It's Mexican inspired, separating two eggs with a barrier of beans and topping each egg with its own zesty salsa. One green, one red—each egg "going its separate way."

2 CUPS JOSÉ'S BLACK BEANS (PAGE 39)	½ CUP TOMATILLO SALSA (PAGE 312)
8 LARGE EGGS, FRIED OR POACHED (SEE PAGES 180 AND 170)	½ CUP PICO DE GALLO (RECIPE FOLLOWS)

❶ On four plates, arrange ½ cup of beans in a line down the center of the plate.

❷ Set 1 egg on each side of the beans.

❸ Evenly divide the salsa and pico de gallo for four servings, and spoon one of the salsas around each egg, so you have a green and a red side.

❹ Serve immediately.

Pico de Gallo

MAKES ABOUT 3 CUPS

2 CUPS SEEDED, ¼-INCH DICE TOMATOES	1 JALAPEÑO, SEEDED AND MINCED
½ CUP FINELY DICED WHITE ONION	JUICE OF 1 LIME, OR MORE TO TASTE
⅓ CUP CHOPPED FRESH CILANTRO, OR MORE TO TASTE	FINE SEA SALT

In a bowl, combine the tomatoes, onion, cilantro, jalapeño, lime juice, and salt to taste. Let the salsa sit for 30 minutes or so for the flavors to marry and then taste again. Add more salt, lime juice, or cilantro if desired.

EGGS BENEDICT

SERVES 4

Some classics never get boring. While not a "simple" recipe, conquering Eggs Benedict will certainly give you a sense of accomplishment and will wow anyone you're feeding. The most important aspect of the recipe is the hollandaise sauce—a French "mother" sauce made from an emulsion of egg yolks and clarified butter. This sauce is best made right before serving, as it can change texture quickly and doesn't store or reheat well.

8 LARGE EGGS, POACHED (SEE PAGE 170)

1 TABLESPOON NEUTRAL-FLAVORED OIL, SUCH AS GRAPESEED OR CANOLA

8 SLICES OF CANADIAN BACON OR GOOD-QUALITY HAM

4 ENGLISH MUFFINS, SLICED

FOR THE HOLLANDAISE SAUCE

½ POUND PLUS 4 TABLESPOONS (2½ STICKS) UNSALTED BUTTER

3 LARGE EGG YOLKS

3 TABLESPOONS WATER

2 TEASPOONS FRESHLY SQUEEZED LEMON JUICE

FINE SEA SALT AND FRESHLY GROUND BLACK PEPPER

❶ Poach the eggs according to the directions, then hold in an ice bath until ready to reheat and serve.

❷ Warm a 10-inch sauté pan over medium-high heat and pour in the oil. When the oil begins to shimmer, add the ham and cook until it browns, 1 to 2 minutes on each side. Set aside until ready to serve.

❸ Prepare the hollandaise sauce. Clarify the butter by melting in a small, heavy-bottomed saucepan. Simmer rapidly for about 10 minutes, until the water has evaporated and the milk solids have coagulated on the bottom and sides of the pan. You will see little brown bits and smell a nutty aroma.

❹ Remove the pan from the heat and let the butter sit for a few minutes to allow the solids to fall to the bottom. Skim the foam off the top and pour the melted butter through a cheesecloth-lined strainer into a small bowl. Let cool.

❺ Combine the egg yolks and water in a saucepan, preferably a pan with sloped sides, called a "saucier." Off the heat, whisk the eggs and water for 30 seconds, whipping in lots of air. Cook the mixture over very low heat, whisking constantly and scraping the sides, until thick and voluminous, 5 to 6 minutes. The whisk will leave tracks that hold for a few seconds. At this point, take the eggs off the heat and whisk rapidly for 30 seconds to cool slightly. Gradually add

the clarified butter in a thin, steady stream, whisking constantly. Be sure the butter isn't too hot or it will break the emulsion.

6 Whisk in the lemon juice and season with salt and pepper. Leave in a warm place while you assemble the dish.

7 To reheat the poached eggs, heat a pot of water just until it's too hot to leave your fingers in. Remove the pot from the heat and place the eggs in the water for 1 minute. Meanwhile, toast the English muffins.

8 To serve, open the toasted English muffins on each plate. Add the ham, poached eggs, and a good drizzle of hollandaise sauce.

SALAD WITH POACHED EGGS

SERVES 2 TO 4

For dinner one evening, try playing with a typical French bistro salad by poaching a few eggs, spooning them onto a bed of greens, and drizzling with Shallot Vinaigrette. If you are inclined to stay traditional, garnish with lardons—¼-inch strips of thick-cut bacon, cooked over medium heat until crisped. Pour yourself a glass of something cold, sit down with a cloth napkin, and notice the happiness your mouth feels when the eggs meet the salty-sweet dressing. You may decide to finish more of your days this way.

4 TO 8 POACHED EGGS, DEPENDING ON HOW HUNGRY YOU ARE

3 OR 4 SLICES OF THICK-CUT BACON, IF THE MOOD STRIKES

EXTRA-VIRGIN OLIVE OIL

SHALLOT VINAIGRETTE (PAGE 231)

2 HEADS OF ASSORTED GREENS, TORN

2 SHAVED RADISHES

FLAKY SEA SALT, SUCH AS MALDON, TO FINISH

❶ Poach the eggs according to instructions (see page 170). Hold them in cold water until ready to plate.

❷ If you're adding lardons, slice the bacon into short ¼-inch strips. Heat a medium skillet over medium heat and pour in enough oil to cover the bottom. Add the bacon and cook, stirring occasionally, until most of the fat has rendered and the strips are browned and crispy, 5 to 8 minutes. Set aside on a plate lined with paper towels.

❸ Make the vinaigrette and toss the greens and radishes with a good drizzle of the dressing. Taste and add more if needed. Arrange on a large serving platter or individual plates. Sprinkle with Maldon salt.

❹ Gently lay the eggs on top of the salad and drizzle with a little extra dressing. Top with lardons if you like.

GOAT CHEESE TART

SERVES 6 TO 8

Goat cheese is more tangy than its cow-created counterparts, making this recipe a slightly zippier alternative to a quiche. A great reward for practicing your dough-making skills, the tart is creamy and beautiful, and can be eaten at any time of the day. Serve hot, warm, or at room temperature with a light salad.

GALETTE DOUGH (PAGE 361), MADE WITHOUT SUGAR

ALL-PURPOSE FLOUR, FOR ROLLING THE DOUGH

3 LARGE EGGS

1 CUP HEAVY CREAM

10 OUNCES GOAT CHEESE, CRUMBLED

FINE SEA SALT

½ CUP CHOPPED FRESH HERBS, SUCH AS TARRAGON, PARSLEY, OR CHIVES

1 OR 2 LARGE HEIRLOOM TOMATOES, SLICED

8 TO 10 SMALL TOMATOES, SUCH AS CHERRY OR SUNGOLD, HALVED

❶ Make the galette dough. Wrap in plastic, and chill for at least 30 minutes.

❷ Preheat the oven to 375°F.

❸ Lightly flour a dry, cool surface. Roll out the dough in a circle, moving away from the center and rotating often, until it's about 14 inches in diameter and ¼ inch thick. Sprinkle with flour to prevent sticking. (For tips, see page 363.)

❹ To transfer the dough to the tart pan, roll it loosely around the rolling pin and unroll it onto a 10- to 11-inch tart pan. Press the dough into the corners and sides, and prick the bottom and sides with a fork to prevent air pockets. There will be excess dough hanging over the edge; leave it for now. Put the tart crust in the freezer for 15 minutes to rest and chill.

❺ Cut the excess dough from the edges. Blind bake the crust: Line the tart crust with aluminum foil and fill it with pie weights, dried beans, or rice to weight it down. Bake for 20 to 25 minutes, remove the weights and foil, and bake for another 5 to 10 minutes, or until golden brown.

❻ While the crust is baking, combine the eggs, cream, and goat cheese in the bowl of a food processor. Pulse until smooth, about 30 seconds. Add a pinch of salt and the herbs, and pulse for another 5 seconds.

❼ Lower the oven temperature to 275°F when you remove the crust.

❽ Pour the filling into the tart crust, evening it out with a spatula. Set the tomatoes into the tart, faceup.

❾ Bake for another 40 minutes, until set and golden.

EGGS EN COCOTTE

SERVES 4

These individually plated charmers make for a special brunch. And while not as skills-intensive as making tarts or soufflés, these eggs, in their delicate ramekins, are just as elegant. Adorned with chopped herbs, they have the power to elicit a collective cheer, even from the non–morning people.

2 TABLESPOONS UNSALTED BUTTER, SOFTENED	FRESHLY GROUND BLACK PEPPER
4 TABLESPOONS HEAVY CREAM	1 TABLESPOON ROUGHLY CHOPPED FRESH FLAT-LEAF PARSLEY
4 TABLESPOONS FRESHLY GRATED PARMIGIANO-REGGIANO	4 OR 5 TORN FRISÉE LEAVES
8 LARGE EGGS	TWO OR THREE 1-INCH CHIVE BATONS
FINE SEA SALT	GOOD CRUSTY BREAD, FOR SERVING (OPTIONAL)

❶ Preheat the oven to 350°F. Bring a medium pot or kettle of water to a boil.

❷ Coat four 8-ounce ramekins or small ovenproof dishes with the butter.

❸ Put 1 tablespoon cream and 1 tablespoon Parmigiano-Reggiano in each ramekin. Gently mix together.

❹ Crack 2 eggs into each ramekin. Season with a small pinch of salt and a few grinds of pepper.

❺ Place the ramekins in a roasting pan. Fill the pan with boiling water until it reaches halfway up the sides of the ramekins. Carefully place the pan in the oven, taking care not to slosh the water, and bake until the whites are just set and the cream is bubbling, 10 to 12 minutes.

❻ Using tongs, remove the ramekins from the roasting pan and set on a wire rack to cool. Sprinkle with the parsley, frisée, and chives, and serve with crusty bread if desired.

CHEESE SOUFFLÉ: THE MOST INTIMIDATING EGG DISH, DEMYSTIFIED

SERVES 6

Despite their reputation, soufflés are not that difficult to make. But on the off chance your soufflé collapses, just do what the mentor of our culinary director, David, taught him: pass it off as intentional and call it a "fallen soufflé." A cheese soufflé is a warming weeknight dinner accompanied by greens with sherry vinaigrette and a hunk of crusty baguette. With butter, what the heck.

3 TABLESPOONS UNSALTED BUTTER, PLUS MORE FOR GREASING THE RAMEKINS

¼ CUP PLUS 2½ TABLESPOONS ALL-PURPOSE FLOUR

2 CUPS MILK

2 CUPS GRATED GRUYÈRE

5 LARGE EGG YOLKS

FINE SEA SALT AND FRESHLY GROUND WHITE PEPPER

6 LARGE EGG WHITES

❶ Preheat the oven to 425°F. Butter six 8-ounce ramekins and place on a baking sheet.

❷ In a medium, heavy-bottomed saucepan, melt the butter over medium heat. When the butter is melted but not brown, whisk in the flour and cook, stirring continuously, for about a minute. It will have the consistency of a roux (see page 160), thick and paste-like. Whisk in a third of the milk to combine, then slowly whisk in the remaining milk until smooth. While constantly whisking, bring to a boil. Reduce to a simmer and cook for 3 minutes, still whisking to prevent lumps from forming. Remove the pan from the heat and whisk in the cheese.

❸ In a large bowl, whisk the egg yolks until uniformly mixed, about 3 seconds. Whisking constantly, very slowly pour the milk and cheese batter into the yolks, taking care not to pour the warm milk mixture into the cool eggs too quickly as that will curdle them. It should take 45 seconds to 1 minute to pour the batter into the yolks. The mixture will be smooth and light yellow. Whisk in a pinch of salt and a few grinds of white pepper. Cover with a lightly greased piece of parchment or plastic to prevent a skin from forming. Set aside.

4 In the bowl of a stand mixer fitted with the whisk attachment, combine the egg whites and a pinch of salt. Whisk on medium-high speed until the whites form soft peaks, about 1½ minutes.

5 Using a silicone spatula, fold a third of the egg whites into the yolk mixture; beat by hand with a whisk until evenly mixed, then gently fold in the remaining egg whites. Spoon the batter evenly into the prepared ramekins, filling each with about 1 cup of the mixture.

6 Place the baking sheet in the oven and bake, rotating the pan halfway through, until the soufflés have doubled in volume and are golden brown, about 14 minutes.

7 Remove from the oven and serve immediately.

SALADS

"A salad with too many walnuts . . . is like a Sunday with too many free hours—you stop appreciating the pleasure they provide."

—APRIL BLOOMFIELD

SALADS HAVE A LOT TO TEACH

about composition: if you've ever been disappointed by a salad that looked like someone just dumped some veggies in a bowl and added a few dried cranberries for good measure, you know what I mean. Contrast that with the salads you've eaten that boasted thoughtful pops of color and bursts of flavor and texture. Salads that have remained favorites over time teach us to think about the base ingredient not just as the bulk of the salad, but also as an *opening note* for creating a well-composed dish. Adding ingredients means creating counterpoints of complementary flavors and textures by adding just enough of what will taste (flavor) and feel (texture) good together.

My mother's deep appreciation of food has always compensated for her limited culinary skills. Take her Waldorf salad, for example. Her version is a multidimensional festival of toasted walnuts, tart apple cubes, tender shredded chicken, diced celery, and golden raisins. Rather than casually throwing them all in the bowl together, she considers her ingredients and how they taste and look and feel once combined. She is generous yet restrained, and just when you start missing the cold, slightly sour apple, you'll find yourself biting into one. Every time I plunge my fork into the bowl, I feel like I am winning a different combination of textures, tastes, and colors.

Composition is the difference between a salad that's essentially a hodgepodge and one that tantalizes. A well-composed salad is a master class in creating joy and surprise in every forkful. Making salad is an opportunity to practice the art of composition, play around with flavors and textures, and figure out how to make what you like to eat and why it appeals to you. Once you know that, cooking becomes a creative and delicious pastime.

Teaching Recipe

BUTTER LETTUCE WITH BLUE CHEESE, DRIED CHERRIES, AND CANDIED WALNUTS

SERVES 4

This salad exemplifies how balancing textures—creamy, chewy, and crunchy—is just as important as flavors—sweet, tangy, and briny. For the blue cheese in this recipe, at Haven's Kitchen we are smitten with the Point Reyes Original Blue. It's bright, peppery, and supercreamy.

HERB BUTTERMILK DRESSING (PAGE 241)

¾ CUP CANDIED WALNUTS
(RECIPE FOLLOWS)

1 LARGE HEAD OF BUTTER LETTUCE

⅓ CUP SOFT BLUE CHEESE, CRUMBLED

¼ CUP DRIED CHERRIES

2 TABLESPOONS FRESH CHIVES,
CUT INTO 1-INCH BATONS

DRESSING & FINISH

❶ Make the buttermilk dressing and the walnuts.

COOKING NOTES

Think ahead about how you'll want to finish a salad and add that final oomph of flavor, color, or texture.

The dressing brings together all the flavors in your salad. In this case, the herb buttermilk dressing is tangy, countering the sweet chew of the dried cherries. The walnuts give a caramelized crunch that adds an addictive flavor and texture to each bite.

Some ingredients are worth making from scratch. These walnuts are among them. Make them in advance, and make extra for snacking. You could also substitute toasted walnuts if pressed for time.

continued

BASE INGREDIENT

② Tear the lettuce into bite-sized pieces.

The base ingredient makes up the bulk of the salad. The other flavors and textures play off the base. We often default to leafy lettuce, but consider grains or beans, vegetable-based salads, or even bread.

If you're not sure where to start, choose a mellow green that's in season and that is hearty enough to hold up to the acid in the dressing.

Tear, don't cut, lettuce into bite-sized pieces that are easy to eat. Using a knife on lettuce bruises the tender leaves.

COUNTERPOINTS

③ Place the lettuce in a large bowl with about three-quarters of the blue cheese, cherries, walnuts, and chives.

Consider counterpoints by thinking about texture like chewy, creamy, crispy, and crunchy elements, and flavor. Crumbled pungent, creamy blue cheese complements mellow butter lettuce, and the handful of tart, chewy dried cherries counters the intense bite of the cheese.

Do not overwhelm the base with too many counterpoints. Remember, a balanced composition is key.

ASSEMBLY

④ Drizzle a few tablespoons of the dressing over the salad and gently toss with your hands until the greens are lightly coated. Add more dressing and salt to taste.

Start with a little dressing and add more if needed. You can't go back once you've added too much, and an overdressed salad is disappointing.

Tossing with your hands evenly distributes the dressing and prevents the lettuce from bruising.

SERVING

5 Place the salad in a serving dish (or wipe the messy sides of the tossing bowl with a moist paper towel) and top with the remaining cheese, cherries, walnuts, and chives, plus a sprinkling of black pepper.

Finish the salad with a final garnish of flavor, color, or texture: It can be a few swipes of citrus peel, a handful of herbs left over from making your dressing, or some reserved counterpoints.

Always consider the final presentation, even when you're eating alone; plate your salad or wipe off the edges of the tossing bowl.

Candied Walnuts

MAKES 1 CUP

Walnuts are cooked in a simple syrup until tender and then fried. This recipe makes enough for the salad plus a few to munch on.

1 CUP WATER

1 CUP SUGAR

1 CUP WALNUTS

CANOLA OR VEGETABLE OIL, FOR FRYING

FLAKY SEA SALT, SUCH AS MALDON, TO FINISH

1 In a small pot, combine the water and sugar and bring to a simmer. Add the walnuts and cook over medium-high heat until tender and slightly translucent, about 15 minutes.

2 Meanwhile, in a separate small pot, pour in enough oil to completely cover the walnuts, but no more than halfway up the sides, and slowly heat to 300°F.

3 When the nuts are cooked, remove them with a slotted spoon and place on paper towels to dry.

4 When the oil is ready, use the slotted spoon to gently place the nuts in the oil. Fry in uncrowded batches until golden brown; this should take less than 1 minute.

5 Use the slotted spoon to remove the nuts from the oil and place on a wire rack to cool. Season with flaky sea salt while warm.

Types of Salad

Salads are a lovely way to begin a meal. They refresh the palate and prepare you for the more robust dishes to come. They are also, as the French showed us, a cleansing finale to a richer, heavier supper. But don't relegate salads to the margins: they shine as a main course as well.

Making a salad is an experiment with ingredients, techniques, and even knife cuts. Roast vegetables; toast nuts. Chiffonade your kale. Cut your carrots on the bias. Brunoise your apples. Salads should showcase seasonal produce and your favorite pantry items, but the assembled ingredients should complement one another with no single one dominating—and that includes the dressing.

LEAFY SALADS

A leafy salad is a staple of summertime, when lettuces are growing strong and fresh. I like Little Gem lettuce, a sweeter, gentler, baby romaine that's crisp enough to hold up to dressings without wilting, and less bitter than some of its sturdier counterparts. In warmer parts of the country, lettuce grows year-round, but even northeasterners can enjoy local-leaf salads nine months of the year. One may pooh-pooh the ubiquity and faddish appeal of kale salad, but its ingenious introduction into our repertoire has extended the seasonality of the green salad way beyond Labor Day: frost makes kale sweeter and more pleasant to eat.

VEGETABLE-BASED SALADS

Some salads don't include a single leaf of lettuce. A vegetable-based salad is a resourceful way to use up the produce lingering in your refrigerator. Vegetable salads are ideal for the colder months when lettuce bows out to thicker-skinned vegetables and those that grow *underground*, where it's nice and warm. You can use raw or roasted vegetables or a combination thereof; a salad composed of sliced celery, grated celery root, and toasted pistachios dressed with extra-virgin olive oil and lemon is a poetic meal. Roasting vegetables, letting them cool, and tossing them with raw vegetables and cooked nutty grains, like our Toasted Farro with Roasted Winter Vegetables and Tahini Dressing (page 216), is a pleasing way to enjoy the duality of vegetables.

SLAWS

Slaws have tremendous potential to be flavorful and sophisticated. In other words, they are not just shaved cabbage and feeble bits of carrots coated in mayonnaise. Slaws are often best made ahead of time; they only get better as they sit and await being eaten. Because of this, a slaw is a smart dish to bring to a potluck or, better yet, a picnic. I've even *planned* a picnic as an excuse to make Thai Cabbage Slaw (page 222).

SALADS WITH GRAINS OR LEGUMES

Salads featuring grains or beans as the main element are hearty and satiating. Like slaws, they are also a nice dish to pack for a big party, lunch at the office, or a long flight. When hosting a brunch, make batches of grains the night before, let them cool and dry out on baking sheets, and then transfer to bowls and refrigerate, uncovered, before you turn in for the night. Leaving them uncovered dries the grains, which prevents mushiness and makes them more amenable to being dressed later on. The next morning, toss the grains with an array of vegetables, fruits, nuts or seeds, and dressings and let them sit for a few hours to marry the flavors. Just before guests arrive, taste the salads and doctor them up with lemon zest, fresh herbs, and cheese.

Make a batch of beans over the weekend and use them as the base for salads throughout the week. Beans add texture and nutrients to salads and love absorbing the flavors of dressings.

Tips for Salad Making

Making salad is an opportunity to master the art of composition and experiment with ingredients. How do you craft a satisfying salad without being slavish to a particular recipe? Consider the following questions to determine a good starting point:

- Are you trying to re-create a salad you've enjoyed? If so, what did you like about it? What are the key elements? What made it work?

- Are you making up a recipe? If so, have you imagined what you want your final dish to look and taste like?

- What ingredients do you need? How do they need to be prepped? Is there work to do ahead of time?

- What ingredients do you have on hand that you can use?

- Will this be a side salad or the main dish?

- Do you want to eat it now or later?

PREPARE YOUR INGREDIENTS

For leafy salads, wash your greens ahead of time. The key is to have them clean and dry. For vegetables, consider the knife cut that will work best with the final salad: celery can be sliced on the bias, diced, or cut into matchsticks depending on the kind of bite you want. Many cooks like to salt their kale before adding it to a salad. For every bunch of kale, massage about ½ teaspoon sea salt into the leaves. The fibers break down just enough to make them more tender without affecting the crunch. If you plan on including beans, remember to soak them beforehand. Toast your nuts and seeds before composing your salad.

THINK ABOUT COUNTERPOINTS

Salads that have remained favorites over time teach us to think about the base ingredient not just as the bulk of the salad, but as an *opening note* for creating a well-composed dish. The trick to composing a salad is considering ingredients that will taste good together, blend well, and bring out the best in one another. Do not throw in everything but the kitchen sink. Avocado and almonds are an example of common salad mates. Too many almonds without enough avocado is hard work on the mouth and makes for a decidedly dry dish. On the other hand, too much avocado can be a letdown as you find yourself digging around for something to chomp on. Balance the dryness of crusty croutons with tart, pickled red onions and juicy tomatoes, and creamier cheese for richness.

GREENS (AND HERBS)

It's best to clean and prepare greens and herbs ahead of time, ideally right when you bring them home, so they are ready to go whenever you may need them—thus tempting you to eat them all week long. Prepped and stored properly in the refrigerator, they can last for up to ten days.

I recommend using a salad spinner to wash and dry greens. It is, along with penicillin and the Internet, one of mankind's best inventions: a spinner saves time, prevents waste, and leads to a superior salad. Follow these steps:

1. Trim the greens, removing stems and anything brown or soft.

2. With the strainer basket in, fill the salad spinner about three-quarters full with cold water.

3. Set the leaves in the water in batches—do not jam-pack them. If some leaves are larger than the spinner, rip them in half.

4. Swoosh the leaves around, being sure to get any sand or dirt out of the crevices.

5. Allow the dirt to settle to the bottom of the spinner bowl and then lift out the strainer with the greens in it. Dump out the dirty water and rinse out any residual grit or sand at the bottom of the spinner.

6. Repeat steps 2 through 5 until your greens are clean and there's no dirt left behind in the bowl.

7. Place the greens—still in the strainer—back into the spinner. Spin, and then lay them out on a dish towel or paper towel until they are mostly dry.

8. Wrap the greens in the towel and refrigerate in the produce drawer. Fresh-cut greens will stay usable for about ten days.

If you don't own a salad spinner, take heart. You can rinse leaves in a clean sink or a bowl filled with water, swish them around a bit to allow the dirt to fall to the bottom, lift out the greens, and then shake, blot, or roll them in a towel and air-dry. Just be sure to get leaves *fully dry*: nothing is a bigger salad-downer than wet, wilted lettuce and watery dressing.

SALAD COMPOSITION: IDEAS AND INSPIRATION

BASE	COUNTERPOINTS		DRESSING	FINISH
LEAFY SALADS				
Arugula or **spinach**	Avocado, sliced	Walnuts, toasted	Shallot Vinaigrette (page 231)	Maldon salt
Kale	Fingerlings, roasted	Panko, toasted	Traditional Caesar Dressing (page 238)	Lemon zest
	Salmon, grilled (see page 261), or Ginger-Garlic Tofu (page 331)	Pumpkin seeds, toasted	Carrot-Ginger Dressing (page 234)	Scallions, thinly sliced
Lettuces: red leaf, green leaf, Boston, romaine, Little Gem, Lolla Rosa	Gorgonzola, crumbled	Croutons (see page 143)	Citrus Vinaigrette (page 231), made with lemon	Lemon zest
	6-minute egg (see page 172), chopped	Almonds, slivered and toasted	Herb Buttermilk Dressing (page 241)	Chives
SLAWS				
Carrot	Feta, crumbled	Sunflower seeds	Greek Yogurt Dressing (page 240)	Za'atar and sesame seeds
Celery root	Parmigiano-Reggiano, shaved	Celery, julienned	Extra-virgin olive oil and **lemon**	Pistachios, toasted
Beet	Goat cheese, crumbled	Pistachios, toasted	Shallot Vinaigrette (page 231)	Orange, supremed
VEGETABLE-BASED				
Cucumber	Golden raisins	Carrot and jicama, shredded	Fish Sauce Vinaigrette (page 232)	Black sesame seeds and cilantro, chopped
Corn	Cherry tomatoes, halved	Marcona almonds, chopped	Green Goddess Dressing (page 242)	Dill, chopped
Asparagus	6-minute egg (see page 172), chopped	Radishes, thinly sliced	Extra-virgin olive oil, champagne vinegar, and **salt**	Sunflower seeds
GRAINS/LEGUMES				
Quinoa (see page 34)	Sweet potato, roasted and cubed (see page 112)	Celery, thinly sliced	Walnut oil, red wine vinegar, and **salt**	Walnuts, toasted and chopped
Garbanzos (see page 226)	Feta	Cucumber, chopped	Citrus Vinaigrette (page 231)	Parsley and red onion, chopped
White beans	Broccoli, roasted	Broccoli, raw, shaved	Miso Balsamic Vinaigrette (page 233)	Black sesame seeds

TYPES OF SALAD

LEAFY SALADS: Hearty greens wilt nicely without getting too soft when tossed with warm potatoes or topped with seared salmon.

VEGETABLE-BASED: Neatly remove corn from the cob by inverting a small bowl into a larger bowl, standing the corn upright, and using a sharp knife to make downward cuts.

SLAWS: The base of a slaw should consist of a finely shredded vegetable that maintains a crunch after being dressed. Great slaws can be made from many grated vegetables, like carrots, beets, celery root, and kohlrabi.

LEGUMES: Beans add a complementary, creamy texture to roasted broccoli. Adding beans to a salad is an excellent way to add protein, making it a satisfying meal on its own.

TOASTED FARRO WITH ROASTED WINTER VEGETABLES AND TAHINI DRESSING

SERVES 6

This salad is all about soft colors, mellow vegetables, chewy farro, tangy tahini dressing, and the pop of black sesame seeds.

½ TO ¾ CUP TAHINI DRESSING (PAGE 237)	3 CUPS ASSORTED WINTER VEGETABLES, SUCH AS BRUSSELS SPROUTS, DELICATA SQUASH, RAINBOW CARROTS, YAMS, CELERY ROOT, RED ONION, AND ROMANESCO OR CAULIFLOWER, CUT INTO BITE-SIZED PIECES
2 CUPS FARRO	
1 SMALL ONION, CUT IN HALF	
2 OR 3 THYME SPRIGS	EXTRA-VIRGIN OLIVE OIL
1 BAY LEAF	1 TO 2 TABLESPOONS BLACK SESAME SEEDS
FINE SEA SALT	

❶ Make the tahini dressing.

❷ Preheat the oven to 425°F and line a baking sheet with parchment paper.

❸ Toast the farro in a large, dry pot over high heat, stirring constantly, until it smells nutty, 3 minutes. Pour in water to cover the farro by about 2 inches and add the onion, thyme, bay leaf, and a large pinch of salt. Bring to a boil, then reduce to a simmer and cook until completely tender, about 40 minutes. Make sure the farro is fully cooked. Add another large pinch of salt and let cool in the liquid for at least 10 minutes. Drain the farro and set aside to cool. Discard the onion, thyme, and bay leaf.

❹ While the farro is cooking, place all the cut vegetables in a large bowl; toss with olive oil to lightly coat and a pinch of salt. Transfer the vegetables to the prepared baking sheet, and place in the oven. Roast until tender, 20 to 30 minutes; most of the vegetables should be caramelized. Remove from the oven and let cool slightly on the baking sheet. Check the seasoning, adding more salt as needed, and transfer to a large bowl.

❺ Add the cooked farro to the roasted vegetables and toss with enough dressing to lightly coat. Taste; add more salt or dressing as needed.

❻ Garnish with black sesame seeds.

BRUSSELS SPROUT SALAD WITH PARSNIP RIBBONS

SERVES 4 TO 6

This salad makes us think about leaves falling, whipping out a scarf for the first time, and the occasional burst of sunshine. The fruit, nuts, cheese, and vegetables play off one another, creating balance and surprise in every bite.

¾ CUP SHALLOT VINAIGRETTE (PAGE 231)

1 CRISP APPLE, THINLY SLICED

1 SHALLOT, THINLY SLICED

4 CUPS BRUSSELS SPROUTS
(ABOUT 1½ POUNDS)

2 PARSNIPS, PEELED

FINE SEA SALT

¼ CUP HAZELNUTS, TOASTED
AND COARSELY CHOPPED

2 TABLESPOONS CHOPPED
FRESH FLAT-LEAF PARSLEY

½ CUP SHAVED MANCHEGO OR
PARMIGIANO-REGGIANO

❶ Make the shallot vinaigrette.

❷ Place the sliced apple and shallot together in a bowl of cold water. Set aside while you prepare the other salad ingredients.

❸ Trim the stems off the Brussels sprouts and discard any outer leaves that fall away in the process. Using a sharp knife, a mandoline, or the shredding blade of a food processor, slice the sprouts as thinly as possible and place in a large bowl.

❹ Peel the parsnips. Using the peeler, shave the parsnips into long, thin ribbons and add to the Brussels sprouts.

❺ Drizzle the vinaigrette over the Brussels sprouts and parsnip ribbons and toss with your hands to coat. Season with salt to taste.

❻ Drain the apple and shallot and add to the bowl. Mix in the hazelnuts and parsley.

❼ Divide the salad among small plates and garnish each with the shaved cheese.

THAI CABBAGE SLAW

SERVES 4 TO 6

This recipe calls for you to grill the cabbage, but if you don't have a grill, don't worry: using raw and thinly sliced cabbage also works well. Mixing red and green cabbage adds beautiful color to the dish, but you can always choose just one or the other. Make this slaw a main course by topping it with Grilled Chicken Paillard (page 271) or Ginger-Garlic Tofu (page 331).

FISH SAUCE VINAIGRETTE (PAGE 232)

½ SMALL HEAD OF GREEN CABBAGE (CUT INTO 2 WEDGES, LEAVING THE CORES INTACT)

½ SMALL HEAD OF RED CABBAGE (CUT INTO 2 WEDGES, LEAVING THE CORES INTACT)

NEUTRAL-FLAVORED OIL, SUCH AS GRAPESEED OR CANOLA

FINE SEA SALT

½ BUNCH OF CILANTRO, ROUGHLY CHOPPED

½ BUNCH OF SCALLIONS (WHITE AND GREEN PARTS), THINLY SLICED

½ CUP ROASTED PEANUTS, ROUGHLY CHOPPED

---

❶ Make the fish sauce vinaigrette.

❷ Preheat the grill until hot, about 30 minutes. (You can also use a grill pan preheated for 15 minutes over high heat.)

❸ Brush the cabbage wedges with oil and season with salt.

❹ Grill the cabbage until charred with visible dark grill marks, about 5 minutes per side. Let cool slightly, then core and thinly slice.

❺ To assemble the salad, place the sliced cabbage in a large bowl. Drizzle on about ¼ cup of the dressing and toss to coat. Taste and add more dressing as needed. Add the cilantro, scallions, and peanuts and toss again; season with salt to taste.

SUMMER PANZANELLA

SERVES 6 TO 8

This panzanella recipe is a classic salad made with ripe tomatoes and cucumbers. The trick is to salt the tomatoes while preparing the other ingredients to extract as much juice as possible.

1 SMALL CIABATTA LOAF (ABOUT 6 CUPS CUBED)	1 ENGLISH CUCUMBER
¼ CUP PLUS 2 TABLESPOONS EXTRA-VIRGIN OLIVE OIL	GRATED ZEST AND JUICE OF 1 LEMON
FINE SEA SALT	½ BUNCH OF BASIL, LEAVES TORN
1½ POUNDS RIPE TOMATOES, IDEALLY A VARIETY OF HEIRLOOMS	½ BUNCH OF FRESH FLAT-LEAF PARSLEY, CHOPPED
1 SMALL RED ONION	½ CUP FRESHLY GRATED PARMIGIANO-REGGIANO

❶ Preheat the oven to 350°F. Line a baking sheet with parchment paper.

❷ Cut or tear the ciabatta into 1-inch pieces. In a large bowl, toss the bread with the ¼ cup olive oil and a pinch of salt until coated. Let the oil soak into the bread for 3 minutes.

❸ Place the bread pieces on the baking sheet and bake until golden brown, 10 to 15 minutes.

❹ While the bread is toasting, prepare the tomatoes by cutting them into fork-sized wedges and tossing them in a large bowl with a few pinches of salt. Salting the tomatoes creates a liquid, which gets absorbed by the croutons, softening them a bit and giving them flavor.

❺ Cut the red onion down the middle from pole to pole, peel, and then cut into thin slices. Soak in ice water until you are ready to toss and plate the salad; this helps maintain the crunch and tempers the pungency. Cut the cucumber in half lengthwise, cut off the ends and discard, then slice into ¼-inch half circles.

❻ Add the croutons to the bowl of tomatoes and toss gently to combine.

❼ Drain the red onion and place in the bowl with the tomatoes. Add the cucumber and lemon juice, and the remaining 2 tablespoons olive oil. Toss gently with your hands.

❽ Add the basil and parsley and toss gently again.

❾ When ready to serve, season the salad with grated cheese and lemon zest.

HOW TO MAKE A SUMMER PANZANELLA

1 Cut the tomatoes in half, pole to pole. Cut a V-shaped notch in the core to remove it. Then slice the tomatoes into bite-sized wedges.

2 Salt the tomatoes before preparing the other ingredients. Salting draws out liquid and creates a flavorful juice that is absorbed by the croutons.

3 While the tomatoes and salt marinate, slice the onion and cucumber.

4 Tossing with your hands prevents bruising of the tomatoes, and ensures that the salad is evenly dressed.

GARBANZO FETA SALAD

SERVES 4 TO 6

Even people with an aversion to beans like garbanzo beans, or chickpeas, for their nutty flavor and firm texture. They can be a bit bland and dry by themselves, though, so this recipe adds flavor, texture, and color with feta, red onion, cucumber, and parsley. Feel free to use canned beans. The vinaigrette is the icing on the cake.

1 CUP DRIED GARBANZOS, SOAKED FOR 8 HOURS, OR ONE 15-OUNCE CAN, DRAINED AND RINSED

FINE SEA SALT

CITRUS VINAIGRETTE (PAGE 231)

1 SMALL RED ONION, THINLY SLICED AND HELD IN ICE WATER

2 PERSIAN CUCUMBERS OR 1 SMALL ENGLISH CUCUMBER, SLICED ¼ INCH THICK ON THE BIAS

¼ CUP CRUMBLED FETA

¼ CUP TORN FRESH FLAT-LEAF PARSLEY

❶ If using dried beans, after soaking, rinse the garbanzos, place in a medium saucepan, and cover with double their volume of water. Bring to a boil, reduce to a simmer, and cook until the beans are tender but hold their shape, about 45 minutes. Remove from the heat, add a large pinch or two of salt, and let sit for 15 minutes. Drain and put in a large serving bowl.

❷ While the garbanzos are cooking, make the vinaigrette.

❸ Drain the red onion and add to the garbanzos. Add the cucumber, feta, and parsley, drizzle on about ¼ cup of the vinaigrette, and toss to combine. Add more dressing and salt to taste. Serve at room temperature or chilled.

Making Dressing

Don't let the idea of making salad dressing intimidate you. Dressings can be assembled using basic pantry staples, are quick to make, and can last for weeks if stored, properly sealed, in the refrigerator.

The dynamic duo of most salad dressings, whether a punchy vinaigrette or a creamy Green Goddess, is fat and acid.

FAT

In most dressings, oil serves as the fat. The best oils for dressing impart their own flavors; take olive oil and walnut oil, for instance. You can also make a richer dressing by using yogurt or avocado as the fat, as in our Green Goddess (page 242).

ACID

Part two of the equation is acid. Acid cuts through the fat in a dressing and adds a sharpness that provides balance in flavor and texture. Some vinegars are intense, like red wine and sherry, and pair better with stronger greens and heartier ingredients. Others, such as champagne, rice, and apple cider, are less assertive. Citrus tends to have sweeter notes, and buttermilk—yes, it's an acid—offers creaminess that you crave in a ranch dressing. (You can refer to our Herb Buttermilk Dressing on page 241.)

SEASONING

Adding salt to the acid before adding other ingredients dissolves it. Other ingredients like mustard, miso, honey, and tahini paste go into the dressing before the oil as well.

SALAD DRESSING

A quick way to dress a salad is to toss it lightly with a drizzle of oil, a squeeze of citrus, or a dash of vinegar and a pinch or two of Maldon. Leaves begin to break down and lose their crispness the moment acid touches them. That's why it's important to hold the acid until serving time—unless you *want* to break down the greens a bit, as is the case when making a slaw or a salad with a hearty green, like kale.

GET THE RATIO RIGHT

Traditional vinaigrettes start with one part vinegar to three parts oil. But this is not a hard-and-fast rule; it's really a matter of personal preference and depends on the salad. Try a 2:1 oil-to-acid ratio, or take a cue from one of our instructors, Ashley Bare, whose favorite trick is to stick with the classic 3:1 ratio but use more than one acid.

Dip a leaf into the dressing to taste it. It's easier to adjust the salt or acid before you've dressed the whole salad.

The first taste of your dressing should be sharp and intense but not burning. It should gradually mellow in your mouth.

MIX, WHISK, SHAKE, OR BLEND

Simple vinaigrettes come together easily with a few turns of the wrist. Creamier dressings need serious whisking or a whiz in the blender.

DRESS THE SALAD

Dress the salad *immediately* before serving. If the salad tastes flat, add another pinch of sea salt or squeeze out a few more drips of lemon. If the dressing is too strong, add another drizzle of oil. Use a *big* bowl. It's hard to achieve a thorough toss when you're trying to keep the salad from flying over the edge. Start by drizzling dressing around the edges of your bowl; then toss gently and briefly, to mix the ingredients and coat them lightly.

CITRUS VINAIGRETTE

MAKES ABOUT 2 CUPS

This dressing can be made with any citrus that you find appealing: grapefruit, lime, lemon, or orange. It lends sunshine to any salad.

1 CUP MIXED CITRUS JUICE, PLUS THE GRATED ZEST OF 1 LEMON	FINE SEA SALT AND FRESHLY GROUND BLACK PEPPER
1 TABLESPOON DIJON MUSTARD	1 CUP EXTRA-VIRGIN OLIVE OIL, OR MORE TO TASTE

1 In a medium bowl, whisk together the juice, zest, mustard, a pinch of salt, and pepper to taste. Slowly whisk in the olive oil until well blended.

2 Finish with additional salt and pepper as desired.

SHALLOT VINAIGRETTE

MAKES ABOUT 1½ CUPS

I'm not sure why, exactly, but every time I make this dressing I get swoons and recipe requests from my guests. Something about the balanced funkiness of the vinegar is infinitely satisfying.

1 SMALL SHALLOT, MINCED	FINE SEA SALT
⅓ CUP VINEGAR, SUCH AS SHERRY, CHAMPAGNE, OR RED WINE	½ CUP NEUTRAL-FLAVORED OIL, SUCH AS GRAPESEED OR CANOLA
2 TEASPOONS DIJON MUSTARD	½ CUP EXTRA-VIRGIN OLIVE OIL

1 In a medium bowl, whisk together the shallot, vinegar, mustard, and a pinch of salt.

2 Slowly whisk in both oils and then season with additional salt as desired.

FISH SAUCE VINAIGRETTE

MAKES ABOUT 1 CUP

This dressing has the bones of nuoc cham, a Vietnamese "mother" sauce. It pairs the brininess of fish sauce with the boldness of sambal oelek, a chile paste (see Resources, page 366). However, if sriracha is your spicy pantry staple, it makes a fine substitute. Use this dressing on roasted vegetables like Brussels sprouts or in a rice noodle salad such as a Vietnamese-style *bún*. Thai chiles pack a punch, so if you are sensitive to heat, skip the pepper.

½ CUP PACKED LIGHT BROWN SUGAR

½ CUP FISH SAUCE

½ CUP FRESHLY SQUEEZED LIME JUICE

1 TEASPOON SAMBAL OELEK

2 GARLIC CLOVES, MINCED

1 RED THAI CHILE, THINLY SLICED (OPTIONAL)

FINE SEA SALT

In a medium bowl, whisk together the brown sugar, fish sauce, lime juice, sambal oelek, garlic, and Thai chile, if using, until the sugar dissolves; add salt to taste.

MISO BALSAMIC VINAIGRETTE

Miso is one of those specialty ingredients that our students often buy for a single recipe and, unfortunately, never use again. They come to us looking for recipes that will save the poor tub from the fate of sitting on the refrigerator shelf for months until one day getting tossed in the trash. You can use miso as a substitute for mustard in salad dressing; though subtle, it adds a salty umami punch. Balsamic can overpower lighter greens, so this dressing shines when paired with darker greens, cooked grains, or roasted vegetables. It also makes a nice marinade for vegetables or fish prior to grilling.

½ CUP BALSAMIC VINEGAR

2 TABLESPOONS WHITE MISO

1 TEASPOON HONEY

½ CUP EXTRA-VIRGIN OLIVE OIL

FINE SEA SALT AND FRESHLY GROUND BLACK PEPPER

In a medium bowl, whisk together the balsamic, miso, and honey to form a smooth paste. Slowly drizzle in the olive oil while continuing to whisk until the dressing is well blended. Season with salt and pepper to taste.

CARROT-GINGER DRESSING

The name of this dressing may conjure images of the little plastic vessels that accompany Japanese takeout, but it's worlds better when homemade. The sweetness of the carrot teases out the spice of the ginger, and that balance is what makes it so addictive.

4 CARROTS, SLICED INTO 1-INCH PIECES

1 SMALL SHALLOT, ROUGHLY CHOPPED
(ABOUT 1 TABLESPOON)

¼ CUP ROUGHLY CHOPPED FRESH GINGER

¼ CUP RICE VINEGAR

2 TABLESPOONS NEUTRAL-FLAVORED OIL,
SUCH AS GRAPESEED OR CANOLA

2 TABLESPOONS HONEY

1 TABLESPOON SESAME OIL

3 TABLESPOONS WATER, OR AS NEEDED

FINE SEA SALT

In a blender, combine the carrots, shallot, ginger, vinegar, grapeseed oil, honey, sesame oil, and water. Blend until smooth, about 1 minute; add more water as needed for desired consistency. Season with salt to taste.

CAESAR

GREEN GODDESS

TAHINI

HERB BUTTERMILK

TAHINI DRESSING

MAKES ABOUT 2 CUPS

The base of this dressing is a tahini sauce (see page 295) that can be thinned out with additional water, olive oil, and lemon juice to preserve the balance of flavors. It's tangy and nutty, and the toasted sesame flavor works beautifully with a roasted vegetable salad. Use this creamy dressing with heartier salads made with beans, raw vegetables, or cabbage too. It's thinner than the "sauce" version, so this dressing is easy to drizzle. Try it on roast lamb, grilled chicken, and eggplant of any persuasion. I went through a six-month phase where I poured it over everything. Everything.

1 CUP TAHINI

JUICE OF 2 LEMONS, PLUS MORE AS NEEDED

2 GARLIC CLOVES

1 TABLESPOON CUMIN SEEDS, TOASTED AND GROUND

¼ CUP CHOPPED FRESH FLAT-LEAF PARSLEY

¼ CUP EXTRA-VIRGIN OLIVE OIL

½ CUP WATER, OR MORE AS NEEDED

FINE SEA SALT

In the bowl of a food processor fitted with the metal chopping blade, blend the tahini, lemon juice, garlic, cumin, parsley, and olive oil. With the motor running, slowly pour in the water, adding only as much as needed to create a dressing thick enough to coat the back of a spoon. It should look like a thick pancake batter. Taste and add salt and more lemon juice if desired. Serve immediately or store, covered, in the refrigerator for up to 4 days.

TRADITIONAL CAESAR DRESSING

MAKES ABOUT 1½ CUPS

Don't mess with a classic.

1 WHOLE GARLIC HEAD PLUS 1 CLOVE	GRATED ZEST AND JUICE OF 1 LEMON
EXTRA-VIRGIN OLIVE OIL	1 TEASPOON WORCESTERSHIRE SAUCE
FINE SEA SALT	½ TEASPOON TABASCO SAUCE
3 OIL-PACKED ANCHOVY FILLETS, RINSED, OR 1½ TEASPOONS ANCHOVY PASTE	1 CUP NEUTRAL-FLAVORED OIL, SUCH AS GRAPESEED OR CANOLA
2 LARGE EGG YOLKS	¼ CUP FRESHLY GRATED PARMIGIANO-REGGIANO
1 TABLESPOON DIJON MUSTARD	FRESHLY GROUND BLACK PEPPER

❶ Prepare the roasted garlic: Preheat the oven to 325°F. Slice off the top ¼ inch of the whole garlic head and place the bulb on a piece of aluminum foil. Drizzle lightly with olive oil and sprinkle with salt, then wrap tightly. Roast for 30 to 45 minutes, depending on the size and age of the garlic. Remove from the oven and unwrap—the garlic will be fragrant and the individual cloves will be soft and golden. If the garlic needs more time, tightly rewrap in foil and roast, checking every 5 minutes, until fragrant and the cloves are soft and golden. Let cool slightly before squeezing the cloves out of their skins. (Roasted cloves can be stored in the fridge for up to a week or in the freezer for up to 3 months.)

❷ In the bowl of a food processor fitted with the metal chopping blade, combine 1 tablespoon of the roasted garlic along with the raw garlic clove, anchovies, egg yolks, mustard, lemon zest and juice, Worcestershire, and Tabasco. Pulse for approximately 30 seconds to form a fairly smooth paste with small bits of anchovy and garlic.

❸ With the food processor running, gradually add the oil in a slow and steady stream. (It should take almost 1 minute to add all the oil.) If the mixture becomes too thick and is no longer spinning around the bowl of the food processor, add a few drops of cold water before adding the rest of the oil.

❹ When the dressing is fully emulsified, turn off the food processor. Stir in the Parmigiano-Reggiano and cold water as needed to thin the dressing to your desired consistency. Season with salt and pepper to taste.

GREEK YOGURT DRESSING

MAKES ABOUT 1¼ CUPS

Yogurt is the main player in this Haven's Kitchen go-to dressing. You might recognize it as similar to tzatziki, but this particular variation is loaded with mint. It's a great match for peppers, romaine, and, of course, cucumbers. It also works well with fritters of all kinds, including the Quinoa Broccoli Patties (page 63).

½ CUP PLAIN GREEK YOGURT

¼ CUP EXTRA-VIRGIN OLIVE OIL

¼ CUP COLD WATER

¼ CUP FINELY CHOPPED FRESH MINT

GRATED ZEST AND JUICE OF ½ LEMON

1 SMALL SHALLOT, MINCED

1 GARLIC CLOVE, MINCED, OR FINELY GRATED ON A RASP-STYLE GRATER

½ TEASPOON ALEPPO PEPPER

FINE SEA SALT AND FRESHLY GROUND BLACK PEPPER

SALADS

❶ In a medium bowl, whisk together the yogurt, olive oil, water, mint, lemon zest and juice, shallot, garlic, and Aleppo pepper until smooth. Season with salt and black pepper to taste.

❷ Store, covered, in the refrigerator for up to 4 days.

HERB BUTTERMILK DRESSING

MAKES ABOUT 2 CUPS

Despite our appreciation for fresh, unprocessed foods, those dry packets of ranch dressing powder are a guilty pleasure among the staff at Haven's Kitchen. There's something about the flavor, comforting but at the same time zippy, and tangy, and a trigger for happy thoughts. This recipe is a from-scratch version that hits the same nostalgic notes.

1 CUP CRÈME FRAÎCHE

½ CUP BUTTERMILK

2 TABLESPOONS FINELY CHOPPED FRESH CHIVES

1 TABLESPOON FINELY CHOPPED FRESH DILL

1 TEASPOON RED WINE VINEGAR

1 SMALL SHALLOT, MINCED (ABOUT 1 TABLESPOON)

½ GARLIC CLOVE, FINELY MINCED, OR GRATED ON A RASP-STYLE GRATER

⅛ TEASPOON CAYENNE

⅛ TEASPOON PAPRIKA

FINE SEA SALT AND FRESHLY GROUND BLACK PEPPER

In a medium bowl, whisk together the crème fraîche, buttermilk, chives, dill, vinegar, shallot, garlic, cayenne, paprika, and a pinch of salt until smooth. Season with additional salt and freshly ground pepper as needed. Chill in the refrigerator for 1 hour before serving.

GREEN GODDESS DRESSING

MAKES ABOUT 2½ CUPS

A stellar example of a dressing that relies on something other than oil for its fat (here, avocado and crème fraîche), Green Goddess is a modern classic. This particular variation is quite thick but can be thinned out with additional lemon juice and cold water.

1 RIPE AVOCADO, PEELED AND PITTED

¼ CUP CRÈME FRAÎCHE

GRATED ZEST AND JUICE OF 1 LEMON, PLUS MORE JUICE AS NEEDED

½ CUP EXTRA-VIRGIN OLIVE OIL

½ CUP COLD WATER, PLUS MORE AS NEEDED

½ CUP CHOPPED FRESH BASIL

½ CUP CHOPPED FRESH CILANTRO

¼ CUP THINLY SLICED SCALLIONS (WHITE AND GREEN PARTS)

¼ CUP CHOPPED FRESH DILL

FINE SEA SALT AND FRESHLY GROUND BLACK PEPPER

In a blender, combine the avocado, crème fraîche, lemon zest and juice, olive oil, water, basil, cilantro, scallions, and dill. Blend until smooth, 1 to 2 minutes. Season with salt and pepper to taste. If the dressing is thicker than you'd like, thin it by mixing in additional lemon juice or cold water, 1 tablespoon at a time.

SALADS

FISH, FOWL & MEAT

"If I am going to eat meat, I want it to be from an animal that has
lived a pleasant, uncrowded life outdoors, on bountiful pasture,
with good water nearby and trees for shade."

—WENDELL BERRY

HAVEN'S KITCHEN WAS ORIGINALLY going to be a vegetarian school. We would teach people how to make legumes and vegetables so satisfying they would never again look longingly at lamb chops or fish tacos. Then one day Mariana, our first intern, approached me. "Maybe," she said, "we teach people how to choose the *right* kind of meat and fish and how to prepare it well." "No," I argued. "Animals are mistreated; fish are going extinct! And what about the *water*? We have to teach people how to eat *outside of the industrial food system*!" Quietly, pensively, Mariana queried, "But if we pretend meat and fish don't exist, then how are we part of the solution?"

And that's how Haven's Kitchen became the proud teaching institution of all things related to butchering, shucking, descaling, nose-to-tailing, spatchcocking, and bone-broth-simmering. The rule that has persisted since that fateful conversation is what I blustered next: "Fine. We'll teach meat and fish, but we will buy it with thought and cook it with care, and teach our students to do the same."

There are many ways to cook a fish, a bird, or a piece of meat—ingredients that restaurant chefs refer to as "protein." Too often, students tell me they're intimidated by cooking meat and disappointed by the results of their efforts. They often ask: How do you know what cooking method to use for a certain cut of beef? Why roast a rack of lamb but braise the shanks? Why does fish cooked in the oven often come out dry? Why do chefs always seem to start something on the stove and then finish it in the oven?

Understanding heat and how it works enables a cook to look at chicken thighs or cutlets, a fillet of salmon, or a lamb shoulder and know, without being wedded to a recipe, what to do with it. Knowing how to approach and then control heat is one of the most powerful techniques a cook can master. The goal of this lesson is to impart enough understanding about *how heat works* that you will feel confident preparing protein. Of course, there are no steadfast rules: It'd be so much simpler if I could tell you that all chicken gets roasted and all fish gets seared. But that's not the case, and it would take all the creativity and most of the fun out of cooking. Instead, choosing what technique will best suit your protein has everything to do with the size and thickness of your ingredient, its fat content, your schedule, and, of course, your preferences.

Dry and Moist

Heat for cooking can be dry or moist; can be generated from above, below, or all around; and can consist of direct or indirect intensity. Knowing what type of heat will bring out the best from your fish, poultry, or meat will result in more delicious, less stressful meals. How tough or thick is the protein? Is it a cut that needs a good long braise, or will a few minutes in a sauté pan do the trick?

DRY HEAT METHODS

Dry heat methods create caramelization and a flavor that we associate with a sear or char. Dry heat cooks protein without liquid, often relying on fat.

There are four methods that rely on dry heat:

1. Broiling

Broiling is best for cooking thinner cuts of meat or fish. Broil already-cooked dishes for a few minutes at the end to give them a nice browned finish.

2. Searing

Searing cooks fish, poultry, or meat on the stovetop over high heat with fat. If searing a protein, refrigerate it, uncovered, until ready to temper, then pat dry before cooking. You want a dry exterior to ensure a seared crust. For thicker and/or tougher cuts of meat or chicken, sear first and either continue to cook it on high heat in the pan or finish it by roasting in the oven.

Fish fillets (as in Sole Meunière, page 264), small whole fish, chicken breasts (both on and off the bone), chicken thighs, and thin steaks are all good candidates for searing.

3. Grilling

Grilling uses a flame source beneath the food. A grill pan is an indoor alternative. It is not a substitute for the direct flames of an outdoor grill, but when heated properly produces a good char.

Whole fish (see page 261), chicken (see page 271), chops and steaks (see page 278), and thicker fish fillets that have more fat, such as salmon, are a grill's best mates.

4. Roasting

Roasting relies on the dry, all-around heat of a very hot oven. When roasting a small cut of meat, you can sear it first on the stovetop, and then transfer it to the oven to finish. If the protein is larger, like our Roasted Leg of Lamb (page 288), start cooking the meat in a very hot (425°F) oven for 15 minutes to brown and caramelize before lowering the temperature to 375°F to finish cooking.

Roasting is the ideal technique for larger cuts of meat, such as brisket, and whole chicken and fish (see pages 268 and 260).

MOIST HEAT METHODS

Moist heat methods cook protein using liquid, often quite slowly. While many cooking methods use moist heat, we most often rely on these four.

1. Steaming

Steaming uses the moist heat from simmering liquid. To steam, first make sure your pot has a tight-fitting lid. Clams and mussels are steamed directly in the pot with a small amount of liquid; they are not completely submerged but are quickly cooked by the vapors. For fish, you'll need a bamboo steamer or steamer basket appropriate for fish.

Oysters, clams, mussels, and fish fillets are best steamed, as they cook very quickly.

2. Poaching

Poaching cooks delicate protein while keeping it from falling apart. To poach, submerge your protein into very hot but not quite boiling liquid. It can be water, stock, or even olive oil. Seasoning the liquid infuses quicker-cooking protein like shellfish or small cuts of fish or chicken with flavor.

3. Braising

Braising cooks tougher cuts of protein slowly by partially submerging them in liquid in a Dutch oven or other heavy pot covered with a snug lid or good wrap of aluminum foil. You can braise on the stovetop over low heat or in the oven at 300°F to 325°F. This low and slow method of cooking breaks down the protein, resulting in a "fall-off-the-bone" texture.

Stock or wine is generally the cooking liquid because it tenderizes and adds flavor.

Tougher cuts of meat like pork shoulder (see Pork Salsa Verde, page 289), brisket, bone-in chicken legs and thighs, and large roasts are made tender when braised.

4. Stewing

Stewing is similar to braising in that it also slowly cooks protein in a flavorful liquid over low heat. Both methods create tender dishes; however, when stewing, you start with small, uniform pieces and completely submerge them in liquid.

Tougher cuts of meat like beef chuck benefit from being stewed (see Beef Bourguignon, page 281).

Tools

6- TO 8-QUART DUTCH OVEN

A 6- to 8-quart Dutch oven is useful for braises and roasts. You'll also use it for making soups and frying fritters. It's on our top tool list because of its incredible versatility and ability to evenly distribute heat—plus it's quite beautiful.

GRILL PAN

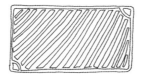

While it's not going to create results quite like an outdoor grill, a grill pan that goes directly on the stovetop will create a char on chicken breasts, fish, and thinner cuts of meat. I like a rectangular version that fits over two burners.

KITCHEN SHEARS

Kitchen shears work better than a knife for certain tasks. I use them for spatchcocking (see page 273) and for cutting cooked chicken breasts into strips or cubes.

FISH, FOWL & MEAT

NONABSORBENT PLASTIC CUTTING BOARD

Reserve your lovely wood cutting board for vegetables and cooked meat. For raw fish, chicken, and meat, I prefer a nonabsorbent plastic cutting board. You can throw them into the dishwasher after cutting raw meat on them.

ROASTING PAN WITH RACK

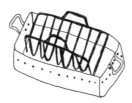

Roasting pans come with a wire rack for chickens and larger cuts of meat. Use it when you want a crisp skin or exterior. Sitting directly on the pan makes for a juicy, moist bottom, not a crisp one.

THERMOMETER

An instant-read stick thermometer takes all the guesswork out of cooking protein. Always insert the thermometer at the thickest part of the protein to accurately gauge temperature. For poultry, 165°F is considered a safe temperature. Remove the protein from the heat when it is five degrees below the optimal temperature, as it will continue to cook while resting.

Fish, Fowl, and Meat Tips

Before we delve into cooking techniques, here are three fundamental tips: bring protein to room temperature before cooking it (this is called tempering); give it a chance to sit before being served (this is called resting); and don't skimp on the salt. Many of our students report that the protein dishes they cook at home end up unevenly cooked and less flavorful than what they've experienced at restaurants. *Tempering*, *resting*, and *seasoning* are the solutions to those problems.

TEMPERING

Bring protein to room temperature by removing it from the refrigerator prior to cooking. This sets it up to cook evenly and sear, or caramelize, better. Moving a cold protein straight to the hot stove cools down the heating surface and slows the cooking; the result is rubbery and overcooked. Depending on the weight and thickness, most meat and poultry will take 30 minutes to 2 hours to temper. Fish tempers more quickly, 15 to 30 minutes. Be mindful of the temperature in your kitchen and adjust the tempering time accordingly. Shellfish does not need to be tempered.

RESTING

Rest any meat, poultry, or heartier fish that's been seared, grilled, or roasted before you carve or serve it. Carving into a leg of lamb or a steak immediately after it's taken off the heat spills a deluge of juices onto the carving board. Resting a protein for 10 minutes redistributes the natural juices within—meaning the protein holds on to more flavor. Resting is also important because it allows for "carryover cooking." Residual heat inside the meat finishes the cooking process.

SEASONING

Salt in any form, if left on too long, draws moisture from your protein and makes it impossible to get a satisfying, crusty sear. That's why we teach our students to add flavor through salt and sauce rather than through marinades. After your protein has tempered, generously shower it all over with sea salt and immediately grill, roast, or sauté. Then, after the meat has rested, salt with another hearty pinch at serving time.

Shellfish

There are two kinds of shellfish: crustaceans, such as shrimp, lobster, and crab, and mollusks, including clams, mussels, oysters, and scallops. (Yes, scallops come in a shell.) Shellfish are a versatile protein that makes a satisfying meal with minimal time commitment.

WHAT AND HOW TO PURCHASE

It cannot be stressed enough that shellfish needs to be *fresh*. Their only odor should be of briny sea air. Purchase shellfish from a reliable source, ideally on the day you intend to cook it.

Always buy live crustaceans. Mollusk shells should be snugly closed. If you see a tight shell peek open, tap it: it should shut immediately. If it doesn't, the mollusk is dead and no longer edible. Shrimp can be purchased frozen, but most of them are farmed under less than desirable conditions. Refer to the Monterey Bay Aquarium Seafood Watch (SeafoodWatch.org) to learn which options are best.

When purchasing shellfish, estimate ¾ pound to 1 pound per person.

Fish

Many of our students are nervous about cooking fish at home—it seems daunting. They wonder what fish to buy, how best to cook it, how to prevent it from sticking, and how to know when it's done.

WHAT AND HOW TO PURCHASE

While your inner Julia Child may fantasize about perusing the fish market stalls in the South of France, selecting a whole Dover sole caught in the Mediterranean that morning, and ferrying it home in your wicker basket, it is much more likely that you will head to your local supermarket to buy a fillet or two. If possible, buy directly from a fisherman at your local farmers' market or from a trusted fishmonger.

Signs of freshness are clear, bulging eyes (not cloudy and sunken); a clean, ocean-like smell; and firm yet elastic flesh that bounces back within seconds of being touched. (Your finger should not leave an indentation.)

When purchasing whole fish, estimate about a pound per person; the actual yield of cooked flesh will be about 6 ounces. For fillets, ask for about half a pound per person.

When buying, let the fishmonger know how you plan to cook the fish and ask what variety would be a good choice. He or she is likely to be a great resource.

Buy whole fish whenever possible. It tends to be fresher. If you prefer fillets, ask the fishmonger to butcher them for you. If you buy precut fillets, make sure they are moist and shiny. Avoid any that are gray, dried out, or limp. Fillets should be from the center of the fish to

ensure an even thickness. The fish thins out around the tail, so that part will cook more quickly than the meat closer to the head. By starting with a piece that's relatively even, you will set yourself up for success.

Finally, let your fishmonger and local market know that you care about sustainability. Explain that you will only buy seafood that is fished or farmed according to sustainable and environmentally safe practices. Contrary to popular belief, buying wild fish isn't always gentler on the environment or better for you than farmed fish. Again, refer to the Monterey Bay Aquarium Seafood Watch.

NOTES ON COOKING

Temper fish by removing it from the refrigerator 15 to 30 minutes prior to cooking; this will bring it to a temperature that's best for cooking but still safe from a microbial point of view.

For dry heat cooking, pat the skin or flesh of the fillet dry before seasoning and cooking. This step is important to ensure that the fish sears and does not stick to your grill or pan.

After removing it from the heat, rest the fish to allow for carryover cooking. When your fish is almost done, the very middle will still be a touch glossy, but the rest should be opaque and flake off easily. It will keep cooking as it rests. Taking it off the heat a little early will prevent dry, overcooked fish.

FILLETING
A COOKED FISH

One of the reasons our students shy away from cooking whole fish is their concern about what to do with it once it's cooked. This can be intimidating, but with a little practice, it takes about three minutes to serve two fillets. And it's almost as impressive as sabering a Champagne bottle.

1. Lay the fish on a cutting board.

2. Cut off the head and tail with a chef's knife and discard.

3. Using a boning or fillet knife, position the knife point away from your body so it's flat against the fish starting from the top of the spine. Following along the spine, press the blade of the knife against the bones to separate the fish fillet from the bone. The knife should skim the surface of the bones, creating a rasping noise as it runs across them. Gently remove the top fillet, and set on a serving plate.

4. Leaving the fish in the same position, use the tail end of the spine as a handle to slowly lift the spine off the bottom fillet. While gently lifting, use your fingers or gently rest the knife on the meat to hold the bottom fillet in place. Discard the spine, and put the fillet on a serving plate.

5. Use your knife to carefully pick out any bones in the fillets.

SPICY COCONUT MILK
MUSSELS
page 257

BELGIAN MOULES

SERVES 2

Belgium may be divided into a French-speaking region and a Dutch-speaking region, but *all* Belgians consider this dish a source of national pride. From September through November, restaurants in windy villages dotting the coast of the North Sea boast platters teeming with briny, creamy, fresh *moules* and *frites*, their other national treasure. Families and friends sit at communal tables, transforming regular weeknight dinners into reunions and celebrations.

Our recipe is a play on the Belgian theme, made with a wheaty ale instead of wine. If you prefer, you can stick with the original and use a crisp Chablis instead. In many cities you can get mussels year-round, but do ask if they've been frozen, as those are not mussels worth eating. Serve with Classic French Fries (page 125) and Roasted Garlic Aioli (page 315) for dipping, or with crusty bread.

1½ POUNDS MUSSELS	¼ CUP HEAVY CREAM
2 TABLESPOONS UNSALTED BUTTER	1 LEMON, CUT IN HALF
2 GARLIC CLOVES, THINLY SLICED	3 TABLESPOONS CHOPPED FRESH FLAT-LEAF PARSLEY
½ CUP BELGIAN-STYLE WHEAT BEER	

❶ Rinse the mussels in cold water, scrubbing the shells and pulling off any visible beards—the hairy strands protruding from the closed shells. The beards are edible, so removing them is a personal preference. If any mussels are open, tap gently; if they close they are alive and are safe to eat. If any open mussels do not close when gently tapped, discard them.

❷ Heat a Dutch oven or other large pot with a tightly fitting lid over high heat. Drop in the butter. When the butter is melted, add the garlic and cook until fragrant and tender, about 1 minute.

❸ Add the mussels gently to avoid cracking the shells. Pour in the beer and cream and immediately cover the pot. Cook for 2 to 3 minutes, gently shaking the pot occasionally, and then peek at the mussels. When about 90 percent of the shells are open in a full yawn, remove from the heat. Discard any shells that did not open. Plate the mussels, squeeze the lemon half over each serving, and garnish with parsley.

SPICY COCONUT MILK MUSSELS

SERVES 2

As an alternative to the classic Belgian-style mussels, this recipe (photo on page 255) takes inspiration from the Thai flavors of ginger, lemongrass, and peppers.

You won't use an entire can of coconut milk here, unless you decide to triple the recipe, but fret not. If you have leftover coconut milk, use it to flavor the rice that you serve with your mussels (see page 31).

1½ POUNDS MUSSELS

1 TABLESPOON EXTRA-VIRGIN OLIVE OIL

1 RED BELL PEPPER, CUT INTO SMALL DICE

1 JALAPEÑO, SEEDED AND THINLY SLICED INTO HALF-MOONS

1 SHALLOT, MINCED

2 GARLIC CLOVES, THINLY SLICED

ONE 4- TO 6-INCH PIECE OF LEMONGRASS, WHITE PART ONLY, SMASHED

ONE 2-INCH PIECE OF FRESH GINGER, PEELED AND GRATED OR MINCED

1 CUP FULL-FAT UNSWEETENED COCONUT MILK

½ TEASPOON FISH SAUCE (OPTIONAL)

1 LIME, CUT IN HALF

2 TABLESPOONS CHOPPED FRESH CILANTRO

❶ Rinse the mussels in cold water, scrubbing the shells and pulling off any visible beards—the hairy strands protruding from the closed shells. The beards are edible, so removing them is a personal preference. If any mussels are open, tap gently; if they close they are alive and are safe to eat. If any open mussels do not close when gently tapped, discard them.

❷ Heat a medium Dutch oven or other large pot with a tightly fitting lid over high heat. Pour in the oil. When it begins to shimmer, add the bell pepper, jalapeño, shallot, garlic, lemongrass, and ginger. Cook until fragrant and tender, stirring occasionally, about 2 minutes.

❸ Add the mussels gently to avoid cracking the shells. Pour in the coconut milk and fish sauce, if using, and immediately cover the pot. Cook for 2 to 3 minutes, gently shaking the pot occasionally, and then peek at the mussels. When about 90 percent of the shells are open in a full yawn, remove from the heat. Discard the lemongrass and any shells that did not open. Plate the mussels, squeeze a lime half over each serving, and garnish with cilantro.

CEVICHE

When we teach fish butchering, students find ceviche a deceptively easy "raw" fish preparation. It requires a supersharp knife and some practice slicing the fish properly, but once both are addressed, you may find yourself making versions of this recipe rather often. A Peruvian delicacy, ceviche is citrusy and satisfying during the hot summer months. You can dress it up as an elegant appetizer and plate it for each guest at your table, or go in a more casual direction and serve it in a bowl with corn chips. It will keep for up to 3 hours sealed in the refrigerator, but note that as it sits in the marinade, the fish will change consistency.

2 POUNDS WHITE FISH, SUCH AS FLUKE OR BASS (WHATEVER IS FRESHEST AT THE MARKET)

1 CUP FRESHLY SQUEEZED LIME JUICE

½ CUP FRESHLY SQUEEZED ORANGE OR GRAPEFRUIT JUICE

1 SMALL RED ONION, THINLY SLICED

2 SERRANO CHILES, SEEDS REMOVED AND FINELY DICED

1 BUNCH FRESH CILANTRO, CHOPPED

1 LARGE PINCH OF FINE SEA SALT

❶ Fillet the fish, remove and discard any bones and skin, and cut the fillets into a medium dice.

❷ Combine the fish, lime, and orange juice in a nonreactive—plastic or glass—container and marinate the fish, chilled over ice or in the refrigerator, for 20 to 30 minutes. The fish should look opaque all the way through.

❸ Strain and discard about one-quarter of the liquid, and then stir in the onion, serrano chiles, cilantro, and salt.

❹ Serve immediately.

ROASTED WHOLE FISH

SERVES 2

You can temper and roast a whole fish in about 45 minutes. No slaving over the hot stove, no minding the heat or sniffing for clues. This recipe uses two one-pound fish to serve two people. You could also buy one two-pounder for two people, and, if serving more, a larger fish. Assume about one pound of uncooked fish per person and add about 10 minutes more cooking time for every additional inch of thickness. Serve it with the Ginger-Garlic Vinegar Sauce (page 311), or Chimichurri (page 300), white rice, and sautéed greens (see page 99).

TWO 1-POUND WHOLE FISH,
SUCH AS BRANZINO OR SEA BASS

EXTRA-VIRGIN OLIVE OIL

FINE SEA SALT

1 LEMON, THINLY SLICED

9 TO 12 SPRIGS OF FRESH HERBS,
SUCH AS THYME, DILL, AND/OR PARSLEY

---

❶ Temper the fish for 15 to 30 minutes and preheat the oven to 450°F. Line a baking sheet with a wire rack.

❷ Rinse the outside of the fish and the internal cavity and pat dry with paper towels. Set the fish on the rack. Drizzle each fish with a light coating of olive oil and season the cavity and skin with a few pinches of sea salt. Place half of the lemon slices and herbs in each fish's cavity and close it.

❸ Place the fish in the oven, roast for 20 minutes, and test for doneness. Use a firm metal spatula to test if the fish loosens easily from the wire rack—the skin should stay attached to the fish rather than the rack. If it is still stubborn, cook it for another 3 to 5 minutes. The cooking time will depend on the thickness of the fish.

❹ When the fish releases easily from the rack, flip the fish by rolling it over on its backbone, keeping the stuffing intact. Cook on the other side for another 5 minutes.

❺ Remove the fish from the oven and allow it to rest for 5 minutes before serving.

GRILLED WHOLE FISH

SERVES 2

Grilled whole fish has a flavor similar to that of roasted fish, but the charring gives a smoky intensity. This recipe is for an outdoor grill. When grilling, *do not flip the fish* until it loosens easily from the grill—when the skin has crisped up enough, it will detach readily. Serve with Summer Panzanella (page 223) and Salsa Verde (page 303) or Sweet Chili Sauce (page 308) for drizzling.

TWO 1-POUND WHOLE FISH, SUCH AS BRANZINO OR SEA BASS	1 LEMON, THINLY SLICED
EXTRA-VIRGIN OLIVE OIL	9 TO 12 SPRIGS OF FRESH HERBS, SUCH AS THYME, DILL, AND/OR PARSLEY
FINE SEA SALT	

❶ Clean the grill by heating it for at least 15 minutes and brushing it down with a grill brush to completely clean the rack. The grate is easier to clean while it's warm. Do not add cooking spray or oil. Preheat the grill for an additional 30 minutes.

❷ Temper the fish for 15 to 30 minutes while the grill heats up. Rinse the outside of the fish and the internal cavity and pat dry with paper towels. Drizzle each fish with a light coating of olive oil and season the cavity and skin with a few pinches of sea salt. Place half of the lemon slices and herbs in each fish's cavity and gently press it together.

❸ When the grill is hot, place the fish on the grate with the cavity side facing you. Leave undisturbed for 7 minutes.

❹ After 7 minutes, use a firm metal spatula to test if the fish loosens easily from the grill—the skin should stay attached to the fish rather than the grill. If it is still stubborn, cook for another minute. Flip the fish by rolling it over on its backbone (the cavity side now faces away from you) and slide it to a fresh part of the grill (the grill will be hotter there). Cook on the other side for 7 minutes.

❺ Remove the fish from the grill and allow it to rest for 5 minutes before serving.

SOLE MEUNIÈRE

SERVES 4

The classic French dish sole meunière illustrates the magic that happens when buttery meets lemony meets briny. Clearly, it worked for Julia Child; rumor has it this dish inspired her to start cooking at the age of forty.

4 FILLETS FLOUNDER, RED SNAPPER, SOLE, OR ANY THIN, WHITE DELICATE FISH, 3 TO 4 OUNCES EACH, SKIN ON	4 TABLESPOONS (½ STICK) UNSALTED BUTTER, CUT INTO SMALL CUBES
1 SCANT CUP ALL-PURPOSE FLOUR	1 LEMON, SUPREMED, JUICE HELD SEPARATELY (SEE PAGE 11)
FINE SEA SALT AND FRESHLY GROUND BLACK PEPPER	1 TABLESPOON CAPERS, RINSED IF SALT-PACKED OR BRINED
NEUTRAL-FLAVORED OIL, SUCH AS GRAPESEED OR CANOLA	1 TABLESPOON FINELY CHOPPED SHALLOT
	1 TABLESPOON CHOPPED FRESH FLAT-LEAF PARSLEY

❶ Remove the fish from the refrigerator 15 minutes prior to cooking to bring it to room temperature (this allows it to cook evenly). While the fish is tempering, set up the sauce ingredients.

❷ Spread the flour on a large plate. Pat the fillets dry and lightly season with salt and pepper on both sides. Holding the tail end of the fillet, dredge it in the flour, gently shaking off any excess.

❸ Heat a large skillet over high heat and pour in enough oil to fully cover the bottom of the pan. When the oil begins to shimmer but is not smoking, hold a fillet by the thin tail end and gently place the thicker end down first on the side of the skillet nearest to you, orienting the tail away from you. You want to start cooking the thicker side first and to divert any potential oil splatters away from you. Add a second fillet to the pan if it will fit, but take care not to overcrowd the pan because then the fish will not properly sear.

❹ When the fillets have browned on the bottom and the outer edges begin to become opaque, 1 to 3 minutes, carefully flip and cook the other side until opaque and cooked through, another 1 to 3 minutes, depending on the thickness of the fish. The fish should flip easily; if it doesn't, let it cook for another 30 seconds and try again. When the second side looks almost entirely opaque, transfer the fish to a warm plate. Cook the remaining fillets.

❺ Wipe out the pan with a dry, clean paper towel. Set the pan back on the stove over medium heat and add the butter. Cook gently until the butter smells nutty and turns golden brown, 1 to 2 minutes. Add the lemon juice, capers, and shallot. Swirl in the lemon supremes and parsley. Taste and adjust the seasoning.

❻ Remove the pan from the heat, gently add the fillets back into the pan, and baste with the sauce.

❼ Serve immediately.

Poultry

Most of our students count on chicken, whether a whole bird, cutlets, thighs, or drumsticks, as the primary source of protein for their meals. With good reason: poultry is amenable to a variety of sauces and preparations, rather uncomplicated to cook, and considered a healthful protein option.

WHAT AND HOW TO PURCHASE

When people hear about the practices used in industrial chicken farming, they often feel morally compelled to give up poultry entirely. However, there are farmers raising birds in an ethical, environmentally sound way. Frankly, it is more expensive for them to let birds roam free on pasture, grazing on what chickens *like* to eat. It is also more labor intensive to buy non-GMO feed and to slaughter using humane practices. However, in the spirit of buying less often but buying well, I argue in favor of quality over quantity.

Look for *pasture-raised*, antibiotic- and hormone-free chickens from small-scale local farms.

HOW TO COOK IT

The joy of cooking chicken is that you can use different cuts to experiment with various types of heat. Dark meat like thighs and legs are the most versatile and reliable. They can be grilled, braised, roasted, and fried—the Pan-Roasted Chicken (page 274) uses three different types of heat in its preparation to make it juicy and crispy. Meat from the breast cooks quickly and is best grilled, pan-seared, or poached to retain its moisture.

ROAST CHICKEN

SERVES 4

In my experience, a roasted bird is the MVP of a home cook's repertoire. Serve it with anything, really, and cook a bigger bird than you need so you have leftovers for the next few days. After all, cold chicken is almost better than hot chicken. Make sandwiches on toasted whole-grain bread with tender lettuce and Roasted Garlic Aioli (page 315). Or shred the chicken and toss it over a bowl of brown rice (see page 31) and crisp greens with Sesame Gremolata (page 301).

ONE 2½- TO 3-POUND CHICKEN	FRESHLY GROUND BLACK PEPPER
FINE SEA SALT	

❶ Temper the chicken for 45 to 60 minutes. Set the oven rack on the lowest track and preheat the oven to 425°F. If your oven has a convection function, turn it on: a fan in the back of the oven circulates the hot air, resulting in a more evenly cooked bird in a shorter amount of time.

❷ Pat the chicken dry and generously season the exterior and the cavity with salt and pepper. When seasoning, hold your hand 8 to 10 inches above the bird to allow for better distribution.

❸ Using a paring knife, remove the wishbone by making a small slice near the neck bone and scrape each side of the bone to remove it from the meat, then using your fingers, pinch and twist the bone at the joint to remove it. Next, remove the wing tips, the last joint of the wing, with a chef's knife, as these will burn.

❹ Truss the chicken with 3 to 4 feet of butcher's twine; it's always best to start with a longer piece than you think you'll need. With the breast up and the legs facing toward you, place the center of the twine behind the neck and pull the twine toward you down the length of both sides of the bird. Press the wings into the breast and secure with the twine. Cross the twine in front of you between the breast and the legs and pull tightly. The breast should plump up and the wings should be tightly pinned to the body. Then cross the twine under the legs and tie them together tightly toward the end of the drumstick. Tie a second knot under the tail to close the cavity.

❺ Place the chicken breast side up in a roasting pan or cast-iron pan and set it in the oven. (A cast-iron pan stays consistently superhot, which makes for a crisper, juicier chicken.) Cook for 40 to 50 minutes or until the temperature registers 160°F in the thickest part of the bird, the area where the thigh and breast meet. Every oven heats

FISH, FOWL & MEAT

differently, but tempered poultry generally takes about 15 minutes per pound when roasted at 425°F.

6 Let the bird rest for at least 15 minutes before carving to allow for carryover cooking and the redistribution of juices.

7 Carve the bird by removing the legs and thighs and cut at the joint to serve the drumsticks. Remove both breasts, slice them on the bias, and serve.

CHICKEN STOCK

MAKES 2 QUARTS

What to do with the leftover carcass from a roast chicken? Freeze it and save it for a rainy Sunday when you have time to make stock. Chicken stock can serve as the liquid for most soups and is a surefire way to make them more flavorful. You can also braise chicken in stock (see page 274), or even cook pasta or rice in it to imbue the starches with flavor.

1 CHICKEN CARCASS

1 LARGE YELLOW ONION, QUARTERED

1 LARGE CARROT, HALVED LENGTHWISE

1 CELERY STALK, HALVED LENGTHWISE

5 FLAT-LEAF PARSLEY SPRIGS

1 BAY LEAF

1 THYME SPRIG

5 WHOLE BLACK PEPPERCORNS

1. Place the chicken, onion, carrot, celery, parsley, bay, thyme, and peppercorns in a 10-quart stockpot with enough water to cover and bring to a boil over high heat.

2. Reduce the heat to low and simmer for 3 hours, skimming periodically with a ladle to remove the fat that rises to the top of the pot.

3. Strain using a mesh strainer and discard the solids. Store for up to 5 days in the refrigerator, or freeze for up to 6 months. See Storage Tips on page 300.

GRILLED CHICKEN PAILLARD

SERVES 2

Although this recipe is written for a grill pan, you can also use an outdoor grill. Just note that the chicken will cook more quickly than on the stovetop, so keep the grill set on medium heat—not too high, or the cutlets will char too much. The serving possibilities are endless: over a bed of arugula or grains with a drizzle of olive oil and a squeeze of lemon or Chimichurri (page 300), or accompanied by roasted potatoes and Salsa Verde (page 303). It's also a great match for Sautéed Green Beans with Garlic (page 100) and Peanut Sauce (page 324). Use a very sharp knife to butterfly the breast.

TWO 1 POUND SKINLESS, BONELESS CHICKEN BREASTS	OLIVE OIL FINE SEA SALT

❶ Lay the breasts on a cutting board and butterfly them: Press your nondominant hand flat on top of a chicken breast with the thinner side toward your pinky finger. Starting at the thick side, slice the breast horizontally in half, so it opens like a book. Be careful not to cut all the way through; you want about ½ inch of muscle holding it together on the thin side of the breast. Butterfly the second breast.

❷ Spread the breasts open, lay them between two pieces of parchment paper, and pound them with a meat tenderizer or a rolling pin until about ½ inch thick. Pounding chicken not only tenderizes the meat, it also speeds up the cooking time and keeps the meat juicy.

❸ Temper the breasts for 10 to 15 minutes. While they come to room temperature, preheat a grill pan over high heat. Drizzle the olive oil over the chicken. This will keep the breasts from sticking.

❹ When the pan is hot, gently lay the breasts on it and generously shower with salt. Make sure there's enough room—about 1 inch—around each breast; this will ensure that the meat gets a proper char and does not steam. Do not touch the chicken for 3 minutes. This allows the meat to form a crust, which will help it release from the pan. Try to flip the breast: if it sticks, the chicken hasn't seared yet. Give it another minute and try again.

❺ Flip and cook the other side for 3 to 4 minutes. When flipping the chicken, move it to a new spot on the pan (which will be hotter).

❻ Remove from the heat and rest for 5 minutes to allow the juices to redistribute. Serve as desired.

continued

If you don't have a grill pan and it's too cold to grill outside, try cooking the chicken in a cast-iron pan. This method is called "under the brick" and produces a juicy chicken with a golden crust. You can use either a clean brick wrapped in aluminum foil or canned foods from your pantry to help weight down the breast. You'll also need a stainless steel or other heavy pan that can nest inside your cast-iron one and extra-virgin olive oil to coat the pan.

❶ Follow steps 1 and 2. In step 3, heat a cast-iron pan over medium-high heat and pour in enough oil to fully cover the bottom. Season the chicken generously with salt. When the oil begins to shimmer, lay the breasts down away from you, to avoid splattering oil in your direction.

❷ Put a small piece of parchment paper on top of the chicken and weight it down with the heavy pan. Place the brick or a can or two as extra weight in the top pan. Cook for about 2 minutes.

❸ Remove the top pan with its weight and the parchment paper and flip the chicken. Replace the parchment, weight it down again, and cook for another 2 minutes.

❹ Remove from the heat, take off the brick, and rest for 5 minutes to allow the juices to redistribute.

TRY SPATCHCOCKING

I'll admit that spatchcocking a chicken sounds either lewd or ominous, but it's actually a brilliant technique and easy to master with a little practice. If you want roast chicken in 30 minutes, spatchcock it. Spatchcocking entails removing the backbone of a whole chicken so it can be flattened. It requires a sharp pair of kitchen shears and a little oomph, but is well worth the work. For a crispy-chicken-skin lover, there is no better way to guarantee the greatest surface area of crispy skin. Finally, you can have white and dark meat that is equally juicy! Try it with roasted fennel and a squeeze of lemon.

HOW TO SPATCHCOCK A CHICKEN

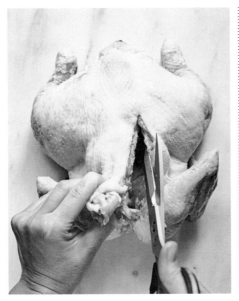

1 Place the bird breast side down on a nonporous cutting board, with the neck facing you. Use kitchen shears to cut down one side of the backbone, straight through the ribs.

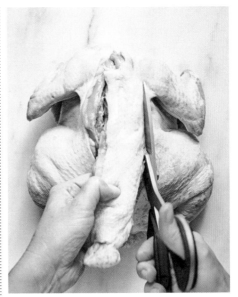

2 Rotate the bird and repeat on the other side.

3 Remove the backbone and flip the bird over.

4 Using your palms, firmly push down on the breastbone to flatten the bird.

PAN-ROASTED CHICKEN

SERVES 4

This variation on a classic coq au vin uses a few different heat methods. Searing the meat renders the fat into a flavorful base for cooking. A good braise cooks the meat to a tender finish. A final blast from the broiler crisps the skin. Serve with rice, roasted potatoes, or a big loaf of crusty bread.

3 POUNDS CHICKEN THIGHS AND LEGS, SKIN ON (ABOUT 8 PIECES)	2 BAY LEAVES
FINE SEA SALT	2 CUPS WHITE, ROSÉ, OR RED WINE
EXTRA-VIRGIN OLIVE OIL	1 CUP CHICKEN STOCK (SEE PAGE 269) OR WATER
½ POUND (2 CUPS) CREMINI MUSHROOMS, TRIMMED AND QUARTERED	1 LEMON, IF USING WHITE WINE OR ROSÉ—DO NOT USE WITH RED WINE
6 GARLIC CLOVES, PEELED AND THINLY SLICED	¼ CUP CHOPPED FRESH PARSLEY, FOR GARNISH
3 THYME SPRIGS	

❶ Temper the chicken by removing it from the refrigerator for 30 minutes prior to cooking. Preheat the oven to 350°F. Use paper towels to pat the chicken dry, then season it generously with salt.

❷ Heat a large, straight-sided ovenproof pan or Dutch oven over medium-high heat and pour in enough oil to fully cover the bottom of the pan. When the oil begins to shimmer, brown the chicken in batches, starting with the skin side down, 4 to 5 minutes on each side. Remove the chicken to a plate and reserve the oil in the pan.

❸ Add the mushrooms to the pan and sauté until browned, 5 to 10 minutes. Season with salt to taste, then add the garlic, thyme, and bay leaves. Cook for 1 to 2 minutes.

❹ Pour in the wine to deglaze the pan, using a wooden spoon to scrape up any browned bits from the bottom of the pan. Cook until the wine is reduced to half.

❺ Return the chicken to the pan, skin side up, in a single layer. Pour in the stock, making sure the chicken is nestled into the liquid, and bring the liquid to a boil.

❻ Place the pan, uncovered, in the oven. Cook for 30 minutes, or until the chicken is tender and cooked through, and the internal temperature is 160°F.

❼ Switch the oven to broil and brown the top of the chicken. Check on it often, every 2 to 3 minutes. When the skin is crisp, not burnt, remove the pan from the oven. Adjust the seasoning with lemon juice and salt to taste. Remove the bay leaves and thyme sprigs and discard.

❽ Garnish with the parsley and serve.

Beef, Lamb, and Pork

For centuries, eating meat was *an event*. Feasts were built around it; coronations and rites of passage called for venison, lamb, or a suckling pig roasted over a fire. Its special status makes sense: meat was always hard to come by, required a lot of effort, and cost much more than it does today. These dishes celebrate their main ingredients, so while meat may be eaten more regularly these days, it can still feel special.

WHAT AND HOW TO PURCHASE

The golden rule is to purchase meat from a reputable rancher or farmer, or from a butcher who supports small-scale meat producers. Such producers are more likely to pasture their animals and feed them a sustainable diet—without antibiotics, hormones, or GMO feed—and follow more humane raising and slaughtering practices. Note that 100 percent grass-fed beef is tougher, with less fat and marbling, than grain-fed meat, and thus may not provide the flavor and texture you desire. In that case, choose meat from humanely raised animals that have been fed a combination of grain and grass.

HOW TO COOK IT

The ideal method for cooking beef, lamb, and pork depends on the cut of the meat. Beef steaks and lamb chops are butchered from the middle part of the animal, which is exercised less, making it tender and flavorful. These cuts respond well to cooking with direct heat—such as grilling—for shorter times to preserve the flavor and texture. Tougher cuts of meat such as beef brisket and pork shoulder come from the forequarter of the animal. They have more connective tissue and so need more cooking time at low temperatures using techniques like roasting or braising.

GRILLED STEAK

A grilled steak with a seasoned char on the outside and a pink and juicy inside makes for a memorable meal. Grilling works best on an outdoor charcoal grill, with a well-marbled steak cut—one where you can see layers of fat and meat. You can use a grill pan as well, but you will get less char and smoky flavor.

The cooking time will vary depending on the cut and thickness of the steak. The best cuts for grilled steak are skirt steak, hanger, T-bone, and rib eye. Cuts like skirt steak cook to medium-rare in 6 to 8 minutes, while cuts like rib eye will take 8 to 14 minutes, depending on the thickness.

To make sure the flavor comes through, keep the steak unadorned: simply season with salt and pepper. No marinade, no rubs. Instead, add flavor with sauce, such as Chimichurri (page 300), or traditional herb butters.

STEAK CUT OF YOUR CHOICE

FINE SEA SALT

FRESHLY CRACKED BLACK PEPPER

---

❶ Temper the steak for 30 minutes to an hour prior to cooking.

❷ Clean the grill by heating it for at least 15 minutes and brushing it down with a grill brush. Then preheat the grill for an additional 30 minutes prior to cooking.

❸ Generously season the steaks with salt and pepper right before placing them on the grill. Don't season too early, as the salt will pull moisture from the meat, creating a tougher texture and causing the meat to steam rather than sear.

❹ Place the steak on the grill. Leave undisturbed for at least 2 minutes. Flip the steak and cook for 2 more minutes. Flip the steak again and continue to cook

for 2 minutes on each side until it reaches the desired doneness. Depending on the cut and thickness, the total cooking time can range from 6 to 14 minutes. Check the temperature and insert a thermometer into the thickest part of the steak. For medium-rare, it should register 120°F.

❺ Transfer the steak to a platter and let it rest for at least 10 minutes before slicing.

❻ Cut with the knife angled against the meat's natural grain. With cuts like skirt steak, the grain may change through the length of the meat.

❼ Finish the steak with an herb butter or chimichurri sauce.

Tarragon Butter

MAKES 1 CUP

½ POUND (2 STICKS) UNSALTED BUTTER, SOFTENED	2 TEASPOONS PERNOD (AN ANISE-FLAVORED LIQUEUR)
3 TABLESPOONS FINELY MINCED FRESH TARRAGON	1 TEASPOON FINE SEA SALT

❶ In a medium bowl, mix the butter, tarragon, Pernod, and salt with a silicone spatula until well combined.

❷ Transfer the butter to a piece of parchment paper or plastic wrap. Use the paper to gather the butter into a log about 6 inches long and 1½ to 2 inches in diameter.

❸ Tightly wrap and store in the freezer until you are ready to use it. It will keep for up to 1 month.

Maître d'Hôtel Butter

MAKES 1 CUP

½ POUND (2 STICKS) UNSALTED BUTTER, SOFTENED	1 TEASPOON FINE SEA SALT
2 TABLESPOONS FINELY MINCED FRESH FLAT-LEAF PARSLEY	GRATED ZEST AND JUICE OF 1 LEMON
	COARSELY GROUND BLACK PEPPER TO TASTE

❶ In a medium bowl, mix the butter, parsley, salt, lemon zest and juice, and pepper with a silicone spatula until well combined.

❷ Transfer the butter to a piece of parchment paper or plastic wrap. Use the paper to gather the butter into a log about 6 inches long and 1½ to 2 inches in diameter.

❸ Tightly wrap and store in the freezer until you are ready to use it. It will keep for up to 1 month.

STEAK CUTS AND WHAT TO DO WITH THEM

STEAK CUT	DESCRIPTION	COOKING TIME	ACCOMPANIMENTS
PORTERHOUSE	Often known as a twofer because it not only serves two, it also contains two cuts: a filet mignon and a strip loin.	8 to 10 minutes	**Tarragon Butter** (page 279)
SIRLOIN	A filet mignon is more tender, but a sirloin has much more flavor. It is a good economical purchase.	10 to 14 minutes	**Summer Panzanella** (page 223)
SKIRT	Thin and affordable, skirt steak is good for a crowd.	6 to 8 minutes	**Tortillas, beans, and Tomatillo Salsa** (page 312)
RIB EYE	The key to a good rib eye is to look for consistent fat marbling, which will give the cooked steak rich flavor and texture.	8 to 12 minutes	Chimichurri (page 300)
FLAT IRON	A tougher steak, flat iron is an economical cut from the shoulder of the cow.	8 to 10 minutes	**Classic French Fries** (page 125) and **Roasted Garlic Aioli** (page 315)

BEEF BOURGUIGNON

SERVES 6 TO 8

Learning to make beef bourguignon is one of our most popular classes. During the fall and winter months, who doesn't like a warming, nourishing, and elegant French stew? As a teaching tool, this one dish packs lots of skills: butchery, knife skills, sauce making, and cooking with wine. Win-win.

Stewing and braising are similar in that both methods cook slowly in moist heat, and thus are most suited to tougher cuts. The primary difference is the size of the meat cuts and the amount of liquid used. Cooking a large cut of meat like a leg of lamb or a pork shoulder partially covered in liquid is considered braising. When the meat is cut off the bone, cubed into uniform pieces, and completely submerged in liquid—as this recipe calls for—the method is referred to as stewing.

8 OUNCES BACON OR PANCETTA, DICED (OPTIONAL)

EXTRA-VIRGIN OLIVE OIL

2½ POUNDS BEEF CHUCK, CUT INTO 1½-INCH CUBES, ANY SILVER SKIN OR SINEW REMOVED

1 POUND (4 TO 6 CUPS) BUTTON MUSHROOMS, TRIMMED AND QUARTERED

1 POUND MULTICOLORED CARROTS, CUT INTO 2-INCH OBLIQUES (SEE PAGE 15)

2 GARLIC CLOVES, SLICED

FINE SEA SALT

1 TABLESPOON TOMATO PASTE (OPTIONAL)

½ CUP COGNAC OR BRANDY

ONE 750-ML BOTTLE OF DRY RED WINE

2 CUPS BEEF STOCK OR CHICKEN STOCK (SEE PAGE 269)

1 TEASPOON FRESH THYME LEAVES

2 BAY LEAVES

1 POUND PEARL ONIONS, PEELED

1 TO 2 TABLESPOONS DIJON MUSTARD

FRESHLY GROUND BLACK PEPPER

❶ In a large, heavy-bottomed pot or Dutch oven, cook the bacon, if using, over medium-high heat until the fat is rendered and the bacon is brown and crispy, about 5 minutes. Transfer to a plate and set aside.

❷ Add olive oil to the rendered fat as needed to cover the bottom of the pot. Add as many pieces of beef as will fit in a single, uncrowded layer. Sear, turning occasionally, until browned on all sides. Transfer the browned beef to a plate and continue searing the remaining beef in batches, adding more oil if needed. Do not crowd the pot.

continued

❸ Reduce the heat to medium and add the mushrooms. Cook, stirring often, until the mushrooms begin to brown; then add the carrots and garlic. Season the vegetables with salt and stir in the tomato paste, if using.

❹ Carefully pour in the Cognac and use a wooden spoon to scrape up the browned bits from the bottom of the pot. Return the beef and bacon to the pot. Add the wine and stock and bring to a boil, then reduce to a simmer. Add the thyme and bay leaves.

❺ Cover the pot and simmer over low heat for 2½ hours, stirring every 20 minutes or so. Alternatively, you can place the covered pot in a 300°F oven for 2½ hours, checking after about 1½ hours and then at about 30-minute intervals.

❻ While the meat is stewing, bring a pot of water to boil, add the pearl onions, and then remove the pot from the heat. Let the onions sit in the hot water for 30 seconds. Drain and let cool. Peel the onions, keeping the hairy bottoms intact.

❼ Add the peeled pearl onions to the stew about 30 minutes before the stew is done.

❽ When the meat is tender but not falling apart, finish the dish by adjusting the seasoning and adding the Dijon mustard and black pepper to taste. Skim any fat off the top with a large spoon and discard before serving. Serve with rice, polenta, or roasted potatoes.

LAMB KOFTA

This is a simplified take on Yotam Ottolenghi's recipe for lamb meatballs. It's a versatile dish to serve: you can wrap them in Grilled Flatbread (page 333), serve them with couscous, a salad of parsley and cucumbers drizzled with olive oil and lemon, and hummus (see page 57) for dunking. For optimal flavor it is important to chop all the ingredients very finely.

1 POUND GROUND LAMB	2 TABLESPOONS FINELY MINCED FRESH MINT
2 SCALLIONS (WHITE AND GREEN PARTS), MINCED	2 GARLIC CLOVES, GRATED
2 TABLESPOONS FINELY MINCED FRESH FLAT-LEAF PARSLEY	1 TEASPOON GROUND CUMIN
	½ TEASPOON GROUND CORIANDER
2 TABLESPOONS FINELY MINCED FRESH CILANTRO	FINE SEA SALT
	EXTRA-VIRGIN OLIVE OIL

❶ Preheat the oven to 375°F. Line two baking sheets with parchment.

❷ In a large mixing bowl, combine the lamb, scallions, parsley, cilantro, mint, garlic, cumin, coriander, and a large pinch of salt. Use your hands to mix the ingredients and evenly distribute the seasonings throughout the meat.

❸ Form the mixture into 1½-inch balls using your hands. Set aside on the prepared baking sheets.

❹ Place a large sauté pan over medium heat and pour in enough oil to cover the bottom. When the oil begins to shimmer, gently place the meatballs in a single layer—you'll need to do this in batches. Note that for meat to sear, the oil must be hot enough; it should sizzle when you place the lamb balls in the pan. Do not crowd the pan, as this will lower the oil temperature and create too much moisture, thus steaming rather than searing the meatballs.

❺ Let the balls sear for 2 to 3 minutes, then rotate them until they are browned all over. Use a spoon or tongs to remove them from the pan and place back on the baking sheets.

❻ When all the balls have seared, bake for 10 to 15 minutes, or until the internal temperature reaches 160°F. Let cool for 5 minutes before serving.

ROASTED LEG OF LAMB

SERVES 6 TO 8

There are days I crave the aroma of roasting lamb: savory, herb-laden waves promising a mouthwatering supper. This recipe is a daylong endeavor, but it requires very little actual work. You can make this recipe with any large cut of lamb, like a shoulder or a rack. Don't scrunch your nose at the anchovies; they've been used by Mediterranean cooks in lieu of salt for ages. They don't taste fishy in this dish—when mixed with the other ingredients, they melt away, creating a savory, rich juice.

ONE 7-POUND LEG OF LAMB, BONE-IN; ASK YOUR BUTCHER TO REMOVE THE AITCH (PRONOUNCED "H") BONE TO AID CARVING

12 GARLIC CLOVES

20 WHOLE BLACK PEPPERCORNS

½ CUP KALAMATA OLIVES

¼ CUP EXTRA-VIRGIN OLIVE OIL

2 WHOLE ANCHOVIES

¼ CUP FRESH ROSEMARY LEAVES

2 TABLESPOONS FRESH THYME LEAVES

2 TABLESPOONS DIJON MUSTARD

FINE SEA SALT

❶ Temper the lamb for 90 minutes and place it in a large roasting pan.

❷ Marinate the lamb while it tempers: combine the garlic, peppercorns, olives, olive oil, anchovies, rosemary, thyme, Dijon mustard, and salt in the bowl of a food processor. Blend until the mixture forms a thick paste.

❸ Make four or five diagonal slashes, each 1 to 2 inches deep, in the lamb and rub the mixture all over the flesh, pressing it into the crevices.

❹ While the lamb finishes tempering, preheat the oven to 425°F.

❺ Roast the lamb until brown, about 25 minutes. Reduce the oven temperature to 375°F and cook the lamb for another 6 hours.

❻ Remove the lamb from the oven, cover it with aluminum foil, and let rest for 30 minutes.

❼ Slice and serve.

PORK SALSA VERDE

SERVES 8 TO 10

In this case, salsa verde refers to the Mexican version, not the Mediterranean one. Zoe Maya features this recipe in many of her Mexican classes at Haven's Kitchen. ZM grew up in Cancún, where she learned to use tomatillo salsa (i.e., "salsa verde") as the liquid for braised pork shoulder. As with all braises, about three-quarters of the meat should be covered by the cooking liquid, and the pot should have a tight-fitting lid. Shred the pork for a savory filling for tacos or as an accompaniment to rice and beans. It's a good idea to make a double batch of the salsa, so you'll have some fresh salsa for serving.

You can make this with a smaller 4- to 5-pound cut while keeping the amounts of the braise ingredients the same. The cook time will be shorter, 3 to 4 hours.

ONE 9-POUND BONE-IN PORK SHOULDER

6 GARLIC CLOVES

¼ CUP PLUS 2 TEASPOONS FINE SEA SALT

3 CUPS TOMATILLO SALSA (PAGE 312)

3 CUPS WATER

1 LARGE ONION, QUARTERED

2 WHOLE ANCHO CHILES

2 ORANGES, QUARTERED

1 LIME, HALVED

2 BAY LEAVES

2 TABLESPOONS CUMIN SEEDS

2 TABLESPOONS CORIANDER SEEDS

LEAVES FROM ¼ BUNCH OF CILANTRO

❶ Temper the pork for 40 to 90 minutes and preheat the oven to 300°F.

❷ Using a paring knife, score the top of the pork shoulder: make six 1-inch-deep cuts across the top and push 1 garlic clove into each hole. Rub the ¼ cup salt into the meat.

❸ Place the pork shoulder in a large Dutch oven or roasting pan. Add the tomatillo salsa, water, onion, chiles, oranges, lime, bay leaves, cumin, and coriander. Cover tightly with the lid or seal with foil.

❹ Cook for 6 hours, or until the meat shreds easily with a fork.

❺ Remove from the oven and shred into large pieces with a fork. Season with the remaining 2 teaspoons salt and baste with the braising liquid, scooping it from the bottom of the pan and pouring it over the meat.

❻ Plate and garnish with cilantro.

SAUCES

"It's always a good idea to follow the directions exactly the first
time you try a recipe. But from then on, you're on your own."

—JAMES BEARD

AS THE OWNER OF A COOKING
school, I entertain a lot of questions about
how to cook better and more often. Much
of the time, I find myself preaching sauce as
a solution. By sauce, I don't mean buttery,
precious French applications—although
those do have their rightful place in the
culinary canon. When I say sauce, I mean
anything that you dip into, toss with, spread,
or drizzle.

Sometimes people don't even ask me for
cooking advice, and I start babbling about
the genius of gremolata, pesto, and romesco.
Sauces elevate your food, making it more
appealing, more complex, and tastier. And
they are the most effective way to satisfy
the flavors you crave. A well-cooked chicken
breast is dependable and, without much
ado, just fine on its own. But consider what
happens when it's drizzled with a nutty
tahini sauce or deep green chimichurri.
Here's why: If there's one simple rule in
food, it is that *opposites attract*. Rich is at
its best when balanced with bright and
acidic. Crunchy is delightful when paired
with creamy. Sour or spicy tastes better
when mellowed with a hint of sweet.
Your mouth loves contrasting flavors and
textures because when combined, they
create a balance of texture and flavor. And
there's no vehicle more capable of creating
balance than sauce. With just one dollop or
drizzle, sauce is the yin to a dish's yang, the
sunshine to its rain.

When thinking about what sauce to make,
first consider your main dish. Then ask
yourself the following questions:

• What taste or texture am I missing in the
meal that would round things out?

• Is there a flavor or cuisine I'm trying to
capture?

• Does the dish need herbiness, tanginess,
heat, brininess, or nuttiness?

• Would something smooth and creamy feel
right, or should the sauce have a bit more
body?

• Do I want a sauce that drizzles like a
dressing or that is more like a dip?

• What color sauce would make the nicest
counterpoint?

It's a gratifying feeling to serve your guests
a platter of (name your favorite dish here)
ladled with a deeply hued, appetizing sauce.
Or pepper your table with a few bowls of
sauce, and encourage your guests to drizzle
and dunk with abandon. Sauces give life to
leftovers, add global flavors to old stand-bys,
and can make you feel like there may just
be an undiscovered culinary wizard inside
of you.

Teaching Recipe

TAHINI SAUCE

MAKES ABOUT 2 CUPS

Most any sauce can be adapted depending on what you're using it for. Let's say you want something tangy for a dip. Reach for Greek yogurt as your base, then add ground toasted cumin seeds, lemon, and salt. The next day, reinvent your dip as a salad dressing by watering it down, but preserving the balance of fat and acid. Lost its kick? Add more lemon and cumin. Just keep tasting and adjusting along the way.

Tahini is a great example of a sauce's versatility. It adds flavor and moisture to anything from lamb to cauliflower. You can make it chock-full of herbs as a spread for sandwiches, or thin it to dress a romaine salad. When serving tahini sauce with blander ingredients like avocado, balance the flavors by spiking it with spicy harissa. The standard recipe is easy to tweak in any direction.

1 CUP TAHINI

JUICE OF 2 LEMONS,
PLUS MORE AS NEEDED

2 GARLIC CLOVES

FINE SEA SALT

½ CUP WATER, PLUS MORE AS NEEDED

BASE INGREDIENTS

❶ In a blender, combine the tahini, lemon juice, garlic, and salt to taste. Blend, slowly adding water until the texture is as smooth as that of pancake batter. Taste, adding more lemon juice, water, or salt as needed.

COOKING NOTES

You don't need to use a blender. Tahini sauce comes together in a bowl using a fork or whisk too.

continued

CUSTOMIZE

❷ Once the sauce itself is balanced—creamy, not watery; tart, but also deeply flavored—you can use it to balance the flavors and textures of whatever you are serving it with.

To make an herby tahini: Add up to ¼ cup chopped fresh flat-leaf parsley or cilantro. Start with 2 tablespoons and work up from there. This adds texture and color to a neutral palette of falafel or roasted lamb.

To make it spiced: Mix in ½ teaspoon ground coriander, ground cumin, za'atar, and/or sumac to balance more mellow dishes or ingredients, or to dress up a fried or hard-boiled egg.

To make it spicy: Mix in 1 teaspoon harissa. Heat is a good counterpoint for oily, rich ingredients like salmon and avocado.

To thin it out: Add more lemon juice or water and a bit more salt. Thin it out when you want it to drizzle more easily—say, as a salad dressing.

To make it thicker: Add more tahini paste and ¼ cup Greek yogurt. Thickened, it works well as a dip for crudités or chips.

SAUCES

Types of Sauces

Why do French fries and ketchup make such a great match? The combination of the salty, crispy fries with a tart, sweet condiment is the embodiment of balance. When making a sauce, ask yourself: What flavor will round out the dish? Something herby, tangy, spicy, briny, or nutty? Once you get the knack for making sauce, feel free to make these recipes your own: Add more garlic here, substitute lemon for lime there, thicken the sauce with herbs or more nuts, or swap in basil or mint for cilantro.

HERBY

These sauces, such as Chimichurri (page 300) and Gremolata (page 301), add vibrancy and pop to roasted vegetables and cold-weather meat dishes. They also provide a refreshing kick in the heat of summer.

TANGY

Tangy sauces like Roasted Garlic Aioli (page 315) and Ginger-Garlic Vinegar Sauce (page 311) are a good balance for fried dishes, as their bold flavors cut through richness and add complexity to subtle ingredients like fish and tofu.

SPICY

Hot sauces provide a satisfying kick. The intensity of spicy sauces varies from the light burn of Tomatillo Salsa (page 312) to the nasal-passage-clearing kick of Habanero Hot Sauce (page 313). Spicy sauces work well with most dishes, but especially those with milder flavors.

BRINY

Since the sixth century, when ancient Romans figured out that fermented anchovy paste mixed with wine made for a tasty gravy (with the added benefit of killing unwanted bacteria), briny sauces, such as Gribiche (page 314) and Olive Tapenade (page 319), have been part of a cook's repertoire.

NUTTY

Nuts and seeds add viscosity, fat, and earthiness to a sauce. They don't overpower; they absorb the flavors of the herbs or spices in the recipe. Nutty sauces, such as Green Cashew Sauce (page 325) and Romesco (page 320), complement grilled chicken and vegetables, grain bowls, and slaws.

SESAME GREMOLATA

PESTO

SALSA VERDE

CHIMICHURRI

Tips for Sauce Making

Sauce making does not need to be intimidating. Follow these simple steps as a template to create your favorite sauce.

1. PREPARE THE INGREDIENTS

Always use the freshest ingredients possible. Herbs should be bright green and perky with no browning. If the herbs are wilted but not brown, you can revive them in an ice bath: submerge them in cold water with ice cubes for 10 minutes. Drain and dry well.

Think ahead: make sure you have the ingredients and determine if you need to boil an egg or roast some garlic.

When you are going to blend sauces, there's no need to remove the stems from leafy herbs like cilantro and parsley; just remove the roots and tougher inch or so at the bottom of each sprig.

2. GET THE TEXTURE AND CONSISTENCY RIGHT

The ideal texture will depend on what you're saucing and your personal taste. Some sauces are meant to be smooth and fully blended; others should remain chunky. A high-speed blender is the best tool for a smooth sauce. You can also use a mortar and pestle to mash garlic down to a paste and then add it with the rest of the ingredients.

Also, add liquids like water, lemon juice, or oil slowly, a little at a time, to ensure that your sauce doesn't get too loose, and check repeatedly for flavor, texture, and balance.

3. TASTE, THEN ADJUST FLAVOR AS DESIRED

After making your sauce, always taste it! If you are happy with the consistency but want to adjust the flavor, stir in salt or acid by hand. Don't overblend.

4. GIVE IT TIME

Sauces sometimes need time to rest and marinate so that flavors blend fully. When cooking any meal, make the sauce first and let it sit until you're ready to serve it.

CHIMICHURRI

MAKES ABOUT 1 CUP

South American gauchos perfected this garlicky, parsley-rich sauce to dollop on *asado* (barbecue). But chimichurri also works well on everything from roasted potatoes to fried fish. There is no one right way to make it, though many families have their own recipe, handed down through generations.

This recipe calls for a food processor. However, you can use a mortar and pestle or a blender. Keep in mind, chimichurri is meant to be chunky, so pulse the items rather than puréeing completely.

2 CUPS PACKED FRESH FLAT-LEAF PARSLEY	JUICE OF 2 LIMES, PLUS MORE AS NEEDED
4 GARLIC CLOVES, MINCED	½ CUP EXTRA-VIRGIN OLIVE OIL
2 TABLESPOONS MINCED FRESH OREGANO	FINE SEA SALT

❶ Place the parsley in the bowl of a food processor with the garlic, oregano, and lime juice and pulse until roughly chopped.

❷ Add the olive oil and a pinch of salt and pulse until chunky, about 15 seconds.

❸ Check the seasoning and add salt and/or lime juice if needed. While it's wonderful freshly made, chimichurri can be refrigerated in an airtight container for up to 3 days.

STORAGE TIPS FOR
SAUCES

To refrigerate sauces: Prevent the top of a sauce from browning or forming a skin by pressing a piece of plastic wrap on the surface of the sauce before covering with a lid.

To freeze sauces: Line a pitcher with a 1-quart freezer bag, ladle the sauce into the bag, and seal it. Freeze for up to 6 months. Lay the bags flat; they'll take up less space and defrost in less time. You can also freeze sauces in ice cube trays, and after they have solidified, pop them into freezer bags. Defrost only what you need.

SESAME GREMOLATA

MAKES ABOUT 1 CUP

The parsley-garlic base of Milanese gremolata is similar to that of a chimichurri, but gremolata is a drier, tighter sauce. Traditionally served with osso buco (a Milanese veal dish), you can dab it on top of roasted vegetables or meat or mix it into scrambled eggs (see page 174). This version uses sesame seeds for textural oomph. You can easily convert it into a lovely "broken" vinaigrette (i.e., not totally emulsified) by adding olive oil and freshly squeezed lemon. Try it over a bowl of crunchy lettuce, a hard-boiled egg, and, if the season is right, a tomato wedge or two.

1 CUP PACKED FRESH FLAT-LEAF PARSLEY LEAVES

GRATED ZEST OF 1 LEMON

2 GARLIC CLOVES, MINCED

⅓ CUP SESAME SEEDS, TOASTED

EXTRA-VIRGIN OLIVE OIL

JUICE OF ½ LEMON

FINE SEA SALT

❶ Place the parsley in the bowl of a food processor with the lemon zest, garlic, and sesame seeds. Pulse until the parsley is minced and the mixture is just combined. Transfer to a bowl and stir in olive oil to reach the desired consistency. Add the lemon juice and salt to taste.

❷ If you do not have a food processor, finely chop the parsley and place it in a bowl with the lemon zest and garlic. Mix in the sesame seeds with the oil to reach the desired consistency. Stir in the lemon juice and salt to taste. If you want the garlic finer, grate it on a rasp-style grater. Store in an airtight container in the refrigerator for up to 3 days.

VARIATION

To make hazelnut or walnut gremolata, replace the sesame seeds with the same amount of toasted chopped hazelnuts or walnuts.

PESTO

A purist would argue that a true Ligurian pesto requires a mortar and pestle, Genovese basil, raw Tuscan pine nuts, freshly grated Parmigiano-Reggiano and Pecorino cheeses, and regional olive oil. But don't miss out on this sauce just because you aren't in Liguria. Try substituting any combination of herbs and greens for the basil. Replace pine nuts with your favorite seeds. You can even skip the cheese.

Pesto works on more than pasta. Try it stirred into warm farro, spread on a sandwich of whole-grain toast and roasted peppers, or tossed with sautéed green beans (page 100), a classic Genovese combination.

---

2 CUPS TIGHTLY PACKED FRESH BASIL LEAVES

¼ CUP PINE NUTS

¼ CUP FRESHLY GRATED PARMIGIANO-REGGIANO

2 GARLIC CLOVES, MINCED

¼ TO ½ CUP EXTRA-VIRGIN OLIVE OIL

GRATED ZEST AND JUICE OF 1 LEMON (ABOUT 2 TABLESPOONS JUICE), OR TO TASTE

FINE SEA SALT

---

❶ Wash the basil by lightly running it under cold water and patting dry, or use a salad spinner. Basil browns quickly so do not wash it ahead of time, and make sure it is thoroughly dry.

❷ Place the basil, pine nuts, Parmigiano-Reggiano, and garlic in the bowl of a food processor. Pulse until roughly chopped; then, while pulsing, slowly add ¼ cup olive oil until the ingredients form a coarse purée.

❸ Taste; then add the lemon zest and juice and salt to taste. If you prefer a thinner texture, add more olive oil or a little water. Pesto will keep for up to 5 days in the refrigerator and can be frozen for up to 3 months in a tightly sealed plastic bag.

VARIATIONS

For the basil: 2 cups herbs or greens, such as kale, parsley, cilantro, spinach, or arugula

For the pine nuts: ¼ cup nuts or seeds, such as walnuts, almonds, pumpkin seeds, or sunflower seeds

For the cheese: Hard aged cheeses, such as Cheddar, Gouda, or Manchego, or nutritional yeast

For the lemon: Sherry vinegar

SALSA VERDE

MAKES ABOUT 1 CUP

Not to be confused with Mexican tomato-based salsa, this one is of Mediterranean origin and made with chopped herbs held together with olive oil. There is no acid in the basic version. Instead, the herbs and oil are balanced with salty, briny capers and anchovies. You can deepen the flavor with another anchovy or two when saucing something mild like vegetables or grains. Serve with polenta (see page 56) and a fried egg (see page 180) and top it off with red pepper flakes.

1 CUP LOOSELY PACKED FRESH
FLAT-LEAF PARSLEY

½ CUP LOOSELY PACKED
FRESH CILANTRO LEAVES

½ CUP LOOSELY PACKED
FRESH MINT LEAVES

1 TABLESPOON CAPERS, RINSED IF
SALT-PACKED OR BRINED, AND MINCED

2 OIL-PACKED ANCHOVY FILLETS,
MINCED

1 GARLIC CLOVE, MINCED

¾ CUP EXTRA-VIRGIN OLIVE OIL

¼ TEASPOON RED PEPPER FLAKES

FINE SEA SALT

❶ Coarsely chop the parsley, cilantro, and mint and place in a bowl. Add the capers, anchovies, garlic, olive oil, and red pepper flakes and mix well.

❷ Taste and add salt if needed. The capers and anchovies might provide enough salinity on their own.

❸ Alternatively, combine all the ingredients in the bowl of a food processor fitted with the metal chopping blade and pulse until combined but still chunky. Store in an airtight container in the refrigerator for up to 3 days.

HOW TO MINCE GARLIC

1 Once you have removed a clove from the bulb, cut the root end off.

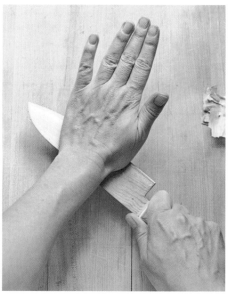

2 Use the flat side of a chef's knife to press down and separate the peel from the clove.

3 If you see a green germ in the middle of the clove, remove it.

4 Continue to slice or mince, depending on the recipe.

PASTA AND NOODLES

Noodles are one of the most reliable and foolproof meals. They're a lovely blank slate, happy to be tossed with olive oil and sautéed vegetables or Crispy Sautéed Mushrooms (page 102) or with a comforting dollop of butter and a handful of Parmigiano-Reggiano cheese. Of course, you can always serve pasta with Fresh Tomato Sauce (page 307) or Pesto (page 302). Knowing a few tricks of the trade can make the difference when prepping a pot of water for pasta.

1. Go big on the pot of water: use a 8- to 10-quart stockpot and fill it three-quarters full of water.

2. Salt the water heavily—at least ¼ cup. It should taste like the sea.

3. That thing about adding oil to the water? Skip it. It's a waste of oil and it doesn't benefit the pasta in any way.

4. Bring the pot of water to a rapid boil before adding the pasta.

5. Make sure *all the pasta is entirely underwater,* with no strands sticking out.

6. Prevent clumping by stirring the pasta at least three times while it's boiling.

7. *Taste* the pasta for doneness. Then drain the noodles in a colander when they are just cooked all the way through: no hard center, but no mush either—the pasta should have just the slightest bite. The pasta package is usually accurate when it comes to timing.

8. Reserve some of the cooking water as you drain. It's good and starchy, and adding a few tablespoons to your sauce will help thicken it.

FRESH TOMATO SAUCE

MAKES ABOUT 1 CUP

Few foods embody summer more than those sultry, nearly bursting tomatoes at
your local farm stand. Almost too soft to hold, overripe tomatoes are best for
making fresh tomato sauce. Salt and oil add other dimensions of flavor to the
sauce and thicken it, so it clings to pasta, arancini, or whatever else it is meant
to adorn. Made with only three ingredients, this sauce requires you to start
with a cold pan; the tomatoes are gently simmered and the olive oil and salt are
added just before serving. Make a double batch and freeze some for glum, dark
winter nights when everyone needs to taste and feel a little sunshine. Serve with
a tube-shaped pasta, like penne, which will capture bits of sauce for extra juicy
satisfaction, or as a dipping sauce for Arancini (page 86).

3 LARGE OVERRIPE BEEFSTEAK TOMATOES	2 LARGE PINCHES OF FINE SEA SALT
2 TABLESPOONS EXTRA-VIRGIN OLIVE OIL	

❶ Using a box grater, grate the tomatoes
over a bowl. Either discard the skin that
doesn't go through the grater or chop it
finely and add it to the bowl.

❷ Add the tomato pulp to a medium sauté
pan, bring to simmer over medium heat,
and cook for about 5 minutes, stirring with
a wooden spoon.

❸ When you see the liquid bubble and
separate from the bulk of the tomatoes,
add the olive oil and salt.

❹ Serve immediately. Store in an airtight
container in the refrigerator, for up to 3 days,
or in ziplock bags in the freezer for up to
6 months (see "Storage Tips for Sauces,"
page 300).

SWEET CHILI SAUCE

MAKES ABOUT 1 CUP

One of our favorite recipes from the kids' classes at Haven's Kitchen is a Southeast Asian–inspired vermicelli salad (see page 328). It inspires young students to eat an array of fresh and pickled vegetables, but equally important, the fun of the noodles and the sweet-meets-spicy chili sauce creates a lot of excitement and laughter in the teaching kitchen. The sweetness of this sauce is a good counterpoint to the heat of the chiles. Drizzle on grain bowls or grilled fish to give them a tasty kick.

½ CUP WATER

½ CUP SUGAR

¼ CUP WHITE VINEGAR

3 GARLIC CLOVES, MINCED

2 HOT RED CHILES (BIRD'S EYE, THAI, HABANERO, OR FRESNO), MINCED

FINE SEA SALT

2 TEASPOONS ARROWROOT

❶ In a small saucepan, combine ¼ cup water with the sugar, vinegar, garlic, chiles, and a large pinch of salt. Bring to a simmer over medium heat and stir to dissolve the sugar.

❷ In a small bowl, dissolve the arrowroot in the remaining ¼ cup water.

❸ When the sugar is dissolved, whisk the arrowroot mixture into the pot. Stir continuously over medium heat until the sauce begins to thicken, about 2 minutes. Remove from the heat and let cool slightly before serving.

❹ Store in an airtight container in the refrigerator for up to 1 week.

SAUCES

GINGER-GARLIC VINEGAR SAUCE

MAKES ABOUT ½ CUP

This recipe starts with the base of a Chinese "mother" sauce—rice vinegar, soy sauce, and ginger—and adds minced garlic and sesame oil. Use it as a dipping sauce for tempura (see page 77), to sauce a whole grilled or roasted fish (see pages 260 and 261), or as a marinade with our fried tofu (page 331). Sesame oil is flavorful, so be prudent if you decide to add more.

¼ CUP RICE VINEGAR	1 TABLESPOON SUGAR
¼ CUP SOY SAUCE	2 GARLIC CLOVES, MINCED
1 TABLESPOON MINCED FRESH GINGER	1 TEASPOON TOASTED SESAME OIL

❶ In a medium bowl, whisk together the vinegar, soy sauce, ginger, sugar, garlic, and sesame oil.

❷ Let the sauce sit for 20 minutes before serving so the flavors have a chance to meld.

❸ Store in an airtight container in the refrigerator for up to 3 days.

TOMATILLO SALSA

MAKES ABOUT 3 CUPS

Also called "salsa verde," this is a staple Mexican sauce with many variations. While many tomatillo salsa recipes call for charring or stewing the tomatillos first, this raw recipe is speedier and preserves the vibrant green color and tartness of the tomatillos. A little more sour than a tomato salsa, this bright-green sauce suits all types of dishes. We use it to braise *and* serve with our Pork Salsa Verde (page 289). It's also a stellar match for black beans, avocado, and all things corn tortilla related.

1 POUND TOMATILLOS, PAPERY HUSKS REMOVED, RINSED AND HALVED

1 SMALL WHITE ONION, CHOPPED

2 GARLIC CLOVES

1 BUNCH OF CILANTRO, BOTH STEMS AND LEAVES

¼ CUP FRESHLY SQUEEZED LIME JUICE

2 SERRANO CHILES, SEEDED AND CHOPPED

FINE SEA SALT

❶ Working in batches, purée the tomatillos, onion, garlic, cilantro, lime juice, and chiles in a blender until smooth.

❷ Season with salt to taste.

❸ Store in an airtight container in the refrigerator for up to 1 week.

HABANERO HOT SAUCE

MAKES ABOUT 2 CUPS

A favorite of Zoe Maya's, this sauce from the Yucatán is bold, flavorful, and deeply hued, making it a killer condiment for fish tacos, grilled chicken, beans, grain bowls, or eggs of any persuasion. Refrigerated in a sealed jar, it keeps for up to two weeks.

5 GARLIC CLOVES	1 CUP WHITE VINEGAR
2 LARGE CARROTS, ROUGHLY CHOPPED	1 CUP WATER
½ ONION, ROUGHLY CHOPPED	2 TEASPOONS FINE SEA SALT
1 OR 2 HABANERO CHILES, STEMS AND SEEDS REMOVED	2 TEASPOONS SUGAR

❶ In a small saucepan, combine the garlic, carrot, onion, chiles, vinegar, and water. Partially cover and bring to a simmer over medium-low heat.

❷ When the liquid reaches a simmer, stir in the salt and sugar. Once the carrots are thoroughly tender, about 10 minutes, remove from the heat.

❸ Let cool slightly, and then pour into a blender and purée until smooth. Season to taste with salt.

GRIBICHE

This French sauce will surprise you. It gets its texture and richness from chopped boiled eggs, balanced by briny cornichons and capers. Traditionally ladled over a French meat stew called pot-au-feu, gribiche is a great stand-in for mayonnaise and can be served over milder dishes from asparagus to grilled fish.

3 HARD-BOILED EGGS (SEE PAGE 173)

1 SMALL SHALLOT, MINCED
(ABOUT 3 TABLESPOONS)

1 TABLESPOON CAPERS, RINSED IF SALT-PACKED OR BRINED, AND MINCED

1 TABLESPOON CORNICHONS, MINCED

1½ TEASPOONS DIJON MUSTARD

3 TABLESPOONS RED WINE VINEGAR

¾ CUP EXTRA-VIRGIN OLIVE OIL

1 TABLESPOON CHOPPED
FRESH CHERVIL

1 TABLESPOON CHOPPED
FRESH TARRAGON

1 TABLESPOON CHOPPED
FRESH CHIVES

❶ Grate the eggs on the finest section of a box grater and set aside in a small bowl.

❷ In a medium bowl, mix the shallot, capers, cornichons, and mustard until well combined. Whisk in the vinegar and then the oil. Mix in the chervil, tarragon, and chives, as well as the eggs. Store in an airtight container in the refrigerator for up to 2 days.

ROASTED GARLIC AIOLI

Provençal aioli is made by whisking the heck out of a raw egg yolk, a bit of salt and olive oil, and lots and lots of raw garlic. The key to achieving a smooth, mayonnaise-like texture, beyond the whisking, is mashing the garlic until it's completely creamy. Roasting the garlic first makes this easier and produces a slightly sweeter flavor. Aioli is traditionally served with raw, steamed, or boiled vegetables. But try it with everything.

Store the aioli in an airtight container in the refrigerator for up to 1 week.

1 WHOLE GARLIC HEAD

½ CUP NEUTRAL-FLAVORED OIL, SUCH AS GRAPESEED OR CANOLA, AND ½ CUP EXTRA-VIRGIN OLIVE OIL, COMBINED, PLUS MORE OLIVE OIL FOR ROASTING THE GARLIC

FINE SEA SALT

1 TEASPOON FRESHLY SQUEEZED LEMON JUICE

½ TEASPOON DIJON MUSTARD

1 LARGE EGG YOLK (RINSE THE EGGSHELL FIRST IF YOU'RE WORRIED ABOUT BACTERIA)

❶ Prepare the roasted garlic: Preheat the oven to 325°F. Slice off the top ¼ inch of the whole garlic head and place the bulb on a piece of aluminum foil. Drizzle lightly with olive oil and sprinkle with salt, then wrap tightly. Roast for 30 to 45 minutes, depending on the size and age of the garlic. Remove from the oven and unwrap—the garlic will be fragrant and the individual cloves will be soft and golden. Let cool slightly before squeezing the cloves out of their peels. Place 3 cloves of roasted garlic in a small bowl and make into a paste. (Roasted cloves can be stored in the refrigerator for up to a week or in the freezer for up to 3 months.)

❷ In a medium bowl, combine the lemon juice, mustard, and salt.

❸ Add the egg yolk and begin whisking. While whisking, slowly drizzle in about 2 tablespoons of the oil mixture, drop by drop, until the mixture begins to thicken and an emulsion forms.

❹ Continuing to whisk, slowly pour in half of the remaining oil mixture in a thin and steady stream. This should take about 1 minute. The mixture should be thick and light in color.

❺ Whisk in 1 teaspoon cold water. In a slow and steady stream, slowly pour in the remaining oil mixture, whisking constantly. It should take about 1 more minute to add the remaining oil.

❻ Fold in the roasted garlic purée and season with salt to taste.

OLIVE TAPENADE

MAKES ABOUT 2 CUPS

Olive tapenade combines all sorts of salty, savory flavors into one sauce. Tapenade balances mellow, slightly sweet foods like salmon or baked potato, and makes a great party dip or sandwich spread (especially with leftover Roasted Leg of Lamb, page 288).

2 CUPS NIÇOISE OR KALAMATA OLIVES, PITTED

1 TABLESPOON ROASTED GARLIC (SEE PAGE 315)

1 OIL-PACKED ANCHOVY FILLET

2 TABLESPOONS EXTRA-VIRGIN OLIVE OIL

1 TABLESPOON CHOPPED FRESH FLAT-LEAF PARSLEY

GRATED ZEST OF ½ LEMON

❶ In the bowl of a food processor, pulse the olives, garlic, and anchovy. Add the olive oil and blend until smooth, about 1 minute.

❷ Add the parsley and lemon zest and pulse to combine, about 10 seconds.

❸ Store in an airtight container in the refrigerator for up to 1 week.

ROMESCO SAUCE

MAKES ABOUT 1 CUP

Romesco is a classic match to *patatas bravas*, a Spanish bar-food snack. The way the mild heat of the peppers combines with the tart sherry vinegar to cut through the fattiness of the almonds is a prime example of balance. Although grilled bread is traditionally used in romesco, you can leave it out. Adjust the recipe by skipping step 1 and adding an extra ¼ cup of almonds.

¼ CUP EXTRA-VIRGIN OLIVE OIL, PLUS MORE TO TASTE

1 SLICE OF SOURDOUGH OR COUNTRY BREAD

⅓ CUP SKINLESS MARCONA ALMONDS

3 GARLIC CLOVES

ONE 16-OUNCE CAN PIQUILLO PEPPERS, DRAINED AND ROUGHLY CHOPPED

½ TEASPOON PIMENTÓN, OR SMOKED PAPRIKA

FINE SEA SALT

3 TABLESPOONS SHERRY VINEGAR, PLUS MORE TO TASTE

❶ Cover the bottom of a large sauté pan with about a tablespoon of the olive oil and heat over medium-high heat. Add the bread and toast it until browned on both sides, 30 seconds to 1 minute per side. Set aside to cool. Cut into ½-inch cubes. (You should have about 1 cup.)

❷ Wipe the pan clean with a paper towel and place back over medium-high heat. Add enough olive oil to coat the bottom of the pan again, about 2 tablespoons.

❸ When the oil begins to shimmer, add the almonds and garlic. Cook, stirring occasionally, until the garlic cloves are golden but not too brown and the almonds are aromatic, 1 to 2 minutes.

❹ Stir in the piquillo peppers and paprika. Season with salt and sauté for an additional minute or so.

❺ Transfer all ingredients—including the cooking liquid, the bread cubes, and the sherry vinegar—to a food processor. Blend until you achieve the desired consistency, 30 seconds to 1 minute. Some people like their romesco supersmooth and creamy, while others like a bit more texture and bite.

❻ Add more salt, vinegar, or olive oil as desired for taste and texture. Refrigerate for 3 to 4 hours to let the flavors meld before serving. Store in an airtight container in the refrigerator for up to 1 week.

ROMESCO SAUCE
page 320

PEANUT SAUCE
page 324

GREEN CASHEW SAUCE
page 325

ROASTED GARLIC AIOLI
page 315

PEANUT SAUCE

MAKES ABOUT 1½ CUPS

This Southeast Asian–inspired peanut sauce works wonders, whether served as a dip for summer rolls or fried tofu, or swirled into rice noodles. Dunk sugar snap peas in it as a snack, baste the Grilled Chicken Paillard (page 271) with it after the first flip, or thin it out with some water or more lime juice to make a savory salad dressing.

1 CUP ROASTED PEANUTS	1 TEASPOON TOASTED SESAME OIL
½ CUP WATER, PLUS MORE AS NEEDED	1 TEASPOON HOISIN SAUCE
2 TABLESPOONS RICE VINEGAR	½ TEASPOON FRESH GINGER, MINCED
2 TABLESPOONS HONEY	FINE SEA SALT
2 TEASPOONS SAMBAL OELEK	JUICE OF ½ LIME, OR TO TASTE

SAUCES

❶ Purée the peanuts and water in a blender until smooth.

❷ Add the rice vinegar, honey, sambal oelek, sesame oil, hoisin, and ginger and blend until incorporated. Season with salt and lime juice to taste.

❸ If the sauce is thicker than you'd like, stir in more water, 1 teaspoon at a time, until the sauce reaches your desired consistency.

❹ Store in an airtight container in the refrigerator for up to 1 week.

GREEN CASHEW SAUCE

MAKES ABOUT 1 CUP

Katie Carey, a chef who's worked at Haven's Kitchen since the day we opened, created this beautifully balanced sauce. The boiled cashews make a creamy, neutral (vegan) base for the cilantro. You might be tempted to eat this sauce alone, with a spoon, but it's a stellar accompaniment for grilled meats, grain bowls, noodles, and stir-fries.

½ CUP RAW UNSALTED CASHEWS	**JUICE OF 1 LEMON**
1 BUNCH OF CILANTRO, STEMS AND LEAVES	**FINE SEA SALT**

❶ Soak the cashews for at least 2 hours (ideally overnight) in at least 2 cups of water. Or place the cashews in a small pot and add enough water to cover by at least 3 inches. Simmer on medium-low heat for 45 minutes. You should be able to easily mush the cashews between your fingers.

❷ Strain, reserving the cooking liquid or soaking in a bowl. Transfer the cooked cashews to a blender. Trim off the bottom inch of the cilantro stems, coarsely chop the stems and leaves, and add to the blender along with about half of the lemon juice, a pinch of salt, and 1 tablespoon of the reserved liquid. Blend, gradually adding more liquid as necessary, until smooth. Season with additional lemon juice and salt to taste. Store in an airtight container in the refrigerator for up to 1 week.

POTATO SALAD WITH GRIBICHE, SHALLOTS, CELERY, AND PARSLEY

SERVES 4

Gribiche can be strong in flavor, thanks to the brininess from the cornichons and the pungent mustard, making it a perfect match for subtle creamy potatoes.

½ CUP GRIBICHE (PAGE 314)	1 SMALL SHALLOT, FINELY MINCED
2 POUNDS FINGERLING OR BABY YUKON GOLD POTATOES	2 CELERY STALKS WITH LEAVES, THINLY SLICED
¼ CUP FINE SEA SALT, PLUS MORE TO TASTE	½ CUP FRESH FLAT-LEAF PARSLEY LEAVES, ROUGHLY CHOPPED

❶ Make the gribiche and refrigerate until ready to use.

❷ Place the potatoes in a large pot and cover with at least 3 inches of water. Add the ¼ cup salt and bring to a boil. Reduce to a simmer and cook until tender, 12 to 15 minutes.

❸ Cool the potatoes in the cooking liquid or, to speed up the cooling, drain them. Return them to the pot, fill it with cold water, and allow to cool. When the potatoes are cool to the touch, drain them again. Slice into roughly 1-inch pieces (or in half if using baby Yukons) and place in a large bowl.

❹ Toss the potatoes with the shallot, celery, parsley, and gribiche. Taste and season with another pinch of salt if needed.

SAUCES

CHILLED VERMICELLI SALAD WITH SWEET CHILI SAUCE

SERVES 4

If you want a light meal with Southeast Asian flavors, look no further. Add Grilled Chicken Paillard (page 271) or Ginger-Garlic Tofu (page 331) for a protein boost. If you're not feeling like sweet chili sauce, try Peanut Sauce (page 324) or Fish Sauce Vinaigrette (page 232) for a more Vietnamese-style *bún*. Top with sliced scallions and chopped peanuts.

½ CUP SWEET CHILI SAUCE (PAGE 308)

ONE 8-OUNCE PACKAGE RICE VERMICELLI

2 CARROTS, JULIENNED OR GRATED

2 PERSIAN CUCUMBERS, SEEDED AND JULIENNED OR GRATED

1 CUP BEAN SPROUTS

1 BUNCH OF FRESH MINT, LEAVES PINCHED OFF AND TORN

1 BUNCH OF FRESH CILANTRO, LEAVES PINCHED OFF AND ROUGHLY CHOPPED

2 SCALLIONS (WHITE AND GREEN PARTS), SLICED THINLY ON THE BIAS

½ CUP PEANUTS, CHOPPED

❶ Make the sweet chili sauce and refrigerate until ready to use.

❷ Bring a large pot of water to a boil. Add the rice noodles, stir, and remove from the heat. Let the noodles soften for about 5 minutes, or as directed on the package. Drain and rinse with cold water. Place in a large bowl.

❸ Toss the noodles, carrots, cucumbers, bean sprouts, and half of the mint and cilantro with the sweet chili sauce.

❹ Garnish with the remaining herbs and the scallions and peanuts and serve.

GINGER-GARLIC TOFU

SERVES 2 TO 4

To make tofu with a satisfying texture—firm with a crisped-up exterior—you first need to expel the extra water in it. Marinating the tofu *after* panfrying it ensures that the tofu crisps, rather than steams, in the pan. Serve tofu on top of a grain bowl, a bed of hearty greens, or vermicelli noodles with Quick Pickled Cucumbers (page 110) and avocado.

ONE 12-OUNCE PACKAGE EXTRA-FIRM TOFU	1 CUP PLAIN RICE FLOUR
GINGER-GARLIC VINEGAR SAUCE (PAGE 311)	NEUTRAL-FLAVORED OIL, SUCH AS GRAPESEED OR CANOLA

❶ Cut the tofu in half crosswise and then slice each half into thirds to create 6 even planks. Line a small baking sheet with paper towels. Place the tofu on the pan and cover with another layer of paper towels. Place another baking sheet on top of the tofu and weight it down with a few cans or a heavy pot. Let sit for 30 minutes. This step removes extra water from the tofu.

❷ While the tofu is pressing, make the ginger-garlic sauce. Pour it into a shallow baking dish or pan large enough to hold all the tofu in an even layer.

❸ When ready to fry the tofu, set up your frying station. Put the rice flour in a shallow bowl large enough to dredge the tofu. Set a wire rack on a baking sheet for cooling the fried tofu and have a spatula or wooden chopsticks handy.

❹ Heat a medium sauté pan over high heat. Pour in enough oil to cover the bottom of the pan by ¼ inch and heat until it begins to shimmer.

❺ Working in batches, dredge the pressed tofu in the rice flour on a large plate. Tap off the excess flour and gently place the tofu in the hot oil, laying it away from you to avoid getting splattered with oil. Gently shake the pan to prevent the tofu from sticking. After about 30 seconds, use a spoon to baste the tofu, gently scooping up hot oil and pouring it over the planks.

❻ Fry until the edges begin to brown and turn golden, about 2 minutes, and then flip using the spatula or chopsticks. Fry for an additional 2 minutes on the other side, or until evenly golden. Remove from the pan. Repeat until all the tofu is fried.

❼ Place the fried tofu in the ginger-garlic sauce before serving.

GRILLED SAUSAGE WITH FLATBREAD, CHARRED SCALLIONS, AND CHIMICHURRI

SERVES 6

Flatbread, while pleasing on its own, takes on a whole new personality when it's smothered in sauce. The combination of chimichurri, sausage, and flatbread creates a meal that is greater than the sum of its parts. Get creative and try other sauces and toppings as well. Let your vegetarian friends build their own meal by serving a few different sauces and grilled vegetables; they will appreciate the gesture.

FLATBREAD (RECIPE FOLLOWS)

1 CUP CHIMICHURRI (PAGE 300)

6 ANDOUILLE OR MERGUEZ SAUSAGES

2 BUNCHES OF SCALLIONS, LEFT WHOLE, ROOTS AND ½ INCH OF THE TOP TRIMMED

1 TABLESPOON OLIVE OIL

FINE SEA SALT

❶ Make the flatbread and set aside, covered with a damp towel.

❷ Make the chimichurri and set aside until ready to use.

❸ Preheat a grill or grill pan.

❹ Grill the sausages, turning occasionally until all sides are lightly charred and the internal temperature reaches 155°F. Transfer to a large serving platter.

❺ Rub the scallions with the olive oil and sprinkle with salt. Grill until charred, about 5 minutes. Transfer to the serving platter.

❻ Serve the flatbread topped with chimichurri, sausage, and a few scallions.

Grilled Flatbread

MAKES SIX 6-INCH ROUNDS

1 CUP ALL-PURPOSE FLOUR,
PLUS MORE FOR ROLLING

1½ TEASPOONS BAKING POWDER

¾ CUP FULL-FAT GREEK YOGURT

1 TO 2 TABLESPOONS WATER

FINE SEA SALT

1 Place the flour and baking powder in a medium bowl and whisk to combine. Add the yogurt, 1 tablespoon water, and a pinch of salt. Using your hands, mix until the dough forms a rough ball and is tacky but does not stick to your hands. Add more water a few drops at a time if the dough is too dry.

2 Knead the ball for 1 more minute with the palm of your hand. Wrap in plastic wrap and let rest for 30 minutes at room temperature.

3 Divide the dough into 6 equal pieces. On a lightly floured surface, roll each piece into a ball, cover with plastic wrap or a damp cloth, and rest for an additional 10 minutes.

4 Preheat your grill or grill pan while the dough rests.

5 Roll each ball into a disk about ⅛ inch thick and 6 inches in diameter.

6 Grill the flatbread in batches until distinct grill marks form, about 1 minute and 30 seconds. Flip and grill until the bread begins to puff up and is lightly charred on both sides. Wrap in a damp cloth until ready to serve.

GEMELLI PASTA WITH ARUGULA PESTO, TOASTED WALNUTS, AND WILTED GREENS

SERVES 4

This recipe is a hybrid, blending a traditional twisted pasta, capable of trapping sauce in all sorts of nooks and crannies, with an unconventional arugula-based pesto. Wilting the arugula adds color and texture to the pasta, and topping it all off with crunchy walnuts transforms this dish into a satisfying meal. Feel free to play with your greens, and if you can't find gemelli, substitute pasta with as many ridges and crevices as possible.

336

SAUCES

1 CUP PESTO (PAGE 302); REPLACE THE BASIL WITH ARUGULA AND THE PINE NUTS WITH WALNUTS	1 POUND GEMELLI PASTA
	3 CUPS ARUGULA
¼ TO ⅓ CUP FINE SEA SALT	¼ CUP TOASTED CHOPPED WALNUTS
	¼ CUP GRATED PARMIGIANO-REGGIANO

❶ Make the pesto and refrigerate until ready to use.

❷ Place a large pot of water over high heat and add enough salt to make it taste as salty as the sea. When the water comes to a rapid boil, add the pasta. Cook, stirring occasionally, until al dente, following the package instructions.

❸ Drain the pasta, reserving 2 to 3 tablespoons of the cooking water, and place in a large bowl.

❹ Toss the warm pasta with the arugula, pesto, and reserved cooking water. Top with the walnuts and cheese and serve.

DESSERTS

"A party without cake is just a meeting."

—JULIA CHILD

THERE ARE PLENTY OF DESSERTS that require exacting attention to detail and total adherence to the recipe. Those delicacies have a lot to teach us about the science of baking. But there are desserts that can teach us other lessons about the final course of the meal. Dessert can teach us to get down with our bad selves, let loose, and have fun with all that's sweet, sticky, fluffy, tart, and luscious. Baking cakes and making dough are about measuring with accuracy, for sure, but they're also about allowing yourself to be creative. And not all desserts have to be pastry-shop-worthy creations that take hours to make. Yes, there might be less flexibility in a flourless chocolate cake recipe than, say, a grain bowl. But like a grain bowl, many desserts can be composed with inventiveness, a minimum of scientific hoopla, and lots of joy.

The same essentials about balance (see Sauces), mise en place (see Fritters), and composition (see Salads) apply to desserts: Think ahead. Prepare your ingredients. Consider your flavor and texture counterpoints. When serving rich chocolate, contrast it with something cold, fruity, or tart to break up the sweetness. When serving mild and chewy meringue, add a counterpoint of juicy or sour. Dessert can also be the foil to the main course while continuing the theme. Coconut Milk Tapioca Pudding (page 364) rounds out a meal rooted in Asian flavors; Flourless Chocolate Cake (page 355) is a coda to a traditional French menu.

Most of the dishes in this chapter are building-block recipes and, with a little practice, can be seamlessly integrated into your cooking repertoire. The lesson here is that making a sublime dessert is not about being a "baker," but rather that cooking is a joyful and adventurous endeavor. It doesn't have to be stressful; you don't need to present a masterpiece.

Sure, you can serve ice cream and bakery-bought cookies for dessert, but when the occasion calls for something more intentional, *make dessert*. If cooking for people shows you care about them, taking the time to make dessert is the literal cherry on top.

Teaching Recipe

PAVLOVA

MAKES EIGHT TO TEN 4-INCH CLOUDS

Once you know how to make meringues, you can take them in many different directions; pavlova can be endlessly transformed. This recipe is topped with berries and whipped cream. But the variations are endless.

The best news? If your meringue, for some reason, cracks or isn't looking right to you, fret not! Roll with it—crumble it into a serving bowl; layer it with the fruit, the cream, and more meringue; and confidently call it by its British name: Eton Mess.

FOR THE MERINGUE

4 LARGE EGG WHITES, AT ROOM TEMPERATURE (SEE PAGE 169)

1 DROP OF LEMON JUICE

1 CUP SUPERFINE SUGAR

FINE SEA SALT

1 VANILLA BEAN, SPLIT IN HALF LENGTHWISE, SEEDS SCRAPED AND RESERVED, OR 1 TEASPOON VANILLA EXTRACT

COOKING NOTES

Egg whites whip better at room temperature.

A drop of lemon juice is the acid needed for the chemical reaction that helps them whip into stiff peaks.

Try to use superfine sugar so it will dissolve completely.

Whenever possible, use vanilla beans scraped from a bean rather than the extract for better vanilla flavor.

FOR THE TOPPING

**WHIPPED CREAM
(PAGE 351)**

FRESH BERRIES

Once you know how to make meringues, you can make many varieties of pavlova, depending on what you're eating for your main course.

Feel free to experiment with substitutions. Try topping with store fruits, toasted nuts, coconut flakes, Poached Pears (page 352), or zingy Lemon Curd (page 346).

OVEN TEMPERATURE

❶ Preheat the oven to 300°F. Line two baking sheets with parchment paper.

Starting at 300°F and lowering the temperature later on makes a nice crust on the exterior.

ALCHEMY OF A MERINGUE

❷ Place the egg whites in the clean, dry bowl of a stand mixer outfitted with the whisk attachment. You can also use a mixing bowl and a handheld mixer.

It is important to use a clean, dry bowl because any trace of fat—including the egg yolk—will prevent the whites from properly forming peaks.

❸ Whip the egg whites on medium speed until they form soft, glossy peaks, 1 to 2 minutes. Add 1 drop of lemon juice and half of the sugar.

Adding too much sugar too quickly could collapse the aeration that you've started to create.

Diced mango, toasted coconut flakes, toasted peanuts, and whipped cream with lime zest

Toasted hazelnuts, cocoa nibs, and whipped cream with espresso

Lemon curd, whipped
cream, and dried lavender

Toasted sesame seeds,
fresh figs, and whipped
cream with rose water

❹ Mix for about 15 seconds to incorporate. Shut the mixer off again and add the remaining sugar, a pinch of salt, and the vanilla. Continue to beat the meringue until stiff and glossy, about 5 minutes.

Remove the whisk attachment, and turn the whisk upright. If the meringue is ready, it won't drip or droop. If it does, whisk it another 3 to 4 minutes.

BAKING

❺ Lift up each corner of the parchment paper lining the baking sheets and place a small smear of meringue underneath.

The meringue acts as a glue to hold the parchment in place.

❻ Use a large spoon to dollop the meringue onto the baking sheets, creating eight to ten 4-inch rounds. Use the back of the spoon to indent each one. The indent will act as a bowl of sorts for the fruit later on.

Keep it rustic, using a spoon for shaping your nests. Or make more precise rounds by piping them onto the baking sheet: Fill a piping bag or a sealable plastic bag. To fill the bag, put it in a large glass or pitcher so it stands upright and fold the sides of the bag over the edges to open it. Pour and scoop in the meringue. After filling the bag, close it and snip off ½ inch from the tip.

❼ Place the meringues in the oven and immediately lower the temperature to 250°F. Bake until the meringues feel dry to the touch. Check after 2 hours.

You may need to alternate racks if you see one sheet cooking more quickly than the other.

Every oven is different. Meringues take a long time.

❽ Turn off the oven but do not open the door! Leave the meringues inside for another hour. Remove from the oven and cool to room temperature.

The meringues will continue to dry out.

FINISH

❾ Transfer the meringues to serving plates. Using a silicone spatula, spread a generous amount of whipped cream onto each meringue. Spoon the fruit (or lemon curd, if using) on top. (If you like, toss the fruit in a bowl with a little sugar first to bring out the juices.) Garnish with mint, nuts, or lemon zest if desired. Meringues can be baked up to 2 days in advance, then stored tightly wrapped or in an airtight container at room temperature.

This is where you have an opportunity to play with different flavors, colors, textures, and serving styles. It also shows us how one dessert can be transformed to suit a range of different menus and profiles.

LEMON CURD

MAKES ABOUT 4 CUPS

Making lemon curd teaches you how to temper eggs into a hot mixture without curdling them, instead creating a thick, rich pudding. Use the curd to top French toast, waffles, or even ice cream. I've been known to dunk a graham cracker into a jar of lemon curd and top it with a mini-marshmallow to make a one-bite lemon meringue pie. Make lemon curd a couple of hours ahead of serving time; it requires some time spent stove-hovering and chilling.

1 CUP SUGAR	4 LARGE EGG YOLKS
4 LEMONS	¼ POUND PLUS 4 TABLESPOONS (2½ STICKS) UNSALTED BUTTER, CHILLED AND CUT INTO ½-INCH CUBES
FINE SEA SALT	

❶ Place the sugar in a small bowl. Using a rasp-style grater, zest the lemons directly over the sugar, letting the lemon zest fall into the bowl. Mix the lemon zest and sugar to release all the fragrant oils from the zest.

❷ Cut the zested lemons in half and juice them into a measuring cup. There should be about ¾ cup.

❸ Combine the lemon juice, sugar mixture, and a small pinch of salt in a small saucepan over medium-high heat. As soon as the liquid boils, remove from the heat and stir until the sugar has dissolved completely.

❹ Whisk the egg yolks in a bowl. While whisking, slowly pour in about ¼ cup of the hot lemon mixture. Once fully combined, add another ¼ cup, and then slowly pour in the remaining mixture while whisking constantly. This tempers the mixture to prevent curdling.

❺ Pour the mixture back into the saucepan and heat over very low heat, stirring constantly with a silicone spatula. Do not let the mixture boil, or it will curdle.

❻ After 8 to 10 minutes, the mixture should begin to thicken. It will heavily coat the spatula. At this point, remove from the heat and add the butter.

❼ Using the spatula, scrape the curd into a blender. Blend on medium speed until smooth.

❽ Transfer the lemon curd to a bowl, cover with a piece of plastic wrap directly on the surface of the curd, and refrigerate until cold, at least 1 hour. Lemon curd can be stored in an airtight container in the refrigerator for up to 1 week.

LEMON CURD TART

MAKES ONE 9-INCH TART, PLUS SCRAPS FOR COOKIES

Pastry dough has scared off quite a few cooks. But with practice and information, you may find yourself enjoying the process of turning butter, sugar, and flour into a sweet, crunchy canvas. This dough, a classic French sablé, makes a crumbly rich crust similar to a killer shortbread cookie. That's why the recipe makes enough for one 9-inch tart plus a little extra. Take those leftover scraps and roll them out as one big cookie or break out your cookie cutters—and bake for 12 to 15 minutes at 350°F.

1¾ CUPS ALL-PURPOSE FLOUR, PLUS MORE FOR DUSTING

1 CUP PLUS 1 TABLESPOON CONFECTIONERS' SUGAR

FINE SEA SALT

½ POUND (2 STICKS) UNSALTED BUTTER, CHILLED AND CUT INTO ½-INCH CUBES

2 LARGE EGG YOLKS

1 VANILLA BEAN, SPLIT IN HALF LENGTHWISE, OR 1 TEASPOON VANILLA EXTRACT

4 CUPS LEMON CURD (PAGE 346), CHILLED

---

❶ Combine the flour, sugar, and salt in the bowl of a food processor fitted with the metal chopping blade. Add the butter and blend on low or pulse until the butter breaks down and the mixture resembles almond meal (ground-up almonds).

❷ Add the egg yolks and scrape in the seeds from the vanilla bean. (Reserve the scraped pod for another use.) Pulse until a ball of dough starts to form.

❸ Dump the dough onto a work surface and gently form it into a disk, being careful not to overwork the dough. Wrap in plastic wrap and refrigerate for at least 30 minutes or up to 3 days.

❹ Preheat the oven to 350°F.

❺ Unwrap the chilled dough and place it on a floured surface. Dust a rolling pin with flour and use it to pound the dough disk until flattened by half its height. Lightly flour the work surface, the dough, and the rolling pin again. Begin rolling out the dough, starting from the middle and working your way out to the edges. Rotate the dough and sprinkle with a bit more flour if it sticks. Continue to roll out the dough until it is a little thinner than ¼ inch. Roll the dough around the pin, then gently unroll it over a 9-inch tart pan. Using your fingers, press the dough into the edges of the pan, allowing excess dough to hang off the sides. Chill in the freezer for 10 minutes, or in the refrigerator for 30 minutes.

continued

❻ Remove the shell from the refrigerator or freezer and, using a knife or sharp kitchen shears, gently trim any overhanging dough and reserve it for making cookies.

❼ Place a large piece of parchment paper or aluminum foil over the dough and fill it with pie weights or dried beans.

❽ Blind bake the crust until the edges are light golden brown, 15 to 20 minutes. (Blind baking is a method of parbaking a pie or tart crust. It ensures a sturdy crust that resists sogginess, especially with wetter fillings or fillings like lemon curd that do not require a long bake.) Remove from the oven and carefully lift out the pie weights along with the parchment or foil. Cool for at least 5 minutes.

❾ Reduce the oven temperature to 300°F.

❿ Pour the lemon curd into the crust and smooth with a silicone spatula. Bake for 10 to 15 minutes, until the curd is lightly set. It may jiggle slightly when it comes out of the oven, but should hold. After it chills, it will set completely.

⓫ Cool the tart in the pan on a wire rack for 1 hour. Transfer to the refrigerator and let cool completely, at least 3 hours. Slice and serve chilled.

PASTRY DOUGH 101

Dough can be intimidating, but these rules should help make the process a bit more manageable. The goal is to keep the dough cool, ensuring a flaky crust. You want to prevent the development of gluten, which happens when flour is overworked.

• Use only very cold butter, and use only the tips of your fingers to work it into the flour. The fingertips stay cooler than the rest of your hands.

• Keep the dough cold! Put it in the fridge for a few minutes if you see it starting to get sticky.

• When rolling out the dough, start in the middle and roll away from your body. Always. You'll have to rotate the dough: roll, then rotate. The rolling pin should always be perpendicular to your body.

• Never pick up the rolled-out dough with your hands (again, hands are warm and you want to keep the dough cold). Roll it up on your pin, and then unroll it over the baking sheet or dish.

WHIPPED CREAM

You will forever be considered a domestic god or goddess once you have fed people freshly whipped cream. It takes just a few minutes to make, and the only ingredients you need are heavy cream and, if desired, sugar or syrup.

HEAVY CREAM	**1 VANILLA BEAN, SPLIT IN HALF LENGTHWISE AND SEEDS SCRAPED (OPTIONAL)**
SWEETENER SUCH AS CONFECTIONERS' SUGAR, SUPERFINE SUGAR, OR MAPLE SYRUP (IF DESIRED)	

❶ If you have time, chill the bowl in which you will whip the cream for 30 minutes. If not using a stand mixer, choose a bowl that's deep enough to accommodate a handheld mixer or a balloon whisk.

❷ Pour at least 1 cup heavy cream into the chilled bowl. Whisk by hand or on medium-high speed until the cream transforms into soft peaks; the cream will gently fall from the whisk when removed from the bowl. If using a mixer, this should take just 2 to 3 minutes. Don't overmix: the cream will seize and harden into butter.

❸ If desired, stir in a little sugar—start with 1 teaspoon sugar per 1 cup of cream and adjust based on your preference. Confectioners' sugar is preferred, but superfine granulated sugar is also fine. Vanilla bean seeds or other types of sweeteners, such as maple syrup, can be folded in instead of or in addition to sugar.

❹ Whipped cream can be made up to 1 day before serving and refrigerated in an airtight container.

POACHED PEARS

SERVES 4

Cold-weather meals eaten around the kitchen table are even cozier with the aroma of a pot of simmering pears. Red-wine poaching imbues the pears with a deep garnet color and makes a beautiful finale to meals of roasts and braises. Poaching in white wine imparts a more delicate flavor, serving as an elegant end to a dinner of grilled chicken or fish. You can experiment with spices. I like to put in a whole cinnamon stick and star anise, an orange peel, a vanilla bean, and fresh ginger. The recipe can be made with other fruits—try rhubarb, hard peaches, or nectarines.

3 CUPS RED OR WHITE WINE (SEE "COOKING WITH WINE," PAGE 354)

3 CUPS WATER

½ CUP HONEY

ABOUT 1 TABLESPOON MIXED WHOLE SPICES AND AROMATICS, SUCH AS CARDAMOM, STAR ANISE, ALLSPICE, OR CLOVES

ONE CINNAMON STICK

1 VANILLA BEAN, SPLIT

ONE 2-INCH STRIP OF CITRUS PEEL (OPTIONAL)

ONE 2-INCH PIECE OF FRESH GINGER, PEELED AND CUT INTO BATONS (SEE PAGE 14)

4 FIRM BUT RIPE BOSC PEARS, PEELED, STEMS LEFT INTACT

ICE CREAM AND/OR TOASTED NUTS, FOR SERVING (OPTIONAL)

❶ Fill a medium pot with the wine, water, honey, spices, cinnamon stick, vanilla, citrus peel (if using), and ginger. Stir to combine and set aside.

❷ Remove the seeds from the bottom of each pear, using either a paring knife to carefully carve them out or a teaspoon to scoop them.

❸ Place the pears in the pot with the liquid, cover, and bring the poaching liquid to a simmer over low heat. Cook until the pears are tender, 30 minutes to 1 hour, depending on the ripeness of the pears.

❹ With a slotted spoon, transfer the pears to a serving bowl. Continue to simmer the liquid for 10 to 12 minutes, or until the sauce thickens enough to coat the back of a spoon. The liquid will reduce to about 1 cup.

❺ Ladle the syrup over the pears and serve alongside a scoop of ice cream. Sprinkle on chopped nuts, if you like.

COOKING WITH WINE

There is some truth in the saying "Only cook with wine that you'd drink"—but not if you only drink expensive wine! I say: "Only cook with a wine that you wouldn't *mind* drinking." If you're going to add sugar and spices to the wine, cooking with a truly special bottle is a waste. For poaching fruits, choose a dry red like Cabernet Sauvignon that's not heavily oaked or an off-dry Riesling—you want the acidity of the alcohol to balance the sugars in the fruit.

The same rule holds true for savory cooking. When making a savory dish like beef bourguignon, it's not necessary to use a Grand Cru Burgundy; a less expensive wine will suffice, as all you really want out of the wine is nice acidity, color, and some structure, or "backbone," as the experts say.

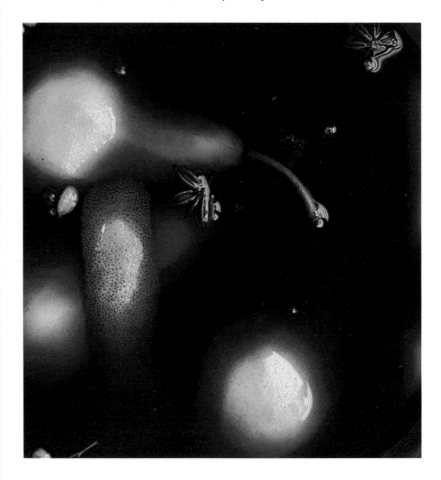

FLOURLESS CHOCOLATE CAKE TO COMMIT TO MEMORY

MAKES ONE 9-INCH CAKE OR EIGHT 6-OUNCE RAMEKINS

French families have some version of this chocolate cake lodged in whatever little corner of the mind is responsible for nostalgia. Pop it in the oven and let the heavenly aroma waft out of the kitchen while you're eating dinner.

My friend Gratianne adapted her family's recipe with almond meal (ground-up almonds), and I love the nutty, marzipan-like flavor it lends. But the recipe is also just fine without it.

¼ POUND PLUS 6 TABLESPOONS (1¾ STICKS) UNSALTED BUTTER, PLUS MORE FOR THE PAN

8 OUNCES BITTERSWEET CHOCOLATE (70% COCOA OR MORE), CHOPPED

5 LARGE EGGS

¾ CUP SUGAR

¼ CUP ALMOND MEAL (OPTIONAL)

FINE SEA SALT

---

❶ Preheat the oven to 375°F. Butter the sides of a 9-inch round cake pan and press a 9-inch round of parchment paper onto the bottom. Alternatively, butter eight 6-ounce ramekins to make individual cakes.

❷ In a small pot, melt the butter over medium heat, stirring occasionally. Remove from the heat and add the chocolate. Stir continually until the chocolate has melted. Set aside to cool.

❸ In the bowl of a stand mixer fitted with the whisk attachment or a mixing bowl if using a handheld mixer, beat the eggs and sugar on medium-high speed until pale yellow and doubled in volume, about 3 minutes.

❹ Using a silicone spatula, fold the melted cooked chocolate mixture into the whipped eggs in three stages so that the chocolate doesn't sink to the bottom and the batter remains nicely aerated.

❺ Fold in the almond meal, if using, and a small pinch of salt, and then pour into the prepared cake pan or ramekins. If using a cake pan, set it on an even surface and give it a quick spin, which will cause the batter to climb up the sides of the pan and bake more evenly.

❻ Bake until the top is set and dry to the touch, 20 to 25 minutes for the 9-inch cake or 10 to 15 minutes for the ramekins.

❼ Let cool in the pan on a wire rack for at least 30 minutes before serving.

CLAFOUTIS

MAKES ONE 8-INCH ROUND

A cross between a Dutch baby (what a great name!) and a custard, clafoutis is a traditional French countryside dessert made by pouring a nutty batter over whole cherries and then baking it. A purist would argue that using anything other than whole cherries—pit *in*—is heresy and does not qualify as a proper clafoutis, but rather a *flaugnarde*. Given that you may not enjoy dodging cherry pits as you eat, ease trumps heritage in this recipe and the cherries are pitted.

Propriety aside, this is a dessert you can bake while you're enjoying the main meal. Once you get the batter down, use it to make a *flaugnarde* with berries, stone fruits, apple slices, or chocolate chips.

1 TEASPOON UNSALTED BUTTER, SOFTENED

1 CUP FRESH OR FROZEN CHERRIES, PITTED

3 LARGE EGGS

1 CUP MILK

1 VANILLA BEAN, SEEDS SCRAPED AND RESERVED, OR 1 TEASPOON VANILLA EXTRACT

½ CUP SUGAR

½ CUP ALL-PURPOSE FLOUR

¼ CUP ALMOND MEAL

1 Preheat the oven to 350°F. Butter an 8-inch ovenproof skillet or pie dish and place it on a baking sheet.

2 Layer the cherries evenly in the bottom of the skillet. Set aside.

3 In a medium bowl, whisk the eggs by hand. Add the milk and vanilla seeds, and continue whisking to combine.

4 Set aside 1 tablespoon of the sugar and add the rest to the milk mixture. Then gently whisk in the flour and almond meal and stir until smooth. Set the batter aside to rest for 10 minutes.

5 Pour the batter over the fruit and sprinkle the reserved 1 tablespoon sugar on top.

6 Bake for 20 to 25 minutes, until golden brown, set, and puffy, rotating the pan after 10 minutes to ensure even browning. To test for doneness, insert a toothpick or cake tester into the center: it should come out clean.

7 Let the clafoutis rest for 10 minutes on a wire rack before slicing. The center will fall slightly as it cools.

FRUIT GALETTE

SERVES 6 TO 8

For me, *galette* is the French word meaning "pastry for the nonbaker," although obviously that is an inaccurate translation. This open-faced pie is purposely rustic and an amenable canvas for any fruit that likes to be baked. This recipe is more forgiving than a pie dough. It is designed to be pliable and sturdy—kind of like the country wife I always imagine making it—and able to hold up the dessert's free-form glory while having some semblance of a pie's flakiness.

We have written the recipe for plums, but you can substitute 4 cups of other seasonal fruits, like blueberries, peaches, or pears. Also, change your spices to complement the fruits—adding cardamom, cloves, or even a little white pepper.

FOR THE DOUGH

2⅔ CUPS ALL-PURPOSE FLOUR, PLUS MORE FOR ROLLING

2 TABLESPOONS GRANULATED SUGAR

FINE SEA SALT

8 TABLESPOONS (1 STICK) COLD UNSALTED BUTTER, CUT INTO ½-INCH CUBES

½ CUP ICE WATER

FOR THE FILLING

4 CUPS PLUMS OR OTHER STONE FRUITS, APPLES, OR PEARS, PEELED AND SLICED

3 TABLESPOONS GRANULATED SUGAR

GRATED ZEST AND JUICE OF 1 LEMON

TO COMPLETE THE GALETTE

1 LARGE EGG WHISKED WITH 1 TABLESPOON WATER

1 TABLESPOON RAW SUGAR (OPTIONAL)

WHIPPED CREAM (PAGE 351)

❶ Make the dough: In the bowl of a food processor, combine the flour, granulated sugar, and a pinch of salt. Pulse once or twice to mix everything. Add the butter.

❷ Pulse until the mixture has broken down to pea-sized pieces, about 5 seconds. If you find the butter is becoming soft, chill the entire bowl for 15 minutes before proceeding.

❸ Slowly add about 6 tablespoons of the ice water, continuing to pulse, until the dough comes together to form a ragged lump. Continue adding the remaining water bit by bit, pulsing to incorporate all the flour. Stop adding water before the dough becomes soft and sticky, and when it has come together in a firm, compact ball.

continued

4 Dump the dough onto a cool surface and form it into a firm, compact disk. This will help when rolling it out into a circle. Wrap in plastic and refrigerate for at least 30 minutes, and up to 3 days. This rechills the butter and lets the dough rest before being rolled out.

5 Preheat the oven to 375°F. Line a baking sheet with parchment paper.

6 Make the filling: In a small bowl, gently mix the fruit, granulated sugar, and lemon zest and juice until evenly distributed.

7 Unwrap the chilled dough and place it on a floured surface. Dust a rolling pin with flour, and use it to pound the dough disk until flattened by half its height. Lightly flour the work surface, the dough, and the rolling pin again. Begin rolling out the dough, starting from the middle and working your way out to the edges. Rotate the dough and sprinkle with a bit more flour if it sticks. Continue to roll out the dough until it is a little thinner than ¼ inch and about 14 inches in diameter. Don't worry if it's not a perfect circle; it's meant to look rustic, and you're going to be folding it. Roll the dough around the rolling pin, then gently unroll it over the prepared pan. Use a pastry brush to dust off excess flour.

8 Arrange the fruit in rows or concentric circles, or for a more rustic look, gently pile the fruit in the center of your dough, leaving a 2-inch border. The important thing is that it forms an even layer.

9 Working around the circle, fold the border around the filling, partially overlapping as you go. Brush the crust with egg wash (the beaten egg and water) and sprinkle with raw sugar.

10 Bake for 35 to 45 minutes, until the fruit is cooked and the crust is golden brown. Let cool on a wire rack for 30 minutes before serving, so the filling has set. Serve with fresh whipped cream.

VARIATION

If you do not have a food processor, you can make the dough by hand.

1 In a medium bowl, combine the flour, sugar, and a pinch of salt. Working quickly, use your fingertips to pinch each piece of butter, smashing it into the flour mixture and breaking it down to pea-sized bits. If you find the butter is becoming soft, chill the entire bowl for 15 minutes before proceeding.

2 Add about 6 tablespoons of the ice water gradually, mixing with your hands or stirring with a wooden spoon until the dough comes together to form a ragged lump. Continue adding the remaining water bit by bit, stirring and then kneading the dough to incorporate all the flour. Stop adding water before the dough becomes sticky, and when it is beginning to come together.

3 Form the dough into a disk. This will help when rolling it out into a circle. Wrap in plastic and refrigerate for at least 30 minutes, and up to 3 days.

4 Follow steps 4 through 10 above.

HOW TO ASSEMBLE A GALETTE

1 The rolling pin should always be perpendicular to your body. Place the pin in the middle of the dough and roll away from you.

2 Rotate the dough. Roll. Then rotate again. If the dough starts to get sticky, pop it back in the refrigerator for a few minutes.

3 Never pick up the rolled-out dough with your hands. When you're ready to lay the dough on a baking sheet, roll it up on your pin, then unroll it over the baking sheet or dish.

4 Fold the edges of the dough over the filling and brush with the egg wash.

COCONUT MILK TAPIOCA PUDDING

SERVES 4 TO 6

Tapioca is made from a root vegetable, much like a yam, called cassava or yuca. Starch from the root is extracted, dried, and formed into little pearls. While tapioca pudding was ubiquitous in American kitchens in the 1950s, this recipe plays on one by Claudia Fleming, the former pastry chef at Gramercy Tavern in New York City. The tropical notes in Fleming's tapioca make it playful, surprising, and perfectly balanced. Soak the tapioca for at least 8 hours to get balls that are cooked through but still chewy and firm. Try all sorts of flavors and textures as toppings: toasted coconut, lime zest, diced fresh or dried fruits, mango or raspberry sorbet, or nuts, such as toasted pistachios, almonds, or macadamias. Serve the pudding warm from the pot or let it cool before garnishing.

⅓ CUP SMALL TAPIOCA PEARLS

ONE 13.5-OUNCE CAN OF FULL-FAT COCONUT MILK

⅓ CUP GRANULATED SUGAR

1 VANILLA BEAN, SPLIT IN HALF LENGTHWISE AND SEEDS SCRAPED, OR ½ TEASPOON VANILLA EXTRACT

FINE SEA SALT

❶ In a nonreactive saucepot, combine the tapioca, coconut milk, sugar, vanilla, and a pinch of salt, cover, and refrigerate overnight.

❷ When ready to cook, uncover the pot and heat the mixture over medium heat. Gently cook, stirring constantly with a spatula or a wooden spoon. After about 4 minutes, when the liquid is hot and has begun to bubble, reduce the heat to low. Continue to stir until the tapioca pearls are translucent, have no crunch in the center, and are suspended in the liquid, 10 to 12 minutes.

❸ Serve warm or cool, with your choice of garnishes (see headnote).

RESOURCES

You will be able to find most of the ingredients and tools used in the book at your local markets and kitchenware and specialty stores. However, I have provided a list of my recommended brands and purveyors for your reference.

INGREDIENTS

Asian Food Ingredients

For sambal olek (Huy Fong), fish sauce (Squid), black vinegar, and other Asian-based ingredients.

Asian Food Grocer
asianfoodgrocer.com

Beans

Rancho Gordo
ranchogordo.com

Grains and Flour

Anson Mills
ansonmills.com

Bob's Red Mill and King Arthur Flour Available at most grocery stores.

Nuts and Dried Fruit

For almonds and cashews, cherries, raisins, and more
nuts.com

Olive Oil

The brands I prefer are Frantoia, L'Estornell, and Nuñez de Prado. Frantoia suits everyday cooking, and is also fragrant enough to use on its own. However, for occasions where you want the olive oil to carry a dish, like in a dressing, I use Spanish-origin oils like L'Estornell and Nuñez de Prado, which are nuttier and fruitier than ones pressed in Italy.

Available at Dean & Deluca
deananddeluca.com

Olives, Capers, and Piquillo Peppers

Despaña
408 Broome Street
New York, NY 10013
Phone: 212-219-5050
info@despananyc.com

Sea Salt

Baleine Fine Sea Salt, for cooking

Maldon Sea Salt, for finishing

Available at most grocery stores.

Spices

Kalustyans is a New York City–based specialty food company and a go-to source for spices and hard-to-find ingredients.

Kalustyans
kalustyans.com

Vinegar

Sparrow Lane
sparrowlane.com

KITCHENWARE SUPPLIES

Baking Supplies

N.Y. Cake: Baking Supplies & Education
nycake.com

General Cookware

Williams-Sonoma
williams-sonoma.com

Specialty Cookware

JB Prince
jbprince.com

ACKNOWLEDGMENTS

Haven's Kitchen has a culture of collaboration, dialogue, and friendly debate. This book is no exception. Though my name may be on the cover, this cookbook was a collective process; staff meals were dominated for a year and a half by discussions of flavor balance, trussing (or not), rinsing, soaking, and salad drying. Along the way we had heated, but mostly fun, conversations about everything from whether a home cook would make a soufflé to the dangers of co-opting "ethnic" dishes to the precise definition of a fritter (we agreed, not unanimously, that burgers do not fit the bill). A huge thank-you to everybody who makes up the Haven's Kitchen community, past and present, including our partners and children, who understand that it's more than a job.

There was, though, a core group that was especially instrumental in its making and without whom this book could have never been written: David Mawhinney, the culinary director at Haven's Kitchen and one of the most gifted cooks I've ever met; Sonjia Hyon, who, among a million other talents, is a wordsmith, the ultimate project manager, and a fierce editor; and Shell Hamilton, who writes otherwise mundane instructions clearly and elegantly and tests, cooks, and photographs recipes meticulously. I am beyond grateful to work with such creative, engaged, and dedicated people. The recipes herein are as much theirs as they are mine.

I'd also like to thank Zoe Maya Jones, Katie Carey, and Ashley Bare, three of our teachers and team members who were all happy to answer questions and offer opinions (and recipes) whenever I asked, whether I stopped them mid-chop or texted them on a Sunday morning.

As confident as we may have been with our recipes, we relied on Maria Zizka to provide her stamp of approval. Her astute feedback was central in finalizing the dishes that appear in the cookbook today.

Much gratitude is also due to Jen Renzi, who was able to take the forest of ideas and theories and recipes in my head and turn them into articulate, readable trees. And to Judy Pray, Sarah Weaver, and Sibylle Kazeroid for pruning and watering those trees and making them beautiful.

I owe so many thanks to Michelle Ishay-Cohen for walking in the door that first week Haven's Kitchen was open and never leaving. Thank you for telling me from the beginning that this cookbook was a worthwhile endeavor and for walking me to the elevator that day and telling me I should stop trying to convince Lia otherwise. And, of course, I am grateful to Lia Ronnen for her faith in this project in spite of my babbling. She was a brilliant guide.

Crazy gratitude to Con Poulos, Ryn Frank, Erica Heitman-Ford, Jane Treuhaft,

Barbara Peragine, Nancy Murray, and all of the other people who worked on the book's photography, illustration, and design. The goal all along was a smart, beautiful book that teaches as much as it inspires, and it is only through your work that we were able to do that.

Thank you to Joan Gussow for starting this whole thing, and to Jenny, Marion, and Krish for turning food into my life's work.

To my parents, thanks for everything, but above all for giving me free rein in the kitchen.

And thanks beyond what words can convey to my friends, to Franklin, and most especially to Kate, Jake, C.C., Julia, and Will, for cheering me along selflessly simply because they know how deeply, completely happy my work makes me.

INDEX

CONVERSION CHARTS

Here are rounded-off equivalents between the metric system and the traditional systems that are used in the United States to measure weight and volume.

WEIGHTS

US/UK	Metric
1 oz	30 g
2 oz	55 g
3 oz	85 g
4 oz (¼ lb)	115 g
5 oz	140 g
6 oz	170 g
7 oz	200 g
8 oz (½ lb)	225 g
9 oz	255 g
10 oz	285 g
11 oz	310 g
12 oz	340 g
13 oz	370 g
14 oz	395 g
15 oz	425 g
16 oz (1 lb)	455 g

VOLUME

American	Imperial	Metric
¼ tsp		1.25 ml
½ tsp		2.5 ml
1 tsp		5 ml
½ Tbsp (1½ tsp)		7.5 ml
1 Tbsp (3 tsp)		15 ml
¼ cup (4 Tbsp)	2 fl oz	60 ml
⅓ cup (5 Tbsp)	2½ fl oz	75 ml
½ cup (8 Tbsp)	4 fl oz	125 ml
⅔ cup (10 Tbsp)	5 fl oz	150 ml
¾ cup (12 Tbsp)	6 fl oz	175 ml
1 cup (16 Tbsp)	8 fl oz	250 ml
1¼ cups	10 fl oz	300 ml
1½ cups	12 fl oz	350 ml
2 cups (1 pint)	16 fl oz	500 ml
2½ cups	20 fl oz (1 pint)	625 ml
5 cups	40 fl oz (1 qt)	1.25 l

OVEN TEMPERATURES

	°F	°C	Gas Mark
very cool	250–275	130–140	½–1
cool	300	148	2
warm	325	163	3
moderate	350	177	4
moderately hot	375–400	190–204	5–6
hot	425	218	7
very hot	450–475	232–245	8–9

Alison Cayne founded Haven's Kitchen—a cooking school, café, and event space in New York City—to inspire and educate people about food and sustainability issues. She serves on the board of Edible Schoolyard NYC and has been featured in such publications as the *New York Times, Vogue,* and *Domino* and on Remodelista.com. Find her on Instagram @havenskitchen.